THE GREAT DEBASEMENT

Currency and the Economy in Mid-Tudor England

THE GREAT DEBASEMENT

Currency and the Economy in Mid-Tudor England

BY

J. D. GOULD

Professor of Economic History
University of Wellington
New Zealand

OXFORD
AT THE CLARENDON PRESS
1970

Oxford University Press, Ely House, London W. 1

GLASGOW NEW YORK TORONTO MELBOURNE WELLINGTON
CAPE TOWN SALISBURY IBADAN NAIROBI DAR ES SALAAM LUSAKA ADDIS ABABA
BOMBAY CALCUTTA MADRAS KARACHI LAHORE DACCA
KUALA LUMPUR SINGAPORE HONG KONG TOKYO

PRINTED IN GREAT BRITAIN

TO MY FATHER

AND TO THE MEMORY OF

MY MOTHER

PREFACE

THE relationship between the coinage, the foreign exchanges and external trade in the early modern period is a topic which has interested me for many years. I had long wanted to investigate the debasement of the English coinage under Henry VIII and Edward VI from this point of view, but the opportunity to do the necessary research in England came only when my University granted me a period of sabbatical leave in 1965–6.

Before I left New Zealand it came to my notice that the topic had meanwhile engaged the attention of another scholar, Mr. (now Dr.) C. E. Challis of the University of Leeds. Correspondence with Dr. Challis revealed, however, that our interests in the debasement differed somewhat, Dr. Challis being concerned more particularly with the administrative and fiscal aspects of mint activity, while I was primarily interested in the effects of changes in the coinage on the external sector. These differences of standpoint seemed to both investigators to make a continuation of their separate researches fully justified. Further, it had long been obvious to me, from evidence published in numismatic journals half a century ago, that existing estimates of the output of base coins during the debasement were seriously astray; and this seemed to suggest that a second recalculation of this output might rather provide reassurance than call for apology. I therefore present in Chapter III my own estimates of mint output during the debasement; these were made independently, save that I owe the reference to the location of Sir John York's accounts to Dr. Challis's article on the Southwark Mint, and the reader may notice that while my estimates agree closely with those of Dr. Challis, they are not quite identical. However, it is proper to draw attention to the fact that credit for first presenting revised, and substantially correct, estimates of mint output during the debasement lies with the two articles by Dr. Challis referred to in footnote 2 on page 5.

In preparing this study I incurred several debts which it is my pleasure to acknowledge. My discussions with Dr. Challis were stimulating and rewarding. I owe more than perhaps their author realizes to brief but typically incisive comments and questions by Professor

H. J. Habakkuk. Dr. H. Van der Wee most generously placed at my disposal the data on which he based his graph of the London–Antwerp exchange rate, while Professor R. de Roover sent me a very interesting graph of the same exchanges in the period 1538–44, which proved instructive even though, in the event, I did not find it necessary to take advantage of his kind permission to reproduce it. Professors E. M. Carus-Wilson and E. H. Phelps-Brown and Drs. P. J. Bowden and C. S. L. Davies are amongst those who answered inquiries by post, while Professor F. J. Fisher introduced me to the Beveridge collection of price material housed at the London School of Economics. None of these scholars is in any way responsible for whatever errors remain in this monograph. Like countless others I owe much to the courtesy and skill of the staffs of the British Museum, the Public Record Office, and the Cambridge University Library, and I express here my indebtedness to the Mercers' Company of London for permission to draw upon the Daybook of Sir Thomas Gresham which is in their possession. Finally, I wish to thank the Council of my University for granting me the sabbatical leave without which this study would have been impossible.

J. D. GOULD

University of Wellington
New Zealand

CONTENTS

LIST OF TABLES

ABBREVIATIONS

The following abbreviations are used in the footnotes:

Add. MSS.	Additional Manuscripts, British Museum.
A.O.	Audit Office Rolls, Public Record Office, London.
APC	Acts of the Privy Council.
Cotton MSS.	Cotton Manuscripts, British Museum.
CPR	Calendar of Patent Rolls.
E.	Exchequer Records, Public Record Office, London.
Harleian MSS.	Harleian Manuscripts, British Museum.
L and P	Letters and Papers, Foreign and Domestic, of the reign of Henry VIII, 1509–47.
SP	State Papers Domestic, Public Record Office, London.

1

THE GREAT DEBASEMENT

THE Great Debasement—the adulteration of the English coinage in the last years of Henry VIII and during the reign of Edward VI—is a unique event in English history. It was the only occasion, throughout the centuries in which England's circulating medium consisted mainly of coins fashioned from the two precious metals, on which the purity and weight of those coins were seriously reduced for fiscal ends. Occasional and progressive deterioration, for which, if it remains gradual and under control, the economist can find something to say, there was; and the fiscal motive, though never on any other occasion dominating policy-making as it did between 1544 and 1551, was rarely absent from the minds of those responsible for the currency. But as Professor Cipolla has written, 'the English currency, although progressively depreciated, displayed throughout the Middle Ages a remarkable degree of relative stability, in striking contrast to the rapid depreciation of Continental currencies'.[1] Oman began his article on the Tudors and the currency,[2] dramatically enough, by pointing out that in the early sixteenth century the English currency had undergone relatively little alteration for over 1,000 years. Nor did the fiscal success of the Great Debasement provide later rulers with an irresistible precedent: even Charles I, in the extremity of his need for revenue, staged a debate on the merits and demerits of debasement before resorting to that expedient, and the outcome of it was a decision to look elsewhere for satisfaction of his needs.[3] The temptation to use the Mint for profit finally disappeared when seignorage was abolished in 1666.

It is not only, however, the uniqueness of the Great Debasement which would have led one to expect historians to show interest in the

[1] C. M. Cipolla, 'Currency Depreciation in Medieval Europe', *Economic History Review*, 2nd Series xv, no. 3 (Apr. 1963), 419.

[2] C. W. C. Oman, 'The Tudors and the Currency, 1526–1560', *Trans. Royal Hist. Soc.*, N.S. ix (1895), 167–88.

[3] Add. MSS. 34324, fol. 67; APC, June–Dec. 1626, pp. 247–8.

episode. It has been widely realized that the adulteration of the coinage between 1542 and 1551 was sufficiently severe to make an impact on several aspects of England's economy and society. The immediate motive for the debasement of the coinage was of course fiscal. When Wriothesley wrote to Paget in September 1545 that 'That office hath marvellously served the King's Majesty'[1] he spoke no more than the truth, but in September 1545 the Mints were far from having revealed their full potential as a major source of revenue, and the best—or worst—was yet to come. It has been suggested, again, that the flood of debased coinage poured out between 1544 and 1551 had a dramatic effect on the price level; I argued myself, indeed, in a recent article that the years of debasement were the only part of the whole period of so-called 'Price Revolution' in which a degree of inflation comparable with our twentieth-century experience occurred.[2] It was suggested, in turn, that this fact must be considered a contributory cause of the popular discontent which marred the middle years of the century, and thus indirectly of the conservative policy, designed amongst other things to avoid a repetition of such tensions, which characterized much of Elizabeth's handling of social and economic affairs and especially the work of her leading economic minister, William Cecil. Finally, many historians have attributed to the Great Debasement a powerful influence on overseas trade—though the effects claimed for it have varied from that of an agent which 'completely demoralized' trade and industry and 'entirely dislocated' commercial and financial relations with foreign countries,[3] to that of a beneficial influence which, in essentially the same way as a modern currency devaluation, stimulated exports and the level of economic activity.[4]

In view of the importance and the many-sided fascination of the topic, it is surprising that in fact there appears to have been no specialist study of it. The closest approach is the article by Oman, which, though valuable in a pioneering way, does not approach the subject from the angle of the modern economic historian and is far from exhausting its analytical interest or, indeed, giving an acceptably accurate outline of events. Similar criticisms must also be raised against the treatments which, of course, are to be found in the stan-

[1] *Letters and Papers of the Reign of Henry VIII* (*L and P*) xx, Part 2, 197.

[2] J. D. Gould, 'The Price Revolution Reconsidered', *Economic History Review* 2nd Series xvii, no. 2 (Dec. 1964), 251.

[3] G. Unwin, *Studies in Economic History* (Macmillan, 1927), p. 149.

[4] F. J. Fisher, 'Commercial Trends and Policy in Sixteenth-Century England' *Economic History Review* x (1940), 95–117.

dard works on the currency and the Mints, such as the well-known volumes by Ruding, Feavearyear, and Sir John Craig.

The first criticism to be made of all these works, as will become clear in the following pages, is that they have seriously underestimated the activity of the Mints, and their fiscal importance, during the debasement years. None has based itself on the mint accounts which are extant in the Public Record Office; directly or indirectly, they have taken their figures of the coinage from the (incomplete) accounts printed in the preface to volume xix, part i, of *Letters and Papers of the Reign of Henry VIII.* All have written as though, throughout the period, only one Mint, that in the Tower of London, was active. In fact, in order to cope with the rush of activity which the debasement of the coins and the monetization of despoiled Church plate provoked, six other Mints were opened or reopened: a second establishment in the Tower; two other metropolitan Mints, at Southwark and in Durham House in Strand; and three in the provinces, at Canterbury, York, and Bristol. The value of the currency issued by these Mints and the revenue they earned for the royal coffers after their establishment in or after 1545 must be added to those of the permanent establishment in the Tower, of which alone previous historians of the debasement have taken note. Naturally, this misapprehension as to the volume of the debased coinage, even had there been no other shortcoming, would in itself have vitiated the occasional attempts of earlier writers to undertake economic analyses of the effects of the debasement, such as Feavearyear's comparison of changes in the level of prices with what he supposed to have been the changes in the magnitude of the supply of money.[1]

This failure of modern historians to search the records—one can more readily here exonerate Ruding, whose old work remains in most respects by far the best, as well as the most readable, account of the coinage—is the more surprising in that numismatists have long ago worked upon and published many of the details of the extant mint records. Thus, for example, a series of articles by Symonds half a century ago had already drawn attention to the documentary evidence for the coinages of the first four Tudors,[2] while another article dating

[1] A. Feavearyear, *The Pound Sterling* (2nd edn., Oxford, Clarendon Press, 1963), pp. 60–1, 68–9.

[2] H. Symonds, 'The Documentary Evidence for the English Royal Coinages of Henry VII and Henry VIII', *British Numismatic Journal*, 1st Series x (1913), 127–71; 'The English Coinages of Edward VI', ibid., 2nd Series i (1915), 123–67;

from 1929 actually printed tables showing the amounts of bullion coined from 1377 to 1550.[1] The numismatists, naturally enough, interested themselves only in the more technical details of the coinage and in the level of activity of the Mints; they did not translate quantities of bullion into value of output, still less go on to ask any of the questions which it would have been natural for economic historians to consider. Still, the latter have no cause to feel proud of their failure to follow up, or even to notice, this lead.

The more serious deficiencies, however, of earlier studies of the Great Debasement are those which are reflected in an inadequate treatment of both the economic mechanisms and the economic consequences of the alterations in coinage. Many of the pages which follow will have to be devoted to an attempt to understand more clearly what determined the level of mint output, and through what mechanism changes relating to the currency exercised an influence on, for example, the foreign exchanges and the volume of exports. This attempt will be seen to involve both theoretical reasoning and empirical inquiry. It also proved necessary to seek to improve our knowledge of changes in the volume of exports during the debasement period. The Exchequer records at the Public Record Office and a few other sources have in fact yielded information which considerably enlarges our knowledge of this subject, though unfortunately still leaving it much less complete than with respect to the period up to about 1545, for which the Enrolled Customs Accounts exist and have been investigated by Professor Carus-Wilson and Miss Coleman.[2] In the event, it seemed necessary to go a little further even than this. The impact of the Great Debasement on England's exports could only be assessed with any confidence in the light of a survey of their trends in the pre-debasement period. Such an exercise has been greatly facilitated by the recent publication by the two scholars referred to of statistics culled from the Enrolled Accounts, and the opportunity has been taken to rearrange some of the material with which the industry of Professor Carus-Wilson and Miss Coleman has provided us in a way which permits a reappraisal of commercial trends in the sixteenth century up to the time of the Great Debasement.

'The Coinage of Queen Mary Tudor, 1553–1558; Illustrated from the Public Records', *British Numismatic Journal*, 1st Series viii (1911), 179–201.

[1] G. C. Brooke and Miss E. Stokes, 'Tables of Bullion coined from 1377–1550', *Numismatic Chronicle*, 5th Series ix (1929), 27–84.

[2] E. M. Carus-Wilson and Olive Coleman, *England's Export Trade 1275–1547* (Oxford, Clarendon Press, 1963).

The reader will realize that this part of the argument of the present study resembles a re-examination of the interpretation of commercial trends in the early and mid sixteenth century as presented in the justly famous article on the subject by Professor F. J. Fisher.[1] It will appear in due course that the present writer has been led to conclusions which differ in some respects from those of the article referred to. It may therefore be as well to state here, to avoid misunderstanding, that this monograph was not conceived originally, even in part, as a critique of Fisher's interpretation of sixteenth-century commercial trends, and that in so far as his article was in this writer's mind during the writing of this monograph, it figured there as an inspiration and as a starting-point rather than as an object of attack. 'Commercial Trends and Policy in Sixteenth-Century England' is one of a series of what I have elsewhere described as 'brilliant pioneer articles' for which we are indebted to Professor Fisher. No historian of the period needs to be reminded how much we owe to these articles. But it is in the nature of pioneer works that they call for, and provoke, subsequent revision; and in part the findings of this essay could be viewed as a modest revision, in one particular area, of Fisher's path-breaking and influential work.

At all events it needs to be borne in mind that the present essay in no sense pretends to offer a balanced and systematic view of all economic aspects of the Great Debasement. It is a specialist study, organized around a specific and fairly narrow problem, which leaves many important economic aspects and consequences of the debasement on one side. A really comprehensive economic appraisal of the Great Debasement still remains to be made; but in the meantime the interested economic historian will certainly benefit by putting Mr. Challis's important contributions[2] alongside the findings of the present study.

If the present study has a narrower aim than that of presenting a systematic economic reappraisal of the Great Debasement in all its aspects, in another respect it has perhaps a wider interest. There seems no reason to doubt that many of the economic relationships here suggested, such as those between changes in mint equivalent and seignorage on the one hand and mint output on the other, or

[1] Fisher, op. cit.

[2] C. E. Challis, 'Southwark Mint 1545–1551', *British Numismatic Journal*, xxxiii (1964), 135–40; 'The Debasement of the Coinage, 1542–1551', *Economic History Review*, 2nd Series xx, no. 3 (1967), 441–66.

between mint regulations and the foreign exchanges, hold *mutatis mutandis* for other periods—hold, indeed, throughout the period in which full-bodied coins of gold or silver constituted the bulk of the circulating medium. The theory of mint affairs and of the foreign exchanges offered in this work, a theory worked out largely by deductive reasoning but held to be validated by the explanatory power which it appears to confer on the investigator of the Great Debasement, should therefore prove useful to economic historians who wish to concern themselves with monetary and allied topics in any part of the medieval and early modern periods. It may reasonably be claimed that our theory will prove useful to such scholars, not only because it is thought to be presented more systematically and clearly than by previous writers (most of whom, indeed, do not appear to have been consciously seized of any 'theory' at all), but also since parts of it, such as the discussion of the determinants of the foreign exchange rate, are novel. I should add that I have myself published at least one earlier study based on a theory of the economic relationships involved which I should now wish to modify. It is hoped, therefore, that the reader may be able to find in this study something of more general value than the reinvestigation of the Great Debasement which is its direct purpose, necessary and overdue as that may nevertheless have been.

2

THE DETERMINANTS OF MINT SUPPLY

THE main aim of this chapter is to analyse the factors which determined the level of activity at the Mints. Before attempting this task, however, it may be useful to recall very briefly some of the more relevant features of the monetary system of the period.

In Tudor England prices were reckoned, as at the present day, in pounds, shillings, and pence. This was 'money of account'. *Real* money, the actual circulating medium, consisted predominantly of gold and silver coins which were rated or tariffed at specified sums in the money of account. In some countries there were no actual coins corresponding to any of the units of the 'money of account', but in England silver pennies had formed part of the circulating medium for many centuries. Shillings, on the other hand, were not minted until the sixteenth century, and there was no coin called 'pound', nor any silver coin of that value (though there were gold 'sovereigns' which usually circulated at a value of one pound).

What I have just referred to as gold and silver coins were not actually made of fine (or pure) gold and silver, but had a small admixture of relatively worthless base metal or alloy. The coins were fabricated at the Mint, which was a royal office. In earlier centuries there were Mints belonging to the Church or to private individuals of standing, and in some parts of Europe this was still the case in the sixteenth century. But by our period the King had established a monopoly of minting in England which was complete save for the work of the counterfeiter and for the issue by tradesmen of 'tokens', or coins of small value and usually of very restricted circulation intended to facilitate everyday transactions in small sums. For most of our period there was only one Mint in England, which was housed in the Tower of London, but during the debasement additional Mints were opened or reopened to cope with the rush of coinage.

The Mint undertook to buy gold and silver from anyone offering those metals to it, payment normally being made in coin of current issue, that is in coin newly fabricated and made according to the standards of weight and fineness in force for the time being. The price payable was fixed for each metal as a certain sum, in money of account, for the pound of fine gold or silver; if metal of some lower degree of fineness was tendered—that is, gold or silver admixed with some alloy—the price was correspondingly reduced. The King exploited his monopoly and aimed to make the Mint an office which not only covered the costs of its own operation but yielded a profit for him. This he did by exacting 'seignorage', a deduction of a specified sum for each pound of gold or silver worked into coin. In simple terms, the mint price was equal to the value of the collection of gold or silver coins into which the pound of fine gold or silver could be fabricated, having regard to the mint standards in force, *less* the deduction made for seignorage. The costs of the Mint, including the salaries and wages of the officers and workmen, were supposed to be met out of seignorage, the balance if any remaining to the King as a profit. Since the fixing of mint standards and of the rate of seignorage were matters falling within the royal prerogative, any profits accruing from the Mint constituted a form of non-Parliamentary revenue, which at times made it a doubly attractive source to tap.

The factors which influenced the quantity of gold and silver offered to the Mint will be analysed in detail in the pages which follow, but one way of increasing this quantity, and, therefore, the level of mint activity, was by 'debasing' the coinage. This meant fabricating the pound of gold or silver into a larger sum than previously, or to put it another way, reducing the gold or silver content of a coin having a specified value in terms of money of account. Since, other things being equal, the yield of seignorage increased *pari passu* with the level of mint activity, it can be seen that the monarch had a direct fiscal incentive to 'debase' the coinage. His temptation to do so was, however, offset by a number of disadvantages of such a policy, amongst which were the unpopularity which tampering with the coinage normally engendered and the fact that debasement was inflationary and might in the long run provoke an increase in the price level which would leave the Crown worse off, in real terms, than before. In the short run, however, debasement often increased royal revenue, and it was frequently resorted to in continental countries, though, as we have seen, the Kings and Queens of England were usually able to avoid the temptation to alter mint standards for fiscal ends.

'Debasement' is actually a loose term, or rather a loosely used term, for while it should properly apply to only one of the three methods by which the relationship between gold and silver and money of account could be altered, in practice—as in the 'Great Debasement' which is the subject of this study—it is often applied indiscriminately to all three. The three methods referred to were: (*a*) to reduce the weight of the coins; (*b*) to reduce the degree of fineness of the gold/alloy or silver/alloy mix from which they were struck (that is, to mix in more base metal with each pound of the precious metal); (*c*) to leave the physical characteristics of the coins unchanged, but to rate or tariff them at a higher valuation in terms of money of account. All of these methods implied that a given weight of fine gold or silver, fabricated into coin, was equivalent to a larger sum in money of account than previously; but the first two methods accomplished this by reducing the gold or silver content of a coin of given denomination, such as a golden half-sovereign or a silver shilling, while the third left the gold or silver content of such coins unchanged but valued them more highly in terms of money of account. Strictly speaking, the word 'debasement' should properly be used only for the second of these practices, which alone involved a deterioration in the purity of the metal used for coining. Contemporaries usually employed the valuable word 'enhancement' to refer to the third, that is rating coins at a higher valuation, and I shall borrow this term in my own exposition. Unfortunately, I know of no one English word, either sixteenth century or modern, which is commonly used to denote the first practice; contemporaries usually spoke of 'making the coins lighter', or some such phrase. There were equally, of course, three methods of 'improving' or 'restoring' the coinage, that is by making coins heavier, by using less base metal in the mixture, or by reducing the money-of-account valuation of coins of a given description.

What is commonly called the 'Great Debasement' was in fact a progressive increase in the valuation of fine gold and silver in terms of money of account in which all three practices were combined in varying degrees. Coins were made lighter; they were made 'baser'; and (though only in the case of gold coins) their valuation was enhanced. Equally, when the debasement finished and the coinage was 'restored', all three possible methods of accomplishing this were used to some degree. These changes will be examined in detail later in this book: for the present, enough has been said about the general monetary background, and we can turn to discuss the factors which influenced the quantity of gold and silver offered to the Mint and, therefore, of new coin struck.

It is perhaps only slightly uncharitable to say that many existing discussions of mint prices, seignorage, and the like are obscure to the point of making it difficult to see why, in the view of their authors, changes in the level of mint activity occurred. Not only older writers such as Ruding but more modern scholars like Feavearyear have written, now of the value of the mint price of fine silver or of sterling silver, now of the weight in grammes of certain particular coins; they have expressed the rate of seignorage sometimes in absolute terms, sometimes as a percentage of what we shall later christen the mint equivalent, and so on. The confusing presentation of the evidence of which such inconsistencies are typical has made it difficult for readers to grasp the mechanics of what is in essence a fairly simple matter. This chapter attempts to cut through this tangle and to present the facts in a quite novel format which, it is hoped, will facilitate an understanding of some of the determinants of mint activity, not only during the Great Debasement, but throughout the period during which full-bodied gold and/or silver coins constituted the bulk of circulating medium.

We begin by drawing the reader's attention to Table I, which presents the essential facts relating to the silver coinage in the period under consideration. (Table II offers similar data for gold coins.) Following column (1), which simply delineates the various periods concerned, we have, it will be seen, seven columns of figures. The first of these, column (2), gives the fine-silver content in ounces and pennyweights of a pound Troy of the mixture out of which newly-minted coins were fabricated in the period in question. (The alloy made up the balance of each pound weight.) The degree of fineness of each issue can, of course, be expressed as a fraction of fine silver by placing the figure in column (2) as the numerator and 12 as the denominator (there being 12 ounces in the pound Troy). Thus, for example, coins of the 1542–4 issue were made from a mixture containing 10 ounces of fine silver and 2 of alloy, and coins of this issue (if faithfully made) could be said to be $\frac{10}{12}$ fine. This was the first issue of 'debased' coins, that is coins containing less than the traditional silver content of 'sterling' silver. Such 'sterling' silver had been issued prior to 1542, when, as we see, the mixture had contained 11 ounces 2 pennyweight (dwt.) of fine silver and 18 dwt. of alloy (there being 20 pennyweight in the ounce Troy). 'Sterling' coins were therefore $11\frac{2}{20}/12$, or $\frac{37}{40}$ fine.

TABLE I

The silver coinages, 1526–1560

(1)	(2)	(3)	(4)	(5)	(6)	(7)	(8)
		Actual fineness			*Fine silver*		
Starting date	*Fineness*	*Total*	*Seignorage*	*To merchant*	*Mint equivalent*	*Seignorage*	*Mint price*
	oz. dwt.	£ *s. d.*	£ *s. d.*	£ *s. d.*	£ *s. d.*	£ *s. d.*	£ *s. d.*
1526	11 2	2 5 0	1 0	2 4 0	2 8 8	1 1	2 7 7
May 1542	10 0	2 8 0	8 0	2 0 0	2 17 7	9 7	2 8 0
Apr. 1544	9 0	2 8 0	8 8½	1 19 3½	3 4 0	11 7	2 12 5
Apr. 1545	6 0	2 8 0	1 0 0	1 8 0	4 16 0	2 0 0	2 16 0
Apr. 1546	4 0	2 8 0	1 9 4	18 8	7 4 0	4 8 0	2 16 0
Apr. 1547	4 0	{2 8 0	1 6 8	1 1 4	7 4 0	4 0 0	3 4 0
		{2 8 0	1 5 4	1 2 8	7 4 0	3 16 0	3 8 0
Apr. 1549	6 0	{3 12 0	1 18 0	1 14 0	7 4 0	3 16 0	3 8 0
		{3 12 0	1 16 0	1 16 0	7 4 0	3 12 0	3 12 0
July 1550	6 0	{3 12 0	1 12 0	2 0 0	7 4 0	3 4 0	4 0 0
		{3 12 0	1 13 0	1 19 0	7 4 0	3 6 0	3 18 0
Apr. 1551	3 0	3 12 0	2 2 0	1 10 0	14 8 0	8 8 0	6 0 0
Oct. 1551	11 1	3 0 0	1 0	2 19 0	3 5 2	1 1	3 4 1
Aug. 1553	11 0	3 0 0	1 5½	2 18 6½	3 5 5	1 7	3 3 10
Aug. 1557	11 0	3 0 0	1 6	2 18 6	3 5 5	1 7½	3 3 9½
Nov. 1560	11 2	3 0 0	1 6	2 18 6	3 4 10	1 7½	3 3 2½

NOTES. (1) Data taken from indentures, or similar instructions to mint officials, where surviving, or from mint Accounts. Indentures or alternative sources of information can be found as follows:

(1526) Harleian MSS. 660, fol. 62.
(1542) E. 101/306/2.
(1544) Hughes and Larkin, op. cit., no. 228 (pp. 327–9).
(1547) E. 101/306/3.
(1549) CPR Edward VI, ii. 303–4.
(1550) (gold only) CPR Edward VI, iii. 345.
(Oct. 1551) Add. MSS. 18759, fols. 69v ff.
(1553) E. 101/307/1.
(1557) CPR Philip and Mary, iv. 194–5.
(1558) CPR Elizabeth I, i. 68–70.
(1560) E. 101/307/1.

(2) There were occasional minor variations in the rate of seignorage and of mint prices (but not of mint equivalent) at some of the provincial Mints.

(3) There was a small issue of 8 oz. silver in 1549 at Canterbury with a mint equivalent of £7. 4*s*. 0*d*. and mint price of £3. 4*s*. 0*d*. This issue was probably struck also at Tower II.

In columns (3), (4), and (5) are shown, respectively, the face value of the collection of coins into which each pound Troy of the mixture was cut; the amount deducted by way of seignorage; and the amount left over to pay the person tendering silver to the Mint. (Column (3) minus column (4), therefore, equals column (5).) Thus for example each pound weight of the mixture $\frac{5}{6}$ fine which was used between 1542 and 1544 was cut into 48 testons (or shillings), 144 groats (4*d*. pieces), or proportionately larger numbers of smaller

TABLE II

The gold coinages, 1526–1560

(1) Starting date	(2) Fineness	(3) Actual fineness: Total	(4) Actual fineness: Seignorage	(5) Actual fineness: To merchant	(6) Fine silver: Mint equivalent	(7) Fine silver: Seignorage	(8) Fine silver: Mint price
	c. *gr.*	£ *s.* *d.*	£ *s.* *d.*	£ *s.* *d.*	£ *s.* *d.*	£ *s.* *d.*	£ *s.* *d.*
1526	23 3½	27 0 0	2 9	26 17 3	27 16 5	2 10	27 13 7
	22 0	25 2 6	3 0	24 19 6	27 8 2	3 3½	27 4 10½
May 1542	23 0	28 16 0	1 4 0	27 12 0	30 1 0	1 5 0	28 16 0
Apr. 1544	23 0	28 16 0	1 4 0	27 12 0	30 1 0	1 5 0	28 16 0
Apr. 1545	22 0	30 0 0	2 10 0	27 10 0	32 14 6½	2 14 6½	30 0 0
		30 0 0	1 19 0	28 1 0	32 14 6½	2 2 6½	30 12 0
Apr. 1546	20 0	30 0 0	4 10 0	25 10 0	36 0 0	5 8 0	30 12 0
		30 0 0	4 0 0	26 0 0	36 0 0	4 16 0	31 4 0
Apr. 1547	20 0	30 0 0	1 0 0	29 0 0	36 0 0	1 4 0	34 16 0
Jan. 1549	22 0	34 0 0	1 0 0	33 0 0	37 1 10	1 1 10	36 0 0
Dec. 1550	23 3½*	28 16 0	1 13 0	27 3 0	29 13 6	1 14 0	27 19 6
Oct. 1551	23 10½	36 0 0	2 9	35 17 3	36 3 9	2 9	36 1 0
	22 0	33 0 0	3 0	32 17 0	36 0 0	3 3½	35 16 8½
Aug. 1553	23 10½	36 0 0	4 0	35 16 0	36 3 9	4 0	35 19 9
Aug. 1557	23 10½	36 0 0	4 0	35 16 0	36 3 9	4 0	35 19 9
Jan. 1559	23 10½	36 0 0	4 0	35 16 0	36 3 9	4 0	35 19 9
	22 0	33 0 0	4 0	32 16 0	36 0 0	4 4½	35 15 7½
Nov. 1560	23 3½	36 0 0					
	22 0	33 0 0					

NOTE. Sources as in Table I, note 1.

* The account of the Southwark Mint, the only Mint to strike gold of this issue, gives the fineness as 23 c. 10½ gr.

coins. The face value of the collection of coins made out of each pound weight of this mixture was therefore £2. 8*s.* 0*d.*, of which 8 shillings was then deducted as seignorage, leaving £2. 0*s.* 0*d.* to be paid out to the person offering the silver.

Columns (6), (7), and (8) relate respectively to the same three concepts, but show the total face value of the coins fabricated, the amount deducted as seignorage, and the amount paid out to the public for each pound weight *of fine silver*. The values are arrived at by multiplying the sums in columns (3), (4), and (5) by the reciprocal of the fraction denoting the fineness of the issue. Thus, each pound weight of the mixture used in the 1545–6 issue was cut into £2. 8*s.* 0*d.* (48 testons, and proportionately). Since this mixture was $\frac{6}{12}$ fine, each pound weight of it consisting of 6 ounces of fine silver and 6 of alloy, a pound of fine silver would have sufficed to make £4. 16*s.* 0*d.* (£2. 8*s.* 0*d.*$\times\frac{12}{6}$) of newly minted 6 oz. coin. Similarly with columns (7) and (8).

Column (8) thus represents the price, in newly minted coin, which would be paid by the Mint to the person tendering one pound weight of fine (12 oz.) silver. Anyone tendering silver of any lower degree of fineness received correspondingly less for it. It seems natural to appropriate to the values shown in this column the term 'mint price'. If, however, we pre-empt this term for use in referring to column (8), in what form of words are we to signify the values shown in column (6), which, to repeat, represent the face value of the collection of coins represented by a pound weight of fine silver *before* deduction of seignorage? (Just as column (3) minus (4) equals (5), so naturally column (6) minus (7) equals (8).) There seems to be no accepted term for the concept conveyed by this column; here I shall suggest, and henceforth use, the term 'mint equivalent'. A higher mint equivalent thus represented a lower fine-silver content, and vice versa.

Armed with an understanding of Table I, we now turn to ask: what would induce private citizens to sell silver, either coined or in the form of bullion, to the Mint? Or, more specifically, what would induce them to offer more when the mint price was increased? It is sometimes suggested that debasing the coinage is akin to trickery, the subject being 'deceived' into selling coin or bullion by an increase in the mint price which, the fact of an adulteration of the fineness of the coin being unknown to the seller, conceals from him that in reality he may be receiving not more but less intrinsic value in return. There is an element of truth in this, in so far as the information contained in columns (2) to (7) inclusive of Table I was normally not published. All the public would know, or at any rate would be told by the authorities, concerning the coinage was the following: first, certain coins would be described and proclaimed current (i.e. legal tender) at such and such values; and secondly, the mint price of fine silver (column (8)) would be publicized. It would, of course, be perfectly easy to weigh a collection of coins so described and in doing so ascertain the value of column (3). But it is impossible to calculate the values of any of the remaining columns from a knowledge of those for columns (3) and (8) alone. Knowing the values for columns (2), (3), and (8), all the others can easily be calculated; so they can if we know (3), (5), and (8) or (3), (6), and (8). But the information placed at the disposal of the public by the authorities denied them knowledge of any columns other than (3) and (8). They did not know, in particular, the fineness of the coin nor how much the authorities held back as seignorage. Hence an increase in the mint price *might* reflect a reduction in the rate of seignorage; but equally, for all the subject knew, it might be combined with an *increase* in the rate of seignorage, the fine-gold or silver content being reduced so as to make this possible.

On its own, however, this is a jejune theory of debasement. It fails to indicate where an additional supply of bullion came from in response to an increase in mint price. It fails indeed to explain why coin or bullion was sold to the Mint at all, considering that so long as seignorage was levied (and the fact that it was—that the Mint was a profit-making office—was always of course perfectly well known, and not least in time of debasement) the person selling to the Mint always got back a smaller quantity of silver (in coined form) than that which he handed over. And above all, it fails to meet the objection that, though the authorities might seek to conceal from the public knowledge of all our columns save (3) and (8)—and they did not, indeed, directly divulge (3)—the others could not in practice long be kept secret. For one thing, there were always gold- and silversmiths capable of assaying coin, of estimating column (2), that is to say, by direct analysis. This was particularly important in respect of coins used in overseas trade, where foreign experts could be expected promptly to assay, if domestic ones did not, the fine metal content of new issues. A second and simpler device (though one costing money) was to take a sample of newly minted coins back to the Mint for recoining. Anyone doing so would find, for example, that he needed £7. 4*s*. 0*d*. of any of the silver coins issued from April 1546 to early 1551 to be credited with a pound weight of fine silver (for which he would be repaid, in coin of the same intrinsic worth, amounts varying from £2. 16*s*. 0*d*. at the beginning of this period to £4. 0*s*. 0*d*. in the second half of 1550). This would reveal to him the value of column (6). Knowing either (2), (3), and (8) or (3), (6), and (8), the whole scheme, as we have seen, is then determinate.

More or less complete knowledge of the whole truth concerning the coinage could, then, never be concealed for long; and glancing at the long period between April 1546 and March 1551 during which the mint equivalent of fine silver remained unchanged at £7. 4*s*. 0*d*., and assuming (which is surely legitimate) that contemporaries were shrewd enough to discount, during a period of wholesale debasement, the possibility of any unheralded improvement of the quality of the coinage, it seems impossible to invoke deception as a satisfactory explanation of the apparent readiness of the supply of silver to respond to the step-by-step increases in mint price which, as we see, were promulgated during those years. Our theory of mint activity, in short, must be one capable of accommodating a more sophisticated public awareness, a more rational behaviour on the part of the Mint's suppliers, than the doctrine of deceiving the public can allow for. This theory we now attempt to offer.

Gold and silver, the scarcer raw materials out of which coinage was fabricated, could come from a variety of sources. Broadly, we may distinguish three: the unworked metal, whether mined within the country or imported; gold and silver previously worked into artefacts other than coins (e.g. plate and ornament) and now melted down for coining; and gold and silver previously worked into coins (whether domestic or foreign) and now melted down for recoining.

It will be convenient to dispose first of the first two cases, which are relatively simple. Unless pieces of uncoined gold and silver circulated as *de facto* currency at values equal to or higher than those which they would command if coined, and except in so far as it was desired to hoard them for future use, we could expect the precious metals either to be put to some industrial or artistic use, or to be brought to the Mint for coining. Gold and silver were hard and expensive to come by, and there was no point in incurring the trouble and expense of acquiring them unless they were to yield some utility, whether direct (as when used for plate or ornament) or indirect (as when worked into coins which conferred purchasing power on their possessors). Gold and silver newly mined or acquired for example by piracy were therefore normally minted or put to some industrial or artistic use, except in so far as they were required for hoarding. This was the fate, also, of foreign gold and silver coins unless they had either a *de jure* or a *de facto* circulation in the host country at a face value at least equal to that which they would command if sold to the Mint and coined into the domestic currency.

The extent to which gold and silver were put to industrial or artistic uses rather than coined was the outcome of a familiar assortment of demand and supply factors. Amongst the most important of the latter was the *real* mint price of the precious metals. We say *real* mint price to draw attention to the fact that what one needs to have regard to is the changing purchasing power represented by the mint price, whether this in money terms changed or not. If, during a period of debasement, an increase in the mint price was accompanied by an equiproportional rise in the level of prices, the real mint price in this sense remained unchanged, and the strength of the temptation to melt down and monetize for example silver plate remained *ceteris paribus* unchanged also. If, however, prices did not rise, or rose less than proportionately, the temptation to divert the precious metals from industrial or artistic use (and probably from hoards) to coinage was thereby increased. The economist might say that the opportunity cost of using gold and silver for non-monetary purposes had increased, thus shifting the supply curve for gold and silver in such cases upwards and to the left.

All this is very obvious. The forces determining the temptation to remint existing coins, however, call for rather closer examination, and it is particularly important to be clear about them, both because coin already in circulation was normally the major source of supply of the precious metals to the Mint during a debasement, and because, as we shall see, such reminting of former issues affected the volume and characteristics of the supply of money in ways which were important in other contexts, for example in determining the level of the foreign exchanges. To the task of analysing these forces we now therefore turn.

Our starting-point is the assumption that, most of the time at least, coins were accepted in everyday transactions at what we shall call their 'fiat value'—the value imposed upon them by Government decree—rather than at their intrinsic (or some other) value. That this was usually so is plain to the student of monetary history in the early modern period. An impressive illustration occurs when we find coins of different intrinsic values (that is, containing different quantities of fine gold or silver) circulating side by side at the same fiat value. An instance of this was provided by the silver coinage in the later years of the debasement period. Between their issue in 1551 and Elizabeth I's recoinage in 1560–1 base 3 oz. testons circulated alongside testons of the 1546 to 1551 issues despite the fact that the fine-silver content of the 3 oz. coins was only half that of the 4, 6, and 8 oz. coins issued in the preceding years. That they did so is proved not only by the fact that they survived, but by the consideration that when Elizabeth's advisers, recognizing the lower silver content of the 3 oz. issue, reduced them in 1560 to *half* of the face value of their 4, 6, and 8 oz. predecessors, the public, to the Government's discomfiture, was unable to distinguish the 3 oz. coin, and experts had to be sent out into the provinces to identify and place a distinctive stamp on these extra-base coins.

It is worth pausing to ask ourselves *why* coins should circulate at a fiat value different from their intrinsic value. This was partly because the first was fixed by law. The way in which the influence of the law would be brought to bear can be shown in a couple of examples. Suppose that in a period of debasement a debtor offered to satisfy his creditor by paying his debt in old, pre-debasement coins which he proposed should be valued for purposes of the transaction in accordance with their intrinsic value rather than their fiat value. The creditor would clearly have an incentive to refuse this offer; while the debtor would have no case in the courts against an action for recovery of debt if his only defence was that he had offered payment in coins so valued. A creditor, on the other hand, offered satisfaction in the form of current coins tendered at their fiat value, would enjoy no support from the law if he insisted that having regard to their gold or silver content these coins should instead be valued, for purposes of repayment, at some value less than their current value; while the debtor, clearly, would have an incentive to resist his creditor's suggestion. The law was thus on the side of fiat value rather than intrinsic value; the strength of its influence in this direction would no doubt reflect the political stability and respect for the law characterizing the society in question.

Convenience, however, was probably a more general and often a more powerful influence making for acceptance of coins at their fiat value. For coin to circulate at any other value would require agreement between both parties to each transaction, and if such agreement were not forthcoming, the party feeling himself to be aggrieved by the proposed value would have the law on his side. The only other objective basis for reaching agreement would seem to be the intrinsic value of the coins as determined by the amount of fine gold or silver contained in them. This would require that in each transaction the fine metal content of each coin should be estimated by multiplying the weight of the coin by its estimated degree of fineness. Clearly this would involve intolerable inconvenience in handling coins of small denomination.

However, occasions did arise when certain coins tended to circulate in accordance with their intrinsic rather than their fiat value. Broadly speaking, such an outcome was most likely in the following circumstances: (*a*) when the gap between intrinsic value and fiat value was exceptionally wide, as during a major debasement; (*b*) in the case of coins of large denomination (especially the more valuable gold coins), where the inconvenience of piece-by-piece assessment of intrinsic value was less conclusive, because of the greater value of the pieces, and in view of the probably greater financial sophistication of those whose business led them to use such coins in their transactions; (*c*) if the coins in question formed only a small part of the total circulation. It may be suggested that a combination of these factors should be invoked, for instance, to explain the tendency of certain gold coins to circulate in England in the later 1540s at values in excess of their fiat values—a phenomenon to whose reality literary evidence, as well as inference from the mint records, testifies.

We return to our assumption that coins were mostly accepted in everyday transactions at their fiat value. This being so, under what circumstances would it be profitable to remint existing coins? First, so far as the private citizen was concerned, this would be the case whenever the *current* mint price exceeded the mint equivalent of the *old* coins already in circulation. Under such circumstances the citizen could increase his purchasing power by taking a collection of the old coins to the Mint to be reissued. For instance, anyone into whose possession sixty-four 9 oz. testons of the 1544–5 issue came would hold in his hands a pound weight of fine silver; for the mint equivalent (of the pound of fine silver) of that issue, as column (6) of Table I shows, had been £3. 4*s*. 0*d*. But given the assumption with which we started this paragraph, these 64 testons would confer only £3. 4*s*. 0*d*. of purchasing power on their owner; whereas by taking them to the Mint he could, from late 1548 onwards, get £3. 8*s*. 0*d*. (rising, in 1550, to £4. 0*s*. 0*d*.) in 4, 6, or 8 oz. coins in return for the pound of fine silver which they contained.

Besides the assumption mentioned in the last paragraph, this conclusion actually depends also on a number of minor conditions, such as: that costs of collection and delivery were sufficiently small; that the period of waiting between delivery at the Mint and repayment was not so long as to outweigh (in interest forgone) the profit expected; that the old coins in question were sufficiently close in actual fine-metal content—wear and adulteration notwithstanding—to the intrinsic value to which their original mint equivalent pointed. A more sophisticated version of the law could easily be devised to meet these additional requirements, but for our present purposes the essence of the matter is that existing coins tended to be reminted on private account when their mint equivalent was less than the mint price of the current issue, provided that the assumption of circulation of both issues at fiat values held good.

This, however, solves the problem satisfactorily only so far as minting on private account is concerned. For the Government (more accurately, perhaps, for the monarch) the matter is somewhat different, in that seignorage constituted a second source of profit (that is, beyond that arising from the excess of new mint price over old mint equivalent). From April 1547, for example, during the minting of 4 oz. coins, the mint price of fine silver was raised to £3. 4*s*. 0*d*.—the same figure as the mint equivalent of the 9 oz. coins issued in 1544–5. To the private citizen, then, there would be no incentive at that time to bring in 9 oz. coins, unless he could find some which were considerably overweight. But for the Government there would be a strong incentive to remint any such coins which came into its possession, since £4 was taken in seignorage, from April 1547, for each pound weight of fine silver used for the minting of 4 oz. silver coins.

In reality, of course, the amount levied by way of seignorage was irrelevant to the profitability of reminting on Government account—all that mattered was that the new mint equivalent should exceed the old by a margin more than sufficient to cover the costs of the operation. Thus whereas the first approximation to a general precept in regard to the supply of gold or silver to the Mint by the private citizen is 'recoin whenever current mint price exceeds mint equivalent of the coins proffered', an equivalent formula applicable to reminting on Government account would be 'recoin whenever current mint *equivalent* exceeds mint equivalent of the coins proffered'—since the Government would reap the benefit of the difference either, as did the private supplier, through a new mint price higher than the old mint equivalent, or through an increased seignorage (or, of course, some combination of the two).[1] Thus, whereas the distribution of mint equivalent between seignorage and mint price was, or could be, vitally important to the incentive to remint on private account, it was irrelevant so far as the strength of Government's incentive to do so was concerned. We have to remember, however, that the work of the Mint itself involved costs which were met out of seignorage, the King keeping only the *net* profits. In addition, therefore, to the costs of reminting on private account referred to above (such as interest forgone and costs of collection) one has to take into account in considering reminting on Government account such costs as the payment of the staff of the Mint and the price of the alloy. The level of these costs per pound of fine silver coined varied

[1] Feavearyear (op. cit., p. 60) clearly fails to recognize that it might be profitable for Government to remint on its own account even when it did not pay to do so on private account.

substantially not only with changes in prices and wages but with the level of mint activity, being relatively high in quiet times and low when the Mint was busy, because of the incidence of relatively inelastic overheads. But during the very busy debasement years mint costs per pound of fine silver coined were relatively low in comparison with rates of seignorage, which always exceeded £3 per pound of fine silver from April 1546 onwards, and reached £8. 8*s*. 0*d*. during the 3 oz. issue of 1551.

Glancing back at columns (6), (7), and (8) of Table I, indeed, one might be inclined to wonder why private reminting should have played any role at all during the debasement period, considering that the figures seem to suggest throughout so powerful an incentive for reminting earlier issues, as they were successively superseded, on Government account.

The answer is that certain circumstances conspired to reduce the Government's opportunity to remint old issues itself, despite its incentive, indeed to some extent in proportion to its incentive, to do so. In the first place, Government could never get its hands on more than a fraction of the money in circulation at any one time, since the proportion of the national income represented by central Government revenues, though not known to us with any precision, was clearly small. Secondly—and this certainly applied with particular force during the fiscally difficult years of the mid sixteenth century—Government's finances were often insufficiently healthy to permit it the luxury of a gap between receipt of revenue and its channelling into the various avenues of expenditure, a gap which the reminting of any coins promising to yield a profit would necessitate. Finally—and this may perhaps have been the most important consideration—there is every reason to believe that, as far as possible, those owing money to the Government (indeed, to anyone) would pay as far as possible in the most debased type of coin (that is, that having the highest mint equivalent) available. Not to do so—to use instead the best silver or gold coins in one's possession to pay one's taxes—would clearly be irrational and would be seen by any financially sophisticated person to be contrary to his own best interests. (And it is probable that in the mid sixteenth century a higher proportion of Government revenue than at the present day was paid by financially sophisticated people.) Thus Government could never get its hands on even that proportion of better coins, that is of those holding out the expectation of greatest profit on being reminted, which its share in the national income made theoretically possible. At the same time the incentive to taxpayers to deny it this opportunity rose *pari passu* with the wish of Government to enjoy it, since the same circumstance —the gap between old and new mint equivalents—simultaneously determined the strength both of incentive and of wish.

We can readily understand, then, that despite the large profits which reminting on Government account promised, as revealed by the sharp upward progression of the mint equivalent shown in column (6) of Table I, the continued activity of the Mints even during the Great Debasement depended on coaxing a continuing supply of precious metals from the private citizen. That this in fact was the case is clear from even a cursory examination of the history of the Mints over that period. Thus although the mint equivalent of £7. 4*s*. 0*d*., which ruled from April 1546 to early 1551, was high enough to make it extremely profitable to remint on Government account *any* of the preceding issues of silver coin, yet as this period of five years progressed the private citizen had to be persuaded to go on supplying by successive reductions in the rate of seignorage and increases in mint price. These manœuvres, as we have seen, would have been *irrelevant* to the incentive to remint on Government account, and therefore unnecessary, had this been capable on its own of exhausting the whole supply of raw material latent in earlier issues. More, we note in the instruments authorizing reductions of the rate of seignorage during this period phrases which confirm the reasons for them which we have deduced from general principles: Sharington, for example, of the Bristol Mint being authorized in the Commission of 20 March 1546 to give the subject 4*d*. an ounce more for fine silver 'for the better furnyture' of his Mint;[1] Peckham, the High Treasurer of all the Mints, permitted in the Commission of 4 May 1549 to increase the mint price from 5*s*. 8*d*. an ounce to 6 shillings 'if the same cann no better chepe be hadd'.[2] Despite all this, and the continuation for some five years of a financial incentive for Government to remint, *inter alia*, the silver issue of 1545–6, plenty of those coins remained in circulation, as we shall see, when for the first time it became profitable to remint them on private account with the 3 oz. issue of 1551. Thus Government was forced to recognize, neither for the first nor the last time, that not everything which would have been

[1] See Sharington's account, E. 101/302/30.

[2] See the account of Martin Bowes, Under-Treasurer at Tower I, where dealing with the coinage of 6 oz. silver Oct. 1549 to June 1550: E. 101/303/5.

profitable was necessarily possible; and we must resist the temptation to suppose, in the light of the greater profits which the reminting of earlier issues brought to Government, that the profits it held out to private citizens were of no, or indeed of inferior, importance in determining the level of mint activity.

This discussion of the determinants of mint supply has so far been couched in terms which would apply either to the gold or to the silver coinage, yet the reader may have remarked that the illustrations have been drawn entirely from the latter. This is not accidental. Though all the relationships so far analysed do indeed hold *ceteris paribus* for gold as well as for silver, an additional complication must now be introduced which, so far at least as this period is concerned, appears to affect chiefly or only the yellow metal. This is the complication which arises from relaxing the assumption that the joint forces of law and of convenience were adequate to ensure that coins should always circulate at their fiat value and at no other.

It is more often necessary to relax this assumption in regard to the gold coins than to the silver coins, because the gold coinage was more likely than the silver to meet two of the three specifications listed on pages 17–18 as being likely to lead to that assumption being invalidated—namely, that the coins in question should be pieces of large denomination, and constitute the smaller part of the circulation. In addition, of course, both gold and silver coins in this period met the first specification, that postulating an appreciable gap between fiat value and intrinsic value. We therefore find a tendency during the Great Debasement for gold coins to be traded at times at values in excess of their fiat value.

The authorities to some extent recognized and attempted to meet this problem. On two occasions the fiat values of the gold coins minted according to the standard of 23 carat 3½ grs. prevailing up to May 1542 were raised (or, to use the useful contemporary expression, 'enhanced') to make them more realistic, having regard to the fine-gold content of these coins, in comparison with the newer sovereigns minted according to lower standards after 1542. Thus the angels minted according to the indenture of 16 May 1542[1] were valued at 8*s.* rather than at 7*s.* 6*d.*, their fiat value since 1526, and two years later a proclamation[2] was published which raised all angels and the

[1] E. 101/306/2.

[2] Paul L. Hughes and James F. Larkin, *Tudor Royal Proclamations* (Yale U.P., 1964), vol. i, no. 228 (pp. 327–9).

older gold coins by a similar fraction (one-fifteenth). Five years later a further proclamation,[1] which began by complaining of the export of gold coins, 'especially the old coin of royals, angels . . . and other of that or like standard', enhanced these older coins again, this time more substantially. The angel went from 8*s.* to 9*s.* 8*d.*, the royal from 12*s.* to 14*s.* 6*d.*, or an increase of 5/24ths.

In some respects the interpretation of these proclamations is puzzling. That of 1544, for instance, appears to have enhanced only the 'angel' gold minted before 1542 to a standard of 23 carat 3½ grs., ignoring the much larger quantity of 'crown' gold of 22 carat minted between 1526 and 1542. The proclamation of 1549, again, raised angels and royals by 5/24ths while explicitly *confirming* the original face value of sovereigns and half-sovereigns, notwithstanding that in the 1542 mint indenture provision was made for the minting both of sovereigns and of angels at the *same* mint equivalent. Perhaps the bulk of the angels to which the 1549 proclamation referred were still 'old' coins (most of which must have survived from pre-1526 issues); or perhaps the preference abroad for angels, which had been minted since 1465, was so marked as to lead to their being the preferred gold for export even when their intrinsic value was no more or actually somewhat lower than that of less well-known gold coins like the crowns and half-crowns minted after 1526.

Another puzzle is the face value of angels between 1542 and 1544. The last sentence of the proclamation attributed to 16 May 1544 provides for debts contracted 'before the first day of this present month of May' to be paid at the rate of 7*s.* 6*d.* the angel; yet the indenture of 1542 clearly shows that newly minted angels of the 23-carat standard were to be issued at 8*s.* 0*d.* Much the most acceptable solution of this and other difficulties would be to suppose that at some stage this proclamation has been wrongly dated, and that it really dates from 16 May 1542. (The numismatist Symonds felt sure that this was the correct solution.) The fact that the day and the month are identical with those of Henry VIII's indenture with Bowes and Rowlett (16 May 1542)—a 364 to 1 against chance, if a coincidence—lends plausibility to such a conjecture, but I know of no diplomatic evidence which would support it. In the tables I compromise by assuming in my calculations that angel gold circulated at 7*s.* 6*d.* the angel in 1542, rising in a linear trend to 8*s.* 0*d.* the angel two years later.

[1] Ibid., no. 326 (pp. 449–51).

However this may be, what is important from our present point of view is that when a coin came to circulate at a value in excess of its original fiat value, whether it did so *de jure* (as above) or simply *de facto*, the mint equivalent attached to that issue was proportionately raised. One might say that the increase in the purchasing power of that coin reduced the incentive to remint it. It also reduced the incentive to export it, and this meant that changes in *de facto* face value might alter the specie export point (that is, the level of the foreign exchange rate at which it became profitable to settle debts abroad by exporting gold or silver rather than remitting money by exchange). Therefore, in applying the foregoing theory of mint supply to the minting of gold, we have to bear in mind that so far as reminting angel gold coins is concerned, the original mint equivalent must be multiplied by the factor representing the difference between their original fiat value and their *de facto* face value (that is, the value at which they actually changed hands amongst merchants) from time to time. We might christen the resulting figure the '*de facto* mint equivalent'.

The question then arises: was the face value of the older gold coins increased only in the two discrete steps imposed by proclamation in May 1544 and in April 1549? Or did it creep up gradually in between these official enhancements, in response perhaps to the increasing mint equivalent of the sovereigns, and other gold coins which were currently being issued from the Mint, and to the increasing scarcity value which the older and better gold coins commanded? The evidence seems to support the conclusion to which reasoning would tentatively point, that is, the second of these alternatives. Indeed, the wording of the proclamation of 11 April 1549 seems in itself to make this quite clear, for it speaks of goldsmiths and others as being 'used now of late . . . to buy and sell the King's majesty's coin, of and for higher price than it is by his majesty's proclamation rated and valued . . .'. The document has the air of making no secret of the fact that the enhancement of certain gold coins by 5/24ths was really merely an official endorsement of a change in their *de facto* face value which had already been accomplished.

Unfortunately, the evidence does not help us to know just how the *de facto* face value of these older gold coins did progressively rise between the dates of these two proclamations. Yet *some* assumption on this point is called for to facilitate the calculation, for example, of the specie export point and the silver/gold ratio. The following procedure has in fact been adopted. First, it has been assumed that the new fiat values established for angels and like gold coins by the proclamations of 1544 and 1549 corresponded very closely with their *de facto* values immediately prior to these proclamations. This assumption is made not merely because there is some presumption that the proclamations, in this respect, were intended to legalize a *de facto* situation, but also because the *de facto* mint equivalents for the old gold coins which these new fiat values implied were at each date close to the actual mint equivalents of the new coins issued from the Mint in the immediately preceding periods. That is to say, the new fiat values established by these proclamations were almost exactly what one would have expected had the older gold coins circulated at that premium above gold coins of recent issue which their intrinsic superiority justified.

What of the *de facto* value of these coins between the dates of the two proclamations? It is tempting to say that, throughout, the value at which they circulated could be expected to have risen in the same proportion as the intrinsic value of newly minted sovereigns declined. But in fact this is inherently unlikely, for it would be some time before the true value of newly minted gold coins became known, and before they became sufficiently numerous to serve as the basis on which older and better coins were valued. (There is no inconsistency here in pointing to the close similarity of mint equivalents of newer and older gold coins at the times of the proclamations themselves, for in May 1544 and April 1549 the mint equivalent of newly-minted gold coins had been unchanged, respectively, for two and for three years, so that there had been time for the *de facto* mint equivalents of the older gold coins, so to say, to catch up.) Moreover, had the *de facto* value of the older gold coins risen in just this fashion, there would never have been any special incentive to cull them either for reminting or for export, as in fact there seems to have been.

In default of better evidence we make the assumption—which it should be stressed is somewhat arbitrary—that between the proclamations of 1544 and 1549 the face value of those older gold coins which were not reminted followed a linear trend, rising gradually, that is, from the lower to the higher value in equal absolute increments within each equal time period. It should perhaps be added that for the purposes for which we most urgently require these values, that is, for calculating the silver/gold ratio and explaining the course of the foreign exchanges, the differences between the values pointed to by this assumption and any other values which cannot be shown to be inherently implausible are small enough not to invalidate the argument they are intended to facilitate.

TABLE III

De facto *mint equivalents of gold, 1526–1550*

(1)		(2)	(3)	(4)	(5)
		£ *s. d.*	£ *s. d.*	£ *s. d.*	£ *s. d.*
1526–42	(23 c. 3½ grs.)	27 16 5	27 13 7		
	(22 c.)	27 8 2	27 4 10½		
1542–4		30 1 0	28 16 0	27 16 5	
1544–5				29 13 6	
1545–6		32 14 6½	30 0 0 30 12 0		30 18 3
1546–7		36 0 0	30 12 0 31 4 0		32 3 0
1547–9		36 0 0	34 16 0		33 7 9
1549–50		37 1 10	36 0 0	35 17 2	

NOTE. For explanation of the columns, see text immediately following.

The effect of making these assumptions, together with that, of course, of the proclamations themselves, is shown in Table III. In this Table we reproduce in columns (2) and (3) the mint equivalents and mint prices of gold coins currently issued up to 1550, as presented already in Table II. In columns (4) and (5) we show the mint equivalents of the older gold coins of 23 carat 3½ grs. fineness, in column (4) as implied by the new fiat values imposed on them by the proclamations of 1544 and 1549, and in column (5) as calculated from the *de facto* values implied by the assumption of a linear trend increase between 1544 and 1549. The values in column (5) are separated from those in column (4) in order to alert the reader to the fact that there is a large degree of arbitrariness in the assumption underlying the former. The values in columns (4) and (5), moreover, necessarily relate to points in time, that is, they were not (on our assumption) constant over the whole periods indicated. They relate, in fact, to the initial dates of the periods in question.

In applying the principles already sketched governing the supply of bullion to the Mint, columns (4) and (5) of Table III should replace column (6) of Table II in respect of those of the older gold coins which came to circulate at *de facto* values corresponding to their intrinsic value rather than their fiat value. A similar substitution is called for, as will appear, in calculating for example the silver/gold ratio. The application of Tables I to III, however, to the actual history of the coinage in the debasement period will not be attempted until some further aspects of our theory of mint supply have been explored.

We now turn to examine briefly a relationship specially likely to affect the supply of the precious metals to the Mint in periods when mint equivalents and/or mint prices of either or both metals were undergoing change: that is, what is usually called the gold/silver ratio (better, to make the order of the words correspond to the usual order of the numbers expressing it, the silver/gold ratio).

It has long been recognized—it was well recognized by contemporaries—that under a bimetallic system (and by this is intended simply a monetary system in which both gold and silver coins are legal tender) the ratio between the two metals was a factor influencing the composition of the supply of money and the role of each metal in mint activity. Of particular importance was the comparison between the ratio in one country and the ratio prevailing in the monetary systems of that country's most important trading partners. Such a comparison might reveal, for example, that in England gold was undervalued in relation to silver by comparison with the Low Countries: that the silver/gold ratio, in other words, was lower in England than in Flanders. This would give an immediate incentive for international balances (e.g. balance-of-payments residuals) to be settled by the export of gold from or the import of silver into England—thus influencing the character of the money supply and of mint activity. But particular emphasis has been laid in recent studies[1] on 'bimetallic flows' which might be set in motion when the disparity between the ratios in two countries was particularly pronounced. What is envisaged by this term is the situation in which the disparity between the ratios in two countries was sufficiently wide to make it worth while incurring the costs and the risks (for contravention of the laws against the export of coin and bullion was here involved) of *exporting* the undervalued metal, in order to buy in and import from another country, where a more 'normal' ratio prevailed, that which was overvalued. It can be seen that when the disparity

[1] J. D. Gould, 'The Royal Mint in the Early Seventeenth Century', *Economic History Review*, 2nd Series v, no. 2 (1952), 240–8; B. E. Supple, 'Currency and Commerce in the Early Seventeenth Century', ibid. x, no. 2 (Dec. 1957), 239–55.

between the ratios was great enough to justify such action, the size of the flows need not be restricted to that necessary to settle balance-of-payments residuals for the nation as a whole, or even, in so far as they were distinct, the trading balances of importing and exporting groups separately. The supply of coins of one of the metals might now be treated as an ordinary exportable commodity; and the whole of it could disappear in a relatively short space of time. In view of its illegal character, it is not surprising that such a type of international exchange tended to leave fewer records than ordinary trade; but it is usually easy enough, where a bimetallic flow of large dimensions was in progress, to find literary evidence which at least apprises us of its existence, if not of its dimensions. It is possible, too, to find corroboration in the mint records; for, naturally, the same circumstances which caused the flow would also generate a telltale disparity in activity in coining the two metals—that which was undervalued ceasing, save for what we shall shortly christen 'compulsory deliveries', to be brought to the Mint, the supply of the other being swollen by the offer of metal whose import had been financed by the export of its undervalued counterpart.

One of these bimetallic flows occurred in the later stages of the Great Debasement, when the realm was largely denuded of gold coin which was exported to pay for the importation of silver. The timing of this flow was not, however, quite what we should have expected in view of the course of the silver/gold ratio as computed by some earlier writers. Oman, for example, in his article on the currency in the period 1526–60,[1] suggests that the silver/gold ratio fell rapidly to about 10·4:1 in 1542, about 6·8:1 in 1545, and to only 5:1 in 1546. 'Gold', he writes, 'disappeared wholesale'—apparently referring to the year 1545–6. And well it might—for, at such ratios, the disincentive to mint and incentive to export gold would be so great that it would be retained in circulation only, one would think, at the point of a gun.

Yet the literary evidence seems to point rather to 1549 and, particularly, to 1550 and early 1551 as the period during which a substantial flight of gold developed, and we shall see that it is precisely in these later years that we need to invoke the export of gold, viewed as one half of a bimetallic flow, in order to explain the big silver coinages of those years. Even more conclusive is the evidence of the mint accounts, which show not only that gold continued to be coined

[1] Oman, op. cit., pp. 177–80.

in substantial quantities until late 1548, but that in the early years of the Great Debasement its output rivalled and even exceeded that of silver.[1] Even allowing for the fact—which we cannot doubt—that part of this activity in gold represented the working of what we shall call 'compulsory deliveries' (such as the coining of confiscated Church plate), it seems impossible not to believe that the spontaneous sale of gold to the Mints continued well beyond the period at which Oman's ratio would require us to suppose it to have become hopelessly uneconomic. It is here submitted that this apparent paradox demonstrates the need for a modification of the 'theory' of bimetallic flows, and this revision we now proceed to offer.

It will be seen that the silver/gold ratios used by Oman, as quoted above, are based upon a comparison of mint equivalents for the two metals: for example, Oman's 'about 6·8 : 1' for 1545–6 is $\frac{\text{£}32.\,14s.\,6\tfrac{1}{2}d.}{\text{£}4.\,16s.\,0d.}$; his 5 : 1 for the period from April 1546 onwards is $\frac{\text{£}36.\,0s.\,0d.}{\text{£}7.\,4s.\,0d.}$. For some purposes computing the silver/gold ratio by dividing mint equivalent for fine silver into mint equivalent for fine gold might be justified. But not for the purpose of explaining bimetallic flows. Consider what a merchant seeking a profit by promoting such flows did. He exported, say, gold coins of a certain issue, the fine-gold content of which (except in so far as reduced by wear) would be indicated by the mint equivalent pertaining to that issue. These he then exchanged for silver coins, or with them he bought silver bullion, in some foreign country at the more 'normal' ratio prevailing there. This silver or these silver coins he then imported to be coined, or to be put to some other use. If the Mint was enjoying an ample supply of silver bullion, we may take this fact as demonstrating that the value of silver in other uses was, at the most, not appreciably higher than its value as bullion brought to the Mint. The values, then, appropriate in computing the silver/gold ratio would be, not the mint equivalents in both cases, but the mint *equivalent* of the exported metal (in this case gold) and the mint *price* of that imported (in this case silver).

This conclusion, however, still calls for a little modification. *Which* gold coins would be exported? In so far as issues of different intrinsic values circulated side by side at the same face value, the

[1] See below, pp. 48–9.

better coins (that is, those with the lowest mint equivalent) would be exported, for their purchasing power would be greater abroad than, but only the same at home as, that of inferior coins of the same denomination. (This is the so-called 'Gresham's Law'.) In the situation, however, where face-value equivalence of coins of differing intrinsic values had broken down, that is, where better coins circulated *de facto* at or approaching the value suggested by their relative intrinsic superiority, the preference for them shown by the merchant culling coins for export would disappear, since their internal and external purchasing powers would now be in the same ratio as that of inferior coins of the same fiat (but lower *de facto*) valuation. Now as we saw above, this divergence between the *de facto* and the fiat value of certain coins can be represented as in columns (4) and (5) of Table III by what one might call, to preserve the consistency of terminology, *de facto* mint equivalents. We shall not err, therefore, in either event if we compute the silver/gold ratio, not on the basis of the mint equivalent of newly minted coin, but on the *de facto* mint equivalent of the best coin of that metal in circulation—which might, or might not, be the same figure.

The formula we propose to use here to compute the silver/gold ratio is, then:

$$\frac{\textit{de facto}\text{ mint equivalent of best gold coins}}{\text{mint price of silver}}.^{1}$$

This differs from the usual formula,

$$\frac{\text{mint equivalent new gold}}{\text{mint equivalent new silver}},$$

(as employed, for example, by Oman), in two respects: the numerator takes account of the possibility that certain superior coins might circulate at a fiat value which under-represented their intrinsic value; the denominator takes account of the exaction of seignorage. It may be noted that in normal times, when mint equivalents had undergone no recent changes and when the rate of seignorage was low, there would be little difference between the ratios suggested by the traditional formula and by that propounded here. During the Great

[1] More accurately, this is the appropriate formula, and the formula employed, when what was in question was the export of gold and the import of silver. When the silver/gold ratio was *above*, rather than *below*, the international level (so that the bimetallic flow was reversed), the appropriate formula is:

$$\frac{\text{mint price gold}}{\textit{de facto}\text{ mint equivalent best silver}}.$$

TABLE IV

Silver/gold ratio, 1526–1551

	Calculated according to the formula											
	De facto *mint equivalent best gold coins* ÷ *Mint price silver*				*Mint equivalent gold* ÷ *Mint equivalent silver*				*Mint price gold* ÷ De facto *mint equivalent of best silver coins*			
	£ s. d.		£ s. d.		£ s. d.		£ s. d.		£ s. d.		£ s. d.	
1526–42	27 16 5	÷	2 7 7	11·7	27 16 5	÷	2 8 8	11·4				
1542–4	28 14 11		2 8 0	12·0	30 1 0		2 17 7	10·4				
1544–5	30 5 10		2 12 5	11·6	30 1 0		3 4 0	9·4				
1545–6	31 10 7		2 16 0	11·3	32 14 6½		4 16 0	6·8				
1546–7	32 15 4		2 16 0	11·7	}							
1547–Oct. 1548	34 6 3		3 4 0	10·7	} 36 0 0		7 4 0	5·0				
Oct. 1548–9	35 11 1		3 8 0	10·5	}							
1549–50	37 1 10		3 12 0	10·3	}							
July 1550	37 1 10		4 0 0	9·3	} 37 1 10		7 4 0	5·2				
Sept. 1550	37 1 10		3 18 0	9·5	}							
July 1551	68 7 0		6 0 0	11·4								
Oct. 1551	36 0 0		3 5 2	11·0					36 0 0	÷	2 8 0	15·0

NOTES. (1) *De facto* mint equivalent of gold 1542–4 to Oct. 1548–9 has been taken as the mean of the values for the terminal dates of each period (see Table III, cols. 4 and 5). For the other periods, the mint equivalent of newly minted gold has been used.

(2) For 1526–42 and 1542–4, values relate to angel gold rather than crown gold, despite slightly higher mint equivalent of former, in view of its greater acceptability abroad.

Debasement, however, the differences were greater, particularly as far as the denominator was concerned, so that the need for the greater accuracy claimed for the present formula is more keenly felt.

Table IV presents silver/gold ratios for the period 1526 to 1550 calculated according to the present and to the traditional formulas. The sharp divergence of the two series in the later 1540s will be noted, and it is contested that the superiority of the present formula is demonstrated by its far greater explanatory power in accounting for changes in the level of the gold output of the Mints and its greater consistency with what we know of bimetallic flows in that period. Specifically, the new formula postpones the fall in the silver/gold ratio to the period from late 1547 onwards, and generates values significantly below the international average only from 1549 onwards. It thus avoids the interpretative difficulty which Oman's figures provoke, namely that of explaining the continuation of large-scale minting of gold at least until late 1547. It can be seen, too, that the new formula puts the lowest value of the silver/gold ratio about July 1550, which is exactly the date which the mint records and literary evidence combine in pointing to as experiencing the sharpest incentive to a bimetallic flow.

Our 'theory of mint supply' is now almost complete. Like many similar economic theories, it undertakes to explain certain economic data (in this instance, figures of mint output) by assuming that light will be thrown on the matter when we can demonstrate how such and such lines of action can be explained in terms of the economic self-interest of those pursuing them. It postulates, that is, the pursuit of gain as the only behavioural assumption, and shows how, given that, the particular economic restraints and opportunities of the time led to the actions in question. It remains, however, to point out that not all of the bullion worked into coin by the Mints was delivered so to say 'spontaneously', in accordance that is with the economic self-interest of individuals or of the Government. Some of it represented compulsory deliveries, as when plate confiscated from the religious houses by Henry VIII was turned over to the Mints conveniently re-established for the purpose at Canterbury, York, and Bristol. The Government's debtors, too, could be induced at times to pay off their debts in the form, for example, of deliveries of plate to the Mint. Mary's dower, ninety-seven chests of Spanish treasure which arrived at the Tower for coining into English money in late 1554, was another striking example of a compulsory delivery.

In a recent article I hazarded the then very tentative suggestion that the monetization of silver and gold in plate and ornament might have constituted an important element of mint activity during the reign of Elizabeth I, and might thus help to resolve the difficulty of reconciling the apparently unfavourable balance of payments which, as some believe, characterized most of that reign with the appearance of a substantial increase during it of the supply of money.[1] On this point the present study throws no new light. But what is certain is that during the Great Debasement there was a substantial monetization of plate and ornament from the suppressed religious houses through what we have termed 'compulsory deliveries'. It might be possible for an assiduous researcher, consulting a wider range of records than the present writer, to form a reasonably precise impression as to the relative magnitude of the contribution which this particular source made to the supply of raw materials to the Mints during the Great Debasement. Here we assert only that it was clearly substantial, particularly perhaps in the case of the strategically placed Canterbury Mint. ('Compulsory deliveries' may help to explain not only why Canterbury was the most active of the Mints outside London, but how it came about that the mint price paid for bullion at the provincial Mints, and especially at Canterbury, several times lagged behind that which had to be offered in order to attract it to the London Mints.)

Compulsory deliveries can sometimes then account for variations in the level of mint supply which the theory sketched above seems powerless to explain. In the Great Debasement period they do some what cloud the issue at times, but not, fortunately, to the point of making it impossible to see our theory in action. We now turn, therefore, to analyse the actual coinage history of the period with the help of the tools fashioned in the foregoing pages.

[1] Gould, 'The Price Revolution Reconsidered', loc. cit., pp. 253–4.

3

THE OUTPUT OF THE MINTS

IT has already been noted that during the Great Debasement seven Mints were operating, for longer or shorter periods. The purpose of opening additional Mints was to cope with the rush of coining which was beyond the physical capacity of the permanent establishment in the Tower, and in the case of the three Mints outside London, to facilitate geographically the collection of the raw material and dispersion of the finished product. We have seen, too, that failure to take note of the activities of these additional Mints has vitiated the quantitative treatment of the Great Debasement by earlier writers.

Fortunately, records survive in the Public Record Office which permit an almost complete reconstruction of the output of the various Mints.[1] Most of the accounts are to be found where we should expect them, amongst the Pipe and Audit Office sections of the Exchequer Records. Their long neglect at the hands of economic historians is the more surprising because, as we have seen, these accounts were known to and worked on by numismatists in the early decades of this century. The accounts for the important Mint at Southwark, which was responsible while it was open for the largest output of any Mint save the permanent establishment at the Tower, are not to be found in the same place; but happily Sir John York, the Under-Treasurer there, took the unusual step of having his accounts enrolled by the Exchequer, and they survive amongst the Memoranda Rolls of the King's Remembrancer. In this relatively unfamiliar and badly calendared location they eluded the search of the present writer, but happily not that of Dr. Challis, to whose resourcefulness we owe our valuable knowledge of Southwark's activities.[2]

It is easy to calculate from these accounts the face value of the coinages issued in the periods and by the establishments covered by them. The accounts were of course concerned with the Mints' incomes

[1] Details are given in the notes to Table V.

[2] C. E. Challis, 'Southwark Mint', loc. cit.

and expenditures, rather than with their level of output as such, and the face value of the coinage struck in a given period does not normally appear. However, since the major item of revenue was seignorage, the accounts do show the quantities of each metal coined and the degree of fineness (column (2) of Tables I and II) together with the rate of seignorage exacted (column (4)). The total seignorage arising from each stream of activity was then calculated and shown. Often the accounts also refer, for each coinage, to the Mint price of fine gold or silver (column (8)), and they show the date of the indenture or other instrument under the authority of which seignorage was levied. From this information the aggregate face value of the various coinages struck in each period can be calculated by multiplying the weight of the mixture worked (the weights shown in the accounts relate to the silver/alloy or gold/alloy mix, not to the fine-silver or gold content) by the face value of the coins into which each pound of such mixture was minted (column (3)). The resulting figures are shown in roman type in Table V. (The other information on the accounts, of course, provides evidence as to the values shown in Tables I and II which is welcome even when it is only confirming what we know from other sources.)

Unfortunately, there are still some gaps in our knowledge of mint output during the Great Debasement as revealed by the sources just described. In the first place, there are no accounts at all for Durham House, which, however, was the most short-lived and the least important of the Mints (it operated only for a few months in 1549, and one may presume that it proved superfluous because during its lifetime the other Mints were not working at full capacity).[1] Secondly, the accounts for the second establishment at the Tower (numismatists,[2] so far as I can discover, have been in error in thinking that there were ever *three* Mints working simultaneously in the Tower) cover only the period from the start of its coinages in July 1545 to the end of 1547; from then until the end of its coining in 1551 accounts are missing. Accounts are also lacking for the permanent Tower Mint between the end of October 1550 and the start of 3 oz. silver coinage in spring of the following year. Finally, the York accounts are not extant beyond March 1550, though this Mint possibly

[1] Cf. H. Symonds, 'Edward VI and Durham House', *Numismatic Chronicle*, 4th Series xiv (1914), 145–6.

[2] The view referred to was espoused, for example, by H. Symonds in his valuable articles.

continued to do a little (and unimportant) work until about the end of Edward VI's reign.[1]

It is possible, however, to fill some of these gaps with approximate estimates. For 1548 this is best done from the accounts of Sir Edmund Peckham, High Treasurer of the Mints, which survive for the whole period May 1544 to May 1554.[2] The office of High Treasurer was established to co-ordinate the activities of the Mints during the period when several were in existence, and to act as accounting superior to the individual establishments, which were placed under the control of Under-Treasurers. In the earlier part of the debasement there was a close correspondence between the sums Peckham is shown as having received from the various Mints, and the amounts which in the preceding period those Mints levied by way of seignorage. It is therefore possible within tolerable limits of accuracy to infer from Peckham's accounts the seignorage generated, and thus the coinage output, at the second Tower establishment (which I shall call Tower II) during 1548.

Unfortunately Peckham's accounts cannot be relied upon in this way after 1548. This is partly because the various Under-Treasurers got too far behindhand in their payments; partly because they were more and more often called upon to dispose of part of their profits other than by handing them over to Peckham; and partly, so far as 1549 is concerned, because the operation which we shall call 'converting testons' disturbed the hitherto fairly close relationship between seignorage levied and profits paid over to Peckham. Fuller details of the method used to infer 1548 output from Peckham's accounts, and of the difficulties which prevent its being employed after 1548, are given in Appendix B. Fortunately it is possible from other evidence to make guesses which enable us to fill one of the other gaps—that relating to the output of 3 oz. silver from Tower II during 1551—so that the only gap of any significance remaining is the output of 6 oz. silver at the two Tower Mints in the last five months of that particular coinage (November 1550 to March 1551). These 'estimated coinages' are shown in Table V but are printed in italic type and enclosed within brackets. That table includes three columns of totals:

[1] This is suggested by the Commission to Gale, Under-Treasurer at York, dated 20 Feb. 1553 (CPR Edward VI, v. 186), and by the payment by Gale to Peckham on 19 May 1554 of a certain sum due upon 'determination' of his account on the last day of February, 1554.

[2] E. 351/2077, 2079, 2080.

one which sums the outputs of the various Mints for those periods where the accounts of all active Mints are extant; a second which totals outputs for those periods for which it has been possible to fill the only gaps in the accounts by estimates made as described above; and a third relating to those periods during which there are gaps which cannot be so filled.

Readers who are troubled by the possibility of error in the estimates made by the writer to fill the gaps in the mint accounts may be comforted if they reflect that the amounts thus inserted are small, save with respect to the 3 oz. coinage of 1551, in comparison with the output calculated direct from mint accounts. They should also be warned against placing unbounded trust even in the much larger part of Table V for which the figures *are* calculated from surviving mint accounts. This general caution is called for, not because of any obscurities in the evidence on which this part of the table is constructed, and not it may be hoped because of the frailty of the writer's arithmetic, but simply because of the unusually low standards of administrative skill and honesty which seem to have prevailed in the control of the Mints during the debasement period. This decline in the quality of administration is only what we should have expected on general grounds. Any period of rapid expansion of a particular economic activity tends to depress qualitative standards, by placing a premium on quantitative performance rather than on maintenance of quality and by calling for an expansion of personnel which brings inexperienced and underskilled workers into the production line. The effect is the same, whether it is a case of the sharp increase in mint activity during the 1540s or of the rapid expansion of factory industry during the first Soviet Five-Year Plans. Nor was this the only reason for the relaxation of standards in the Mints during the Great Debasement. An even more insidious influence was the sharply increased temptation to dishonesty in the recording of and accounting for production to which the phenomenal increase in seignorage subjected the senior mint officers. This increase meant that officials who made coins which they did not account for could pocket the inflated sums which the King levied on each pound of metal struck. That they did not always succeed in resisting this temptation is clear from the most notorious and widely discussed lapse from probity, that of Sir William Sharington, first Under-Treasurer of the Bristol Mint.[1]

[1] H. Symonds, 'The Bristol Mint of Henry VIII and Edward VI', *Numismatic Chronicle*, 4th Series xi (1911), 331–50.

Table V

The output of the mints, 1542–1552

A. GOLD

Period	*Fineness*	*Tower I*	*Tower II*	*Southwark*	*Bristol*	*Total* (1)	*Total* (2)	*Total* (3)
	c. gr.	£	£	£	£	£	£	£
1.7.1542 to 31.3.1543	23	15,581	—	—	—	15,581		
1.6.1544 to 31.3.1545	23	165,917	—	—	—	165,917		
1.4.1545 to 31.3.1546	22	206,070	69,300	96,750	—	372,120		
1.4.1546 to 31.3.1547	20	107,580	37,470	111,690	6,390	263,130		
1.4.1547 to 30.9.1547	20	107,190	18,750	83,640	6,120			
1.10.1547 to 31.12.1547	20				—			
1.1.1548 to 30.9.1548	20	132,330	(*16,500*)	69,630	—			434,160
1.10.1548 to 31.12.1548	20		*		—			
1.1.1549 to 31.10.1550	22	48,212	*	28,560	—			76,772
1.11.1550 to 31.12.1550	22	*	*		—			
1.1.1551 to 31.3.1551	23 10½	*	*	2,765	—			2,765
1.4.1551 to 30.9.1551	23 10½	—	*		—			
1.10.1551 to 31.3.1552	22	3,597	—	—	—	3,597		

B. SILVER

Period	*Fine-ness*	*Tower I*	*Tower II*	*South-wark*	*Durham House*	*York*	*Canter-bury*	*Bristol*	*Total* (1)	*Total* (2)	*Total* (3)
	oz.	£	£	£	£	£	£	£	£	£	£
1.7.1542 to 31.3.1544	10	52,927	—	—	—	—	—	—	52,927		
1.6.1544 to 31.3.1545	9	149,287	—	—	—	—	—	—	149,287		
1.4.1545 to 31.3.1546	6	176,155	66,173	98,047	—	48,696	51,142	—	440,213		
1.4.1546 to 31.3.1547	4	120,240	73,754	105,386	—	68,966	43,066	40,399	451,811		

1.4.1547 to 30.9.1547	4	27,871	19,406	16,716	—	25,056	13,651	16,411			
1.10.1547 to 31.12.1547	4	87,365	(*28,710*)	80,179	—	18,336	63,871	—		397,572	
1.1.1548 to 30.9.1548	4				—			—			
1.10.1548 to 31.12.1548	4	14,026	*	27,982	—	1,056	20,784	—			
1.1.1549 to 31.3.1549	4	—	*		—	—					88,681
1.4.1549 to 30.9.1549	4	—	*	—	*	—	9,478	14,347			
1.10.1549 to 31.10.1549	4	—	*	—	—	1,008	—				
1.11.1549 to 30.11.1549	4	—	*	—	—	—	—	—			
1.12.1549 to 31.12.1549	4	—	*	—	—	—	118	—			118
1.2.1549 to 28.2.1549	8	—	—	—	—	—	9,024	—	9,024		
1.4.1549 to 30.4.1549	6	3,478	*	—	*	—	—	—			3,478
1.5.1549 to 30.6.1549	6	—	*	—	*	—	—	1,102			1,102
1.7.1549 to 30.9.1549	6	—	*	—	*	—	43,326	—			
1.10.1549 to 31.12.1549	6	146,297	*	27,396	—	—		—			
1.1.1550 to 30.6.1550	6		*	32,522	—	—	—	—			401,072
1.7.1550 to 31.10.1550	6	98,496	*	53,035	—	—	—	—			
1.11.1550 to 31.3.1551	6	*	*	102,272	—	—	—	—			102,272
1.4.1551 to 31.7.1551	3	80,748	(*80,000*)	92,207	—	—	—	—		252,955	
1.10.1551 to 31.3.1552	11 1/20	41,640	—	—	—	—	—	—	41,640		

C. CONVERTING TESTONS

	4	35,040	*	46,998	*	90,182	40,329	32,585			245,134
	6	78,678	*	76,167	*	—	30,654	1,938			187,437
	8	9,355	*	24,430	*	—	7,392	—			41,177

[*See notes to Table V at foot of p. 40*]

Sharington was removed from office after being implicated in the rising of Lord Seymour of Sudeley, for the financing of whose cause he worked his Bristol Mint illegally. Sharington later confessed to having issued large sums in testons without authority, to having minted clipped and underweight coins, and having burned the records and falsified the accounts. His dereliction was exposed because it had served an unsuccessful political cause. To what extent his fellow Under-Treasurers committed similar and better-concealed falsifications for motives rather more venial, in terms of Tudor public morality, than rebellion against the State, it is impossible to know with certainty. Some accounts, certainly, were not made up until long after the activity they were supposed to summarize had ceased; and the round sums sometimes received 'in determination of' an account have a suspicious air of compromise about them. It is by no means certain indeed that all the counterfeit coin which appeared in response to the temptations which high rates of seignorage held out came from abroad. Yet it is also possible to be too suspicious. It will be argued later[1] that the debased coinage was at least made faithfully close to the standards of fineness laid down from time to time in the instruments controlling the Mints. (The cynic could justly point out that

NOTES TO TABLE V

(1) Amounts calculated from mint accounts in roman type.

(2) Amounts estimated as described in Appendix B in italic type and between brackets.

(3) — signifies mint closed or inactive in issue shown.
 * signifies mint possibly active in issue shown but account missing.

(4) Total (1) sums amounts produced within period where all relevant mint accounts are extant.
 Total (2) sums amounts produced within period where gaps in accounts have all been filled by estimates calculated as described in Appendix B.
 Total (3) sums amounts produced within period where there are gaps in accounts which have not been filled by such estimates.

(5) Mint accounts are to be found as follows:
 Tower I: E. 101/302/22 (1542–4)
 E. 101/302/27 (1544–7)
 E. 101/303/5 (1547–June 1550)
 E. 101/303/7 (July–Oct. 1550)
 E. 159/331 TRINITY 41 (Apr. 1551–Mar. 1552)
 Tower II: E. 101/302/29
 Southwark: E. 159/331 TRINITY 41
 York: E. 101/296/18
 Canterbury: E. 101/302/25
 Bristol: E. 101/303/30 (1546–7)
 E. 101/303/6 (1549–50)

[1] See below, pp. 60–2.

in the light of the high rates of seignorage it would be more profitable, as well perhaps as safer, to under-record mint activity than to issue coins of somewhat less than the stipulated weight or fineness.) Further, the evidence of Elizabeth's recoinage makes clear that the levels of output suggested by the mint accounts of the debasement period are of the right order of magnitude; about as much debased coin was left, broadly speaking, as we should have been led to expect, starting from the indicated debasement output and allowing for the subsequent reminting or disappearance elsewhere of part of these issues. Thus if the evidence on output is, as a whole, suspect to a degree which makes the additional uncertainty introduced by the estimates made to fill gaps in the records a relatively easy thing to bear, yet there seems to be no warrant for rushing to the other extreme and refusing to accept the mint accounts even as evidence of orders of magnitude of the output of coinage during the debasement period.

What does this evidence point to? What modifications, in particular, to previous accounts of the level of output does it call for? We see, for example, that for the first year or two of the debasement period, when only the original Tower Mint was working, Feavearyear's figures of output[1] are correct. Thereafter his table showing output for the period up to September 1547 is correct only for the permanent Tower establishment under Sir Martin Bowes (which it will be convenient to refer to as Tower I). As a result of ignoring the existence of the other Mints which began work in or after 1545, Feavearyear greatly underestimates output for the period April 1545 to September 1547, during which silver output, for example, was probably about a million pounds rather than the less than a third of a million which he suggests. In the case of gold, the figure yielded by the mint accounts is about twice Feavearyear's £420,000. In 1548 and the first half of 1549 the level of mint activity, particularly in regard to silver, gradually declined, until by the summer of the latter year the coining of the 4 oz. silver had almost ceased and Peckham could complain to Smythe that there was little bullion left in the Mint.[2] Activity revived, as we shall see, when the Mints began turning out new and lighter 6 oz. coins with bullion partly supplied as the consequence of a 'bimetallic flow'. Feavearyear surmises, from the evidence of Elizabeth's coinage—he does not divulge his actual reasoning from this evidence—that some million pounds 'of this

[1] Feavearyear, op. cit., p. 62. [2] SP 10/7, fol. 98.

money' (presumably the 6 oz. coins) were minted from the summer of 1549 to the summer of 1551. This, curiously, seems to be a decided overestimate. The last stage of the debasement was the issue of 3 oz. silver coins in 1551, where Feavearyear takes the puzzling figure of £130,000 from the *Journal* of Edward VI. Surviving mint accounts show that Tower I and Southwark alone produced about £173,000 of 3 oz. coin; and taking the second Tower establishment into account, it is probable that upwards of a quarter of a million pounds of this coin was minted in all.[1]

In 1551 a serious attempt was made—it had been preceded by a few more futile gestures in the direction of reform from 1548 onwards —to restore the coinage to something like its original weight and purity. The indenture of October 1551[2] which authorized the striking of this reformed coinage had been preceded by proclamations[3] calling down the debased testons and smaller silver coins to one half of their previous fiat value. Unfortunately for Edward's intentions, this was not far enough. In the language of the 'theory of mint supply' which we have already sketched, the new *de facto* mint equivalent of the silver issues of April 1546 onwards was still higher (£3. 12*s*. 0*d*.) than either the mint price or the mint equivalent of the new sterling coins. Only the 6 oz. issue of 1545–6, with its lower original mint equivalent of £4. 16*s*. 0*d*. (now, effectively, £2. 8*s*. 0*d*.), was worth reminting, and the remaining silver coins of this issue doubtless constituted part of the raw material for the fine-silver coinages of the last years of Edward's reign, and perhaps of that of Mary and of the first two years of Queen Elizabeth I.

Edward's attempt to reform the coinage thus failed primarily because he did not call down the baser silver coins to a fiat value at which they could have been profitably reminted on private or Government account, and because he could not afford to subsidize their transformation into sterling silver. That intelligent contemporaries realized that this was the crux of the problem of reforming the coinage is shown by the letter of William Lane, the London merchant, to Cecil in January of 1551, in which he stated that 'to newe fyne owre base quyne from the delaye (?) cannot be done withowte more charge than may be borne of the kynge or the comons'.[4] Elizabeth

[1] For a discussion see Appendix B.

[2] Add. MSS. 18759, fols. 69v ff.

[3] Hughes and Larkin, op. cit., nos. 376 (p. 525) and 379 (pp. 529–30).

[4] Printed in R. H. Tawney and Eileen Power (eds.), *Tudor Economic Documents* (Longmans, 1965) ii. 183.

overcame the difficulty by her greater ruthlessness in depressing the fiat value of the base silver still further, much to the disgust of the poor who, without doubt, were the greatest sufferers, and by the better-contrived administrative preparations which her advisers made. But Edward's attempt at reform does not quite deserve the neglect which, by comparison with the recoinage of 1560–1, has been its fate. Still less does one feel able to endorse the claims made by Mrs. Dewar on behalf of Mary's so-called reform of 1553 (wrongly attributed by Mrs. Dewar to 1554),[1] which in fact merely repeated, with the most trifling alterations, the provisions of Edward VI's last mint indenture.

Our narrative, however, has run ahead of analysis, and it is best at this point to turn back to analyse mint output during the debasement years with the help of the theoretical framework already erected in Chapter 2.

Stages of the Debasement: (1) Silver, 1542–1551

As shown in Chapter 2, it became profitable to remint existing coins whenever the current mint price exceeded the mint equivalent of earlier issues still in circulation. (This, to repeat, (*a*) ignores such costs as those of collection; (*b*) assumes that earlier coinages still conformed to the mint equivalent at times of issue, that is, that the coins had not become excessively worn or clipped; and (*c*) assumes that the Government could impose acceptance of coins at their fiat value rather than their intrinsic value.)

In Table VI, the data on mint equivalents and mint prices already presented in Tables I and II are reproduced in simplified form, with a system of boxes and connecting lines designed to show the possibilities of reminting earlier issues on private account. In the light of this it becomes possible to distinguish several stages in the history of debasement issues. First, the silver coin will be considered.

(*a*) The first debasement of the silver coin, that is, to 10 oz. in the issue of 1542–4, offered no incentive to remint silver coins of the 1526–42 issue except on Government account, and the rate of output in this period was in fact very modest.

(*b*) From June 1544, however, the new mint price exceeded the mint equivalent of the 1526–42 issues, so that the public as well as the Government now had an incentive to treat the latter as a supply

[1] See Appendix A.

TABLE VI

Reminting of gold and silver coins on private account, 1526–60

	GOLD							SILVER								
Period	Issue	Equivalent			Price			Issue	Equivalent			Price			De facto mint equivalent after 1551		
	c.	£	s	d	£	s	d	oz.	£	s	d	£	s	d	£	s	d
1526-42	22	27	8	2	27	4	10½	11$\frac{1}{10}$	2	8	8	2	7	7			
1542-44	23	30	1	0	28	16	0	10	2	17	7	2	8	0			
1544-45	23	30	1	0	28	16	0	9	3	4	0	2	12	5			
1545-46	22	32	14	6½	30 30	0 12	0 0	6	4	16	0	2	16	0	2	8	0
1546-47	20	36	0	0	30 31	12 4	0 0	4	7	4	0	2	16	0	3	12	0
1547-48 }	20	36	0	0	34	16	0	{ 4	7	4	0	3	4	0	3	12	0
1548-49 }								4	7	4	0	3	8	0	3	12	0
1549-50 }	22	37	1	10	36	0	0	{ 6	7	4	0	3 3	8 12	0 0	3	12	0
1550-51 }								6	7	4	0	4 3	0 18	0 0	3	12	0
1551 }								3	14	8	0	6	0	0	7	4	0
October 1551	22	36	0	0	35	16	8½	11$\frac{1}{10}$	3	5	8	3	4	7			

Note The boxes and arrows show where it was possible to remint profitably on private account.

of raw material for recoining. The output of 9 oz. coins of the 1544–5 issue was in fact much larger. From April 1545 the incentive to bring in the pre-1542 coins increased with a further rise in the mint price for the 6 oz. (1545–6) and 4 oz. (1546–7) issues to £2. 16*s.* 0*d.*, which nearly doubled the margin over the pre-1542 mint equivalent.

(*c*) The adoption of a 4 oz. fineness in April 1546 with a new mint equivalent of £7. 4*s.* 0*d.* did nothing, immediately, to increase the incentive to the public to bring silver to the Mint, since seignorage was so increased as to leave the mint price unchanged. But it did of course enhance the incentive to remint earlier issues on Government account, and it gave increased scope for subsequent reductions of the rate of seignorage designed to entice a greater offer of silver to the Mint by the citizen. When in April 1547 the mint price was raised to £3. 4*s.* 0*d.* it became profitable for the first time for the public to bring in one of the issues of the debased coins, namely the 10 oz. issue of 1542–4. Then, when seignorage was reduced again and the mint price rose to £3. 8*s.* 0*d.*, it became profitable for the private citizen to deliver 9 oz. silver also for reminting.

It seems improbable, however, that much of the 9 oz. silver coinage remained to act as raw material for the 4 oz. coins after the mint price of fine silver was raised to £3. 8*s.* 0*d.* This was not done, apparently, until the last quarter of 1548 in the case of the London Mints, and until 1549 in the case of Canterbury and Bristol (York, apparently, never paid this price for its silver at all). A glance at Table V, showing the output of silver coin, reveals that by the dates in question the output of 4 oz. silver was almost exhausted anyway; only small quantities of 4 oz. coins were minted at a seignorage of £1. 5*s.* 4*d.* (i.e. a mint price of £3. 8*s.* 0*d.*). The implication seems to be that by late 1548 much of the 9 oz. silver had already been reminted on Government account, since private reminting of 9 oz. coins was not profitable until mint price rose to £3. 8*s.* 0*d.*

(*d*) By late 1548 or early 1549, therefore, the supply of silver was drying up. There were no longer many 10 oz. or 9 oz. coins to be enticed even by a mint price of £3. 8*s.* 0*d.*, and the larger 6 oz. issue of 1545–6 was not worth reminting on private account at any time before the last stage of debasement, the 3 oz. issue of 1551. But a new source of supply nevertheless opened up to provide the bulk of the raw material for the 6 oz. issue of 1549–51. (The mint equivalent of this coin was the same as that of the 4 oz. silver which preceded and overlapped with it, and also of the small 8 oz. issue struck in early 1549, the differences in the fineness of these coins being exactly cancelled out by offsetting differences in their weight.) This new source of supply arose because, as we have seen, the reductions in the rate of seignorage which brought the mint price of silver from £2. 16*s*. 0*d*. in April 1546 to £4. 0*s*. 0*d*. in 1550, the mint equivalent meanwhile remaining unchanged at £7. 4*s*. 0*d*., equally led to a fall in the silver/gold ratio, which for the first time during the whole debasement period began in late 1548 to fall appreciably below the ratio in neighbouring countries. This disparity in silver/gold ratios not only greatly reduced the inflow of gold to the Mint, but also led to a bimetallic flow in which much of the gold in circulation left the country in the course of 1549, 1550, and early 1551. Apart from the compelling evidence of the mint accounts, which show that from early 1549 onwards the previous fairly even balance of gold and silver output was replaced by a decided preponderance of silver, there is supporting evidence of this outflow of gold in the period indicated. We may therefore say that the large 6 oz. silver output which gathered momentum in mid 1549 depended to a large extent on a supply of the white metal paid for by the export of gold coins.

(*e*) Early in 1551 this source, too, threatened to dry up, for there was now no longer any substantial quantity of gold left to export, and what was left tended increasingly to circulate at values substantially in excess of the authorized values, thus of course reducing the incentive to export it. In these circumstances the advisers of the boy King conceived their last desperate round of debasement, the introduction of 3 oz. silver with a mint equivalent of £14. 8*s*. 0*d*. Coupled with this went, naturally, the levying of an extraordinarily high rate of seignorage, but even so the new mint price (£6. 0*s*. 0*d*.) was for the first time high enough to make it profitable on private as well as on Government account to bring in the earlier 6 oz. issue, that of 1545–6, the mint equivalent of which had been £4. 16*s*. 0*d*. However, the issue of 3 oz. silver was discontinued, for reasons which are somewhat obscure and not at present relevant, before this potential supply had been nearly exhausted.

Our theory of mint supply thus seems capable of accounting for most of the changes in the silver coinage and the rate of mint output of silver. We have seen how successive increases in the mint price from June 1544 to 1550 tapped the supply residing, first in the pre-1542 coins, then in the 10 and 9 oz. issues of 1542–4 and 1544–5 respectively, and finally in the 6 oz. coins of 1545–6. A passage in the

Journal of Edward VI dating from 6 September 1551[1] states explicitly that 'few or none were left of nine ounces fine', and, by failing even to mention the 10 oz. coins and those of the pre-1542 standard, implicitly confirms our reasoning that by that date virtually all of these earlier issues had been either exported or reminted into coins of baser quality.

The evidence of Elizabeth's recoinage,[2] on the other hand, confirms—and this, again, is equally what we should expect—that the base coins still in circulation in 1560 were exclusively of those issues with mint equivalents of £7. 4*s*. 0*d*. or of £14. 8*s*. 0*d*.—that is, the 4 oz. coins of 1546–9, the 6 oz. coins of 1549–50, and the very small 8 oz. issue of early 1549, on the one hand, and the 3 oz. coins of 1551 on the other. We should have expected these coins to have survived because at no subsequent date, even after the 'calling down' of 1551, did the mint equivalent or the mint price of subsequent issues exceed the *de facto* mint equivalents of these base coins. At no stage, therefore, was there any financial incentive to remint any of these coins either on public or on private account.

The only issue which calls for any more detailed explanation is the earlier 6 oz. issue of 1545–6. Even here there is no question where the supply of silver which went to the making of these coins came from. Leaving on one side what we have called 'compulsory deliveries' and the reminting of a small quantity of 1542–5 coins on Government account, it came from the melting down of pre-1542 sterling silver coins. But there *is* some question where it went to. Some part of the silver contained in the 6 oz. 1545–6 coins was reminted in the 1551 issue of 3 oz. coins—the first, as we have seen, in which the earlier 6 oz. coins could profitably be sold to the Mints by the public. But only a small part; for the whole 3 oz. issue contained but some 18,000 lb. of fine silver, whereas the 1545–6 issue had contained over 91,000 lb. of the metal. More, as we shall see, had probably been reminted on Government account during the years 1546 to 1551, and it can be estimated with some confidence that the 'converting testons' operation of 1548–9 absorbed some 31,000 lb. of these coins (that is, the equivalent of about 15,500 lb. of fine silver). It is likely, too, that some 6 oz. coins were exported during the period of low exchange rates in 1551. The remainder was probably reminted into

[1] *The Journal of King Edward VI,* Clarendon Historical Society Reprints Series ii (1884–5), p. 45.

[2] See pp. 68–9 and Table VII below.

sterling silver during the last coinages of Edward VI, and perhaps during those of Philip and Mary and of the first two years of Elizabeth's reign. Let us recall that in the summer of 1551 the debased testons were cried down (and smaller coins equiproportionally) from 1*s*. to 9*d*. and then to 6*d*. To reduce the fiat value of these coins by fifty per cent was the same as halving their mint equivalents. Even this reduction left the base coins of the 1546 and later issues too poor in silver to be worth reminting, as we have just seen. But the 1545–6 6 oz. issue, whose original mint equivalent of £4. 16*s*. 0*d*. was effectively reduced in 1551 to £2. 8*s*. 0*d*., was now worth bringing in; and those earlier 6 oz. coins which had not already disappeared did so at some time between late 1551 and late 1560, leaving Elizabeth and her advisers with the problem only of the baser issues of 1546 and onwards. It is in this way that we explain the facts that whereas there *were* some of the 1545–6 issue still in existence after the 3 oz. experiment had been discontinued, as the passage in Edward's *Journal* dated 6 September 1551 makes clear, they had disappeared by the time the base coins were reminted by Elizabeth I in 1560–1.

Stages of the Debasement: (2) Gold, 1542–1551

There seems to be a rather general belief that the Great Debasement was essentially an episode which concerned the silver coinage. It is true, indeed, that the silver coins underwent a markedly greater degree of adulteration. Their mint equivalent (which, as we have seen, is in effect the reciprocal of the fine-silver content) rose from £2. 8*s*. 8*d*. for the 1526–42 issues to £7. 4*s*. 0*d*. between 1546 and 1551, an almost threefold rise, and then doubled again to £14. 8*s*. 0*d*. in thc 3 oz. issuc of 1551. By contrast, the mint equivalent of newly minted gold coins rose only from the £27. 8*s*. 2*d*. of the 22 carat 1526–42 issues to £37. 1*s*. 10*d*. in 1549–50, an increase of only a third.

Yet if we look rather at the volume of output, gold is seen to have played a role which makes its relative neglect seem undeserved, at least in the period prior to the commencement of 6 oz. silver coinage in 1549. The value of new gold coins issued exceeded that of silver in the year 1544–5; it continued to do so, in respect of the two Tower Mints, in the following year, and lagged only a little behind silver at Southwark. Only the fact that York and Canterbury, which were not authorized to strike gold, were now contributing to the supply of new silver coins brought the total for that metal above the value of the gold output. In the following year silver for the first time took a decisive lead in the value of mint output, but it lost this again for a time after the substantial increase in the mint price of gold arising from the reduction of the gold seignorage in April 1547. From late 1548 the position seems to have been that the output of new coins of both metals declined markedly, most of the Mints devoting a considerable proportion of their time to the recoining of testons into coins of smaller denomination, an activity which had been authorized by commission in February 1548 but which did not start, except briefly at Southwark and York, until the beginning of 1549. Then, in the summer of that year, the production of the new 6 oz. silver coins began in earnest, the raw material being provided in large part (as we have argued) by a bimetallic flow which of course implied a compensating export of gold. In such circumstances, as we should expect, the minting of new gold coins shrank to very small proportions, though thanks no doubt to compulsory deliveries there was always some activity in the metal. Gold issues thus played, thanks to the fall in the silver/gold ratio, only an insignificant role in the last two and a half years of the Great Debasement, whose reputation as an episode primarily in the history of the silver coinage became for the first time justified.

How can we reconcile the large role of gold coinage up to late 1548 with the fact, already noticed, that its mint equivalent was much less tampered with than that of the silver? The case appears to be that gold coins were apt to respond more sensitively to relatively smaller proportionate changes of mint price. It was, after all, the *absolute* profit held out by the reminting of a given coin, not that profit as a percentage of the face value of thc coin, which chiefly counted; it was no more troublesome or costly to cull and present to the mint a pre-1542 angel than a 10 oz. teston (though some other costs, chiefly the cost of interest forgone if the seller had to wait an appreciable time for repayment, *would* be proportionate to the value of the coin). And since the larger gold coins were so much more valuable than the bulk of the silver circulation, even the smaller proportionate rises in their mint equivalents and mint prices might represent larger absolute increases than in those of the silver. It is probable, moreover, that gold coins responded more sensitively than silver even to a given *absolute* rise in their price. For gold coins, particularly the larger gold coins, were by and large familiar tender only amongst well-to-do people, and especially in international trade; and the greater sophistication of those whose business took place in such areas would ensure a promptness of response to marginal inducements which was absent in the world of the poor dealing only in the smaller silver pieces and in trade tokens. We have seen that between 1551 and Elizabeth's recoinage, silver coins of the 1546–51 issues on the one hand and of the 1551 3 oz. issue on the other circulated side by side at the same fiat values, despite the fact that the fine-silver content of the former was precisely double that of the latter. More, that when Elizabeth's advisers, recognizing this fact, fixed a new fiat value for the 3 oz. coins only half that chosen for their richer counterparts, 'thunlerned and uplandyshe people', as the Earl of Bedford complained to Cecil,[1] were unable to distinguish between them, and professional moneyers had to be sent out into the provinces to put stamps upon the two sorts. It is impossible to conceive of two sets (say) of gold angels, one with an intrinsic value twice that of the other, continuing for long to circulate side by side at the same fiat value; indeed, we have seen evidence already that the *de facto* face value of the older gold coins tended to rise, during the Great Debasement, in response to the reduction in the intrinsic value of newly minted gold coins, even though that reduction fell far short, proportionately speaking, of what was inflicted on the silver. And this was so partly because by and large it was not 'unlerned and uplandyshe people' who dealt in gold coins. The situation thus bore some similarities to the contrast one can observe at the present day between the financial sectors (say, the stock or foreign exchange markets) of a highly developed economy, in which dealers make (or lose) money by responding to the smallest fractional differences in quotations, and the complex of widely varying and ill-integrated interest rates which one finds in underdeveloped economies.

The relatively small (though absolutely large) alterations made to the mint equivalent and mint price of gold during the debasement years were, then, sufficient to ensure the continuation of a lively activity in reminting old gold coins. In one way, indeed, there was a more frequent inducement to remint gold than silver. This can be seen by glancing at Table VI. Applying the criteria governing reminting on private account which have already been discussed, it is evident that it would have been profitable to remint the 1526–42 issues after the mint changes of May 1542; that coins of the 1542–5 issues, in turn, could profitably be reminted into the 22 carat gold

[1] SP 12/13, fol. 127.

of 1545–6 once seignorage relating to that issue had been so reduced as to permit the mint price to rise to £30. 12*s*. 0*d*.; and, finally, that it would have paid to bring these 22 carat coins in, in their turn, when mint price rose to £34. 16*s*. 0*d*. in April 1547. Thus it was possible for the private citizen to make a profit on each of *three* successive occasions from reminting the gold originally contained in the pre-1542 coins. In the case of silver, on the other hand, only *two* such operations were possible: pre-1542 coins could profitably be reminted on private account in any debasement issue from the 9 oz. coin of 1544–5 onwards, and the 9 oz. issue could again fetch a profit by redelivery after the mint price of silver reached (and subsequently exceeded) £3. 8*s*. 0*d*. in the 4, 6, and 3 oz. issues of late 1548 onwards.

The tendency for the *de facto* value of the older gold coins to rise in sympathy with the reduction in the intrinsic value of the newer issues, a tendency twice legitimated, as we have seen, by proclamations announcing increases in their fiat value in 1544 and in 1549, does make necessary some modification of this argument in regard to some of the older, pre-1542 gold issues. If the assumptions underlying Table III are correct, such coins could *not* be profitably reminted on private account from 1544 onwards, except for a relatively brief period after April 1547 when their *de facto* mint equivalent again fell short of the mint price relating to new issues. What probably happened is that the bulk of the pre-1542 gold coins were reminted during 1542–5, a minority of the heavier coins surviving by becoming an élite currency circulating at values in excess of their fiat values. (These would be the 'old' gold coin which survived in this fashion right through to Elizabeth's recoinage.) Meanwhile the remainder of the pre-1542 coins went three times through the Mints, only to disappear in the massive gold export of Edward VI's reign.[1]

The changes in mint equivalents and prices authorized by the Commission of 16 March 1547 sustained gold output at a high level for most of 1547, the rate of output then gradually falling off in the ensuing couple of years until by the summer of 1550 possibly only compulsory deliveries were keeping the Mints active on gold at all. The more detailed chronological breakdown of gold output at Tower I which the mint accounts permit us to make shows the monthly rate of output of gold coins there jumping from £11,953 in the period April to December 1546 to £21,438 from the resumption of gold coining (at the new rates) between May and September 1547.

[1] Cf. pp. 79–80 below.

Thereafter gold output fell gradually to a monthly figure of only £1,114 in the late summer of 1550. This fall marked the virtual end of gold's role at the Mints during the Great Debasement. The continued fall in the silver/gold ratio occasioned by the successive increases in the mint price of silver imposed an increasingly prohibitive disincentive on the minting of gold and indeed inaugurated, as we have suggested, a bimetallic outflow which by the summer of 1550, at the latest, had assumed major proportions.

In such circumstances it would be natural to expect that the *de facto* value of at any rate the older and better gold coins, always favoured in overseas trade, should have gone on rising above their fiat value even after the proclamation of April 1549. Unfortunately, it is difficult to find much evidence on this point, and what little there is is not entirely easy to interpret. Thus, it is no surprise that the Government's attempt in late 1550 to reduce the fiat value of French crowns to 6*s*. 4*d*. (they had been made legal tender in England at 7*s*. by the proclamation of 4 August 1550)[1] proved unavailing, and that the Government had tacitly acknowledged this fact at least as early as the following March, when we find a warrant issued by the Privy Council for the payment of a certain sum in French crowns 'after the rate of 7*s*. 4*d*. the peece'.[2] In January 1551, indeed, the merchant William Lane had pointed out in a letter to Cecil[3] that the fiat value imposed on French crowns was being ignored in practice; they were bought up, he tells us, for 7*s*. 3*d*. and 7*s*. 4*d*., to be exported like all other gold. (Lane also asserts that in June, July, and August of the preceding year £100,000 of gold had been exported while silver flowed in.) Still, even a *de facto* value of 7*s*. 4*d*. does not suggest a runaway inflation in the value of gold coins in early 1551. The Johnson letters, on the other hand, give evidence of *de facto* values for the old English gold coins which *do* imply an absolute breakdown of fiat values by summer of the same year; for example, they state that in July 1551 (the period, significantly, when the foreign exchanges were at their lowest levels) angels could not be bought in London for 18*s*. 4*d*. whereas a few days earlier bankers had been glad to take 17*s*. 0*d*. for some 'old and very good' ones.[4] These were presumably angels of the pre-1542 issues, whose fiat value had been raised, as we

[1] Hughes and Larkin, op. cit., nos. 367 (pp. 509–10) and 364 (pp. 498–9).
[2] APC 1550–2, p. 230. [3] Tawney and Power, loc cit.
[4] B. Winchester, 'The Johnson Letters, 1542–1552' (London Ph.D. thesis, 1953), letter no. 700.

have seen, to 8*s*. 0*d*. by the proclamation of 16 May 1544 and to 9*s*. 8*d*. by that of 11 April 1549.

It is in any event necessary, one might argue, to assume that the *de facto* value of gold coins completely liberated itself, so to say, from their fiat value, merely to explain the fact that some of them survived. It is clear from numismatic evidence that some of them did so; and Stanley, Elizabeth's Master of the Mint, in attempting as a preliminary to the recoinage exercise to estimate the size of the circulation of various categories of coins, put that of 'sovereigns, half-sovereigns, angels, half-angels and crowns' at £100,000 in 1559.[1] Had the market value of such coins in England remained at their fiat value throughout 1550 and 1551, the level of the silver/gold ratio and advantage in settling international obligations by the export of gold would surely have led to the disappearance abroad of those old gold coins which had escaped earlier reminting. All that enabled a minority of them to escape this fate was the fact that, once they had become a sufficiently small and as it were élite fraction of the total circulating medium, their domestic purchasing power released itself from the constraints of fiat value and rose to a level which sufficiently offset the strong inducements operating to export them. The significance of this fact in relation to the foreign exchanges we shall examine in the next chapter.

Stages of the Debasement: (3) From 1551 to the Recoinage

It is impossible, but fortunately for our purposes unnecessary, to reconstruct in great detail the history of the currency in the last years of Edward VI and in the reign of Queen Mary. Mint accounts appear to have survived only for the permanent Tower Mint in the six months of Sir John York's control there (October 1551 to March 1552) and for two years of that of Thomas Egerton (Christmas 1553 to Christmas 1555).[2] It has generally been agreed—and the writer knows of no reason for doubting the truth of the claim—that the Mint was virtually inoperative in the later years of Mary and Philip's reign. (In September 1556 the Privy Council stopped the allowance for the diet of the mint officers 'forasmoche as there have not byn of long tyme any coynage'.)[3] We also have Stanley's account from 1 January 1559—effectively, one would suppose, the beginning of

[1] Add. MSS. 40061, fols. 11–12. [2] E. 159/41; A.O. 1/1670/497.
[3] APC 1554–6, p. 348.

Elizabeth's reign as far as the Mint was concerned—until, and including, the recoinage.[1] During all this period, mint equivalents and mint prices for both metals remained virtually unchanged at about the levels established by Edward VI's indenture of 5 October 1551.[2]

Egerton's account for 1553–5 points to the minting of some £59,000 worth of fine gold and some £138,000 of sterling (11 oz.) silver, to which should be added another £17,592 of silver coins made out of Spanish royals. The account of Sir Edmund Peckham, High Treasurer of the Mints, for April 1552 to May 1554, which also survives,[3] suggests substantial coinages between Mary's accession and the start of Egerton's surviving account. By this time, as already explained, it is impossible to use Peckham's accounts to calculate the production of coins; clearly this particular account shows Peckham receiving from the Under-Treasurer money which in fact does not all represent income from seignorage. Even excluding amounts apparently relating to the Irish coinages (excluded from the present study) and to the reworking of base coin, the amounts Peckham received from Egerton between September 1553 and the end of that year, totalling over £30,000, would have represented an impossibly large output with seignorage now at only 1*s.* 5½*d.* per pound of 11 oz. 1 dwt. silver (face value £3) and 4*s.* per pound of gold (face value £36). Nevertheless, it seems reasonable to suppose that the Mint was indeed active between Mary's accession and the following Christmas, and that it was during this interval that perhaps most of the balance of the fine gold and sterling silver coined in Mary's reign, which Stanley's 1559 estimate of the circulation put at £370,000, was struck.

Stanley's estimate, prepared in connection with preliminary considerations on reforming the coinage, is interesting.[4] He placed the value of the base coins in circulation at £1,200,000, which was nearly a third too high judging by the evidence of the recoinage (though perhaps not all the smaller base coins were actually hauled in by the recoiners' net). Most of his overestimate related to the 3 oz. coins, whose circulation he put at £300,000 instead of the indicated £123,723. His estimate for the 'best sort' of base coins (i.e. those with an original mint equivalent of £7. 4*s.* 0*d.*) was £900,000, only about an eighth too high. In addition to the base silver coins, Stanley surmised that there was some £620,000 in 'fine monies' in circulation, made up as follows:

[1] SP 65/6.
[2] Add. MSS. 18759, fols. 69v ff.
[3] E. 351/2080.
[4] Add. MSS. 40061, fols. 11–12.

	£
(*a*) Sovereigns, half-sovereigns, angels, half-angels, and crowns	100,000
(*b*) Spanish rials and pistolets and French crowns	50,000
(*c*) Fine gold and sterling silver coined under Edward VI	100,000
(*d*) The same, coined under Mary	370,000
	£620,000

The separation of (*a*) from (*c*) and (*d*) suggests that the coins referred to in (*a*) were of pre-1551 issues, some of them probably of the pre-1544 issues (though half-sovereigns, under that name, were not coined until 1544). The separation would seem to have no point were this not so; and certainly there was no sterling silver coined under Edward VI before 1551. It has been suggested already in what manner some of the earlier gold issues may have managed to survive the fall in the exchange rate and in the silver/gold ratio in 1550–1. At all events the estimate makes clear that Stanley supposed a large part of the fine-gold and sterling-silver coinages of the last years of Edward VI and of Mary's reign to have survived to 1559. While there is no reason to take his precise figures *au pied de la lettre*, it seems inconceivable that so strategically placed an official should have been completely mistaken as to the survival of many of these good coins, and we must therefore reject the suggestion of Feavearyear that in Edward's reign 'the price of silver was much too high to permit coins as fine and as heavy as his new ones to stay in circulation', and must feel, too, that his rather slighting remarks about Mary's treatment of the coinage do her something less than justice.[1] There is, indeed, nothing in our theory of mint supply to make it necessary to suppose that the fine gold and silver of these reigns should have disappeared wholesale, save in so far as they would have been the natural target if it proved necessary to resort to the export of specie for balance-of-payments reasons. The course of the exchange rate in the period in question, however, and the comparative absence of the usual literary evidence which was normally generated by massive specie flows combine to make it seem unlikely that a great deal of good coin was lost in this way. Some, of course, was gained, as when Mary's dower arrived at the Mint in October 1554. Indeed, it seems clear that we need to assume a reasonably adequate circulation of good coins

[1] Feavearyear, op. cit., pp. 73, 74.

precisely in order to be able to explain the level and overall stability of the exchanges in this period.

The money supply (leaving aside foreign coins) between 1551 and the recoinage therefore consisted of three sets of coins minted to substantially different standards. There was in the first place 'fine' gold and silver, largely but not we may think wholly minted in and after late 1551, the older and better of these coins being rated at a fiat value enhanced from the original one so as to offset their greater intrinsic value. Secondly, there was 'base' silver, constituting the bulk of the circulation in terms of face value, which consisted largely (especially after the 'converting testons' operation of 1549–50) of groats and smaller coins. The groat was originally worth 4*d.* but was reduced in 1551 to 2*d.* (and smaller coins proportionally). Included as a special class within the 'base' monies, thirdly, were the 3 oz. coins of 1551, difficult to distinguish from the 6 oz. issue of 1549–51 and circulating, it seems, at their appointed fiat values despite the fact that their intrinsic value was only half that of the 8 oz., 6 oz., and 4 oz. coins which had preceded them.

These three standards of coin coexisted with little apparent difficulty. The base silver could not profitably be reminted (save for the remnants of the 6 oz. issue of 1545–6), because its mint equivalent, even after the 'calling down' of 1551, was higher than either the mint equivalent or the mint price of newly issued sterling silver. These good coins, in turn, could not be reminted because the issue of base coin had been discontinued. Nor were they unduly prone to be exported, because, as we shall see, the foreign exchanges were based upon *their* value and not on that of the base silver. The basest (3 oz.) silver did not drive out the better partly, no doubt, because it was so difficult to distinguish but also because, in any event, it was but a small part of the circulation. It was therefore tolerated, in so far as recognized, as no more than an occasional nuisance. The best and oldest gold coins, on the other hand, had been protected from their less valuable successors by 'enhancements' of their face value which made their *de facto* mint equivalents identical with those of post-1551 fine gold coins. And finally the apparent difficulty posed by the somewhat too low silver/gold ratio represented by the mint equivalents of the new post-1551 fine-gold issues and the mass of base silver (about 10·4:1) was rendered harmless by the discontinuation of minting of silver coins of that fineness. Gold could *not*, therefore, be exported, despite the ratio, to finance an import of cheap silver. At the same time the silver/gold ratio for newly minted coins (about 11·6:1) was perfectly reasonable in terms of international comparisons. This insulation of the international sector from the potentially disruptive effect of the base silver was rendered more complete by the fact that this coin was in any event predominantly, after 1551, of too small a denomination (2*d.* and less) to enter in any large way into the calculations of those who dealt on the level of the foreign exchanges and international capital movements. Its chief function, as Edward VI's *Journal* said in a slightly different context, was 'to serve for the poor People, because the Merchants make no Exchange of it'. Such small base coins thus found their chief and (largely insulated as they were from other sectors) not too disruptive role in facilitating the everyday business of 'thunlerned and uplandyshe people'.

The one difficulty which the multiplicity of standards did present lay in the temptation which it offered to the counterfeiter. The higher mint equivalents of the 1546–51 silver issues meant that there was a possibility of gain if silver, instead of being delivered to the Mints to be worked into sterling coins, could be worked into counterfeit base coins instead. Further, since the foreign exchange rate tended to be based on the mint equivalents of fine gold and sterling silver there was an incentive to settle international obligations by importing silver, either in the form of counterfeit coin, or of bullion to be worked into such coin in England.

It is hard to know just how great a problem this was. The promotion of counterfeiting and its disadvantageous implications for the balance of payments were offered as the second of the 'summary of reasons' for reforming the coinage which Elizabeth I publicized in 1560.[1] In third place in the same document stood the allegation that the 'great quantities' of good gold and silver coins minted in the later years of Edward VI and under Philip and Mary had been largely driven out of circulation (and in part exported) because of the base silver. The student of Tudor history knows well, however, the danger of placing too much reliance on evidence contained in documents of this type, which, like preambles to statutes of the day, were designed more to win acceptance for the measures they introduced than to present an objective analysis of the circumstances which had really prompted them. The third 'reason' is not easy to reconcile with

[1] Quoted in R. Ruding, *Annals of the Coinage of Great Britain* (3rd edn., 1840), p. 334.

Stanley's confidential and expert assessment, in 1559, of the circulation of post-1551 fine gold and sterling silver; and it is hard to reconcile the considerable mint output up to late 1555 with the belief that silver was being diverted wholesale into the hands of counterfeiters. Moreover, as we shall see, evidence from the recoinage does not suggest that counterfeit money had been fabricated on an overwhelmingly large scale; neither the amounts of base coin delivered to the Mints nor the fine silver they appear to have contained lend support to such a view.

Actually, the temptation to counterfeit the base silver was not all that great, for after the 'calling down' of the testons in the summer of 1551, the *de facto* mint equivalent of all save the 3 oz. coins was £3. 12*s*. 0*d*., or only some 8*s*. above the mint price for the new sterling issues. Bearing in mind that the base silver predominantly consisted of groats (now worth 2*d*.) and smaller coins, the costs and danger of striking, transporting, and distributing such coin must have been considerable and the net gain, therefore, not particularly tempting. Certainly the incentive to the counterfeiter had been very much greater during the debasement period itself, with the very high levels of seignorage then prevailing, and this consorts well with the evidence of the recoinage that it was the issues of 1546 to 1550 which had chiefly attracted his attention. Had the counterfeiter been very active after 1551 one would have expected him to devote his skills chiefly to imitating 3 oz. coins, which had the same fiat value as, but only half the silver content of, their 8 oz., 6 oz., and 4 oz. predecessors. This seems not to have happened, for the amount of 3 oz. coin in existence in 1560 seems to have been just about what we should have expected had their been no illegal additions to the quantity of them struck by the Mints in 1551. Perhaps, then, we should avoid too much emphasis on the temptation which the post-1551 coinage situation held out to the counterfeiter, conceding it only, perhaps, as a subsidiary cause of the idleness of the Mints from late 1555 onwards.

The Edwardian and Marian settlement of the coinage thus represented a not too unsatisfactory compromise. The mass of base coin was largely 'neutralized' and prevented from thwarting the gradual build-up of a satisfactory circulation of good coins in the larger denominations. But equally, the Government was unable itself to subsidize the reminting of the base coin, and apparently lacked the wit or the resolution to take the measure which would cause this to be possible without subsidy. This is what Elizabeth did. Calling down the base silver to three-quarters of its 1551 fiat value, or three-eighths of the original (three-eighths and three-sixteenths respectively in the case of the 3 oz. coins), she caused the *de facto* mint equivalents of these coins to fall for the first time below the mint price of current sterling issues and thus made it possible, and indeed profitable, for the Crown to remint them without subsidy. The public holding these coins were in effect made to pay for the job (together with a typical rake-off for the Crown) by a ruthless reduction of their fiat values not only below those which had prevailed for more than nine years, but for the first time below their intrinsic values too.

The face value of the base coin reminted was some £668,000. Prior to the 'calling down' of these coins in late 1560 their face value would have been about £954,000.[1] The base coins, melted down and brought to the resumed sterling standard of 11 oz. 2 dwt., provided raw material for some 247,411 pounds Troy of sterling silver, equivalent to a total face value of new coins of £742,233. It can be seen that the undervaluing of the base coin had been sufficient to leave a gross margin of some £75,000, out of which the Government paid the costs of the operation and was left with an acceptable profit. Conyers Read's statement that Elizabeth's profit came mainly from the undervaluing of the better testons,[2] though literally true, is not true in the sense in which it seems to have been intended and in which it would normally be read. The sole source of the profit for the whole operation was the prior crying-down of the base coins to fiat values below their intrinsic values. The 3 oz. coins were no more undervalued by this act than the rest, since their newly appointed fiat values were exactly half those of the 8 oz., 6 oz., and 4 oz. coins of similar pre-1560 denomination and this faithfully reflected the fact that their original mint equivalent had been precisely double that of these earlier issues. The sense in which Conyers Read's statement is literally true is that, the profit arising and arising only from the undervaluing of *all* the base coins, more of the total profit could have been said to come from the better coins (not actually 'better *testons*', as Conyers Read writes, since the greater part of the base silver was in coins of smaller denomination) simply because there were many more of them.

[1] The values suggested for 1560 are calculated by applying *de facto* mint equivalents to the weights of base coin recorded as received at Stanley's and at Fletewood's Mints, increased to allow for the extent to which coins of the various issues were underweight as revealed by Fletewood's accounts (see p. 60 below).

[2] Conyers Read, 'Profits on the Recoinage of 1560–1', *Economic History Review* vi, no. 2 (Apr., 1936), 189 (fn.).

In the more natural sense of Conyers Read's words, the truth was the reverse of what he asserts. The base coins by and large did not contain quite as much fine silver as their original mint equivalents would strictly have led one to expect. This could be due to the fact that the fine-silver content of the coins when they came out of the Mint was below specification; that the coins had subsequently suffered from wear or clipping; or that included in the coins accepted by the Mints during the recoinage were counterfeit coins made to a lower standard. The extent to which the coins suffered in one or more of these ways varied from one issue to another. The surviving recoinage account for Fletewood's Mint[1] permits us to calculate the extent to which the coins of various issues which he received fell short, on average, of the weight to which their original mint specifications pointed. It lists the base coins of each fineness received both by weight and by tale (i.e. face value). It is easy to calculate from the latter what their original weight should have been, and, therefore, how much the actual weight of the coins received fell short of it. It seems that the few 8 oz. coins received by Fletewood were about 2 per cent under weight, the 3 oz. about 2½ per cent, the 6 oz. about 3½ per cent, and the 4 oz. about 4½ per cent. Similar figures do not appear on Stanley's account, which (contrary to Conyers Read's assertion that it is missing) can be found amongst the State Papers.[2] But there is in the Exchequer records an incomplete receipt book which appears, from the name of one of the signatories, to apply to Stanley's Mint,[3] and this lists the weight and face value of what must have been a substantial and (presumably) random sample of the base coin received there. 8 oz. coins are not mentioned; under weight percentages for 3 oz. and 4 oz. coins are very similar to those calculated from Fletewood's account; but the document suggests that the weight of the 6 oz. coins received by Stanley fell some 5 per cent short of the correct weight, rather than only 3½ per cent as at Fletewood's Mint.

This evidence, however, permits us to assess only the extent to which the base coins were *under weight*. The problem of the extent to which their fineness may have fallen short of that laid down by the mint regulations remains. At Stanley's Mint, and apparently at

[1] E. 351/2185.

[2] SP 65/6.

[3] E. 101/303/20. One of the signatories, John Bull, served both recoinage Mints, but the other, William Humphrye, appears to have been confined to Stanley's establishment; cf. the indentures with Fletewood and Stanley in E. 101/307/1.

Fletewood's too, the Mint Masters were debited with silver of a fineness 1½ dwt. short of the nominal one for each type of coin: for example, Stanley was recorded as having received 114,340 pounds weight of 5 oz. 18½ dwt. silver (that is, in coins supposed to contain 6 oz. of silver in the pound), making 56,455 pounds of fine silver ($114{,}340 \times \frac{5\text{ oz. }18\frac{1}{2}\text{ dwt.}}{12\text{ oz.}} = 56{,}455$). Presumably the difference was chiefly intended to take account of the probability that the base coins were generally of less than their stipulated degree of fineness. The Masters were then credited with an output of sterling coin reflecting this supposed fine-silver content of the base coin they melted or had melted for them, so that if the coin actually averaged a higher degree of fineness than that assumed, the Masters were that much in pocket; and if a lower, that much out of pocket. Since no complaints seem to have been voiced regarding this arrangement, one must assume that over the whole range of base coins, at least, the allowance of 1½ dwt. was large enough to compensate for the actual shortfall in the purity of the coins compared with their authorized degree of fineness. 1½ dwt. is a little less than 1 per cent of 8 oz.; exactly 1¼ per cent of 6 oz.; less than 2 per cent of 4 oz.; and exactly 2½ per cent of 3 oz. If, then, we could accept this allowance of 1½ dwt. as an accurate reflection of the actual shortfall of the purity of the coins, it would suggest that even the worst coins were only 2½ per cent below their stipulated degree of fineness, and that on the whole the base silver which was recoined was something less than 2 per cent under its specified degree of purity. Combining this with the (weighted) average of 4 per cent by which the coin as a whole fell short of its stipulated weight, this would lead to the conclusion that the actual fine-silver content of the base silver received during the recoinage was some 94 per cent of what it should have been, had the coins retained their true and original weights and degrees of fineness as laid down in the various mint indentures. Since the mint equivalent of Elizabeth's sterling silver (£3. 4*s.* 10*d.*) was some 20 per cent above the *de facto* mint equivalent of the base coins after she had called them down in 1560 (£2. 14*s.* 0*d.*), it can be seen that the Queen left an ample margin to cover the costs of the operation, throw out a minor *douceur* in the form of a 3*d.* in the pound allowance for those delivering base silver before 25 April 1561,[1] and still rake in an acceptable profit.

In fact, of course, we cannot believe that the fineness of all the

[1] See her proclamation of 29 Nov. 1560 in Tawney and Power, op. cit. ii. 198.

base silver coins—8 oz., 6 oz., 4 oz., and 3 oz. alike—should have fallen short of their official purity by just the same figure, 1½ dwt. This allowance has a decidedly conventional air about it. But as we have suggested, the absence of complaint from the mint officials leads us to believe that the actual fineness of the coins was within rather than beyond this tolerance—that the coins were on average, that is to say, less than, rather than more than, 2 per cent below their stated degree of fineness. This conclusion is consistent with the favourable outcome of the assay of the base silver made by Edward VI's officials late in 1551, when plans to reform the coinage were under consideration.[1] Like most of the references to the coinage in Edward VI's *Journal*, the passage referring to this assay is infuriatingly obscure, but at least it seems clear that the base coins had been found to be not appreciably worse than the mint officers, presumably apprised beforehand of the technical data relating to them, had expected. There have also been modern assays of surviving coins[2] which confirm that the charge of issuing coins of less than the authorized degree of fineness is not one which can generally be preferred against mint officials of the debasement period. The years between 1551 and the recoinage might, of course, have seen some deterioration in the *weight* of these coins, but not, presumably, of their fineness. It thus seems likely that the fine-silver content of the base silver coins received at the Mints during the recoinage was above, rather than below, 94 per cent of that to which their original mint equivalents pointed. That being so, Elizabeth's 'margin' was surely an ample one.

Several reflections follow from all this. First, in calling down the base silver to new fiat values *below* its intrinsic values, Elizabeth made it profitable not only to remint it but to export it. Hence the proclamation of 9 October 1560[3] which, only a fortnight after that calling down the base coins, referred to the collection and melting of testons for export and provided for the punishment of those continuing the practice and for the rewarding of informers. The superior strength of Elizabethan administration is clear, amongst other things, from its success in dissuading private citizens from exporting the cried-down silver for their own profit, and forcing them instead to deliver it to the Mints for that of the Government.

[1] *The Journal of King Edward VI*, p. 46.

[2] See Symonds, 'Coinages of Henry VII and Henry VIII', pp. 165–6; H. W. Morrieson, 'The Silver Coins of Edward VI', *British Numismatic Journal*, 2nd Series ii (1916), 141.

[3] R. Steele, *Tudor and Stuart Proclamations* (Oxford, 1910) i, no. 531.

Secondly, we may here conveniently note that the surviving mint accounts, if I correctly interpret them, do not necessarily give us the true values of sterling silver struck out of the reminted base coins. We have seen that the extent to which these coins differed from their authorized degrees of fineness was only conventionally allowed for in the accounts by recording each category of base coin as 1½ dwt. baser than its original true quality. Now the amounts of sterling coins issued with which the Mint Masters were debited were computed indirectly from the amount of fine silver alleged to have been yielded by the melted-down base coins. But this amount in itself was only indirectly assessed by multiplying the recorded (and presumably actual) weight of each type of coin delivered by the *conventional* degree of purity attributed to it. Whatever departure from reality this conventional fineness implied, therefore, was carried forward into the weights of fine silver and of sterling silver, and the face value of the resulting sterling coins, as shown in the accounts. It is in this sense that we have reasoned that the Mint Masters had a vital interest in the adequacy of this conventional 1½ dwt. allowance, for if it had been on average inadequate, they would have been held responsible for a greater output of sterling silver than the fine-silver yield of the base coins in fact sufficed to permit.

In the third place, even though we do not know for sure how far each base issue fell short of its authorized degree of fineness, it is improbable that whatever difference there were would reverse the implication of the evidence as to the extent to which the various issues were below their authorized weights. That implication is, that it was the 4 oz. and 6 oz. coins, rather than their 3 oz. successors, which fell furthest below their authorized fine-silver contents. For this, several explanations come readily to hand. The 4 oz. and 6 oz. coins had been longer in existence and therefore longer exposed to normal wear and to the attentions of the clipper. The latter, too, would find them a more worthwhile target; clearly there was a better prospect of gain in shearing a given quantity off a 6 oz. coin than off a 3 oz. coin, indistinguishable from the former save in having only half its fine-silver content. The earlier issues, moreover, had continued to be struck for long enough to enable counterfeiters to begin their work, whereas the output of 3 oz. coins was discontinued almost before they could have got started. Finally, the minting of 3 oz. coins was confined to the two Tower establishments and to Southwark; and technical and administrative standards were probably always better at the London Mints than at the provincial Mints which had made substantial contributions to the output of the pre-1551 base issues.

All this, in turn, validates our contention that Conyers Read's attribution of the profits on the recoinage primarily to the under-valuing of the 'better testons' is misguided (save in the literal sense explained above). For what Elizabeth did was to establish new fiat values which correctly reflected the difference between the authorized fine-silver contents of the 8, 6, and 4 oz. coins on the one hand, and of the basest, 3 oz., coins of 1551 on the other. But the evidence reviewed above seems to suggest that it was the better base coins, rather than the 3 oz. silver, whose fine-silver content was furthest below that called for by the technical data in the mint indentures. That being so, it was precisely the 3 oz. coins which Elizabeth's new fiat values most undervalued in relation to their *actual* intrinsic value in 1560; and these coins thus presumably contributed more, pound for pound, to covering the costs of the recoinage, and to Elizabeth's profit on it, than did their superior fellows of the pre-1551 issues.

The success of Elizabeth's recoinage, then, was a triumph not of cleverness but of ruthlessness and organization. There is evidence that, as one might expect, it provoked hostility from the poor, who, as chief users of the small base silver coins, in effect bore the burden of the operation. For nearly ten years the base silver had coexisted alongside good silver and gold coins with little inconvenience to anyone. Ten years was a long time in terms of sixteenth-century expectations of life; and it is not surprising that after nearly a decade of monetary stability the poor no longer viewed the base coins with the hostility they had provoked in the years of violent price increases at mid century.

Our final commentary on the recoinage relates to the amounts of the various issues of debased coin brought to the Mints in 1560–1. The evidence on this is summarized in Table VII. Columns (2) and (3) show the total weight of the coins of each issue received, respectively, at Stanley's and at Fletewood's Mints. Column (4) totals these two figures. Column (5) shows the face value of each of these weights at the original mint equivalent, that is, what that amount of each issue would have been worth when originally struck. The values in Column (6) are half those in the preceding column, and show the effect of the 'calling down' of the base silver by Edward VI in 1551. Column (7) similarly shows the face value of the same coins after Elizabeth's proclamation of 27 September 1560. All of these columns are

TABLE VII

Statistics of recoinage, 1560–1561

(1)	(2)	(3)	(4)	(5)	(6)	(7)	(8)	(9)
	Weight			*Face value at official weights*			*Face value at real 1560–1 weights*	
Fineness	*Stanley*	*Fletewood*	*Total*	*Original*	*After 1551 reduction*	*After 1560 reduction*	*Original*	*After 1560 reduction*
	lb.	*lb.*	*lb.*	£	£	£	£	£
8 oz.	211	255	466	2,237	1,118	839	2,282	856
6 oz.	114,340	71,194	185,534	667,922	333,961	250,471	692,147	259,555
4 oz.	164,540	217,472	382,012	916,829	458,414	343,811	960,030	360,012
3 oz.	41,738	26,997	68,735	247,446	123,723	46,396	253,531	47,537

NOTES. (1) For explanation of Table, see text, pp. 64–6.
(2) Weights of coin received (*a*) at Stanley's Mint, SP 65/6; (*b*) at Fletewood's Mint, E. 351/2185.

calculated as though, on average, coins of each issue had been of their authorized weight when delivered for reminting in 1560–1. As we have seen, this was not so; and in column (9) we recalculate the values shown in column (7) to take account of the degree to which each issue was, on average, under weight, as revealed by the evidence of Fletewood's account. (A check on this working is possible. Fletewood's account gives the total of base coins received by tale as well as by weight, while Stanley's account shows the total paid out to subjects —which is presumably the same as the total of the base coin tendered at that Mint. Summing these two, and subtracting the face value of the small quantity of Irish coins received, one reaches by this route a value for column (9) of about £667,200, which compares excellently with the total of £667,958 in column (9).) A similar recalculation of column (5) appears in column (8).

How do the values in column (8) compare with the amounts of each type of coin originally issued, as revealed by the calculations presented earlier in this chapter? Before confronting the two sets of figures, two further aspects of mint activity may conveniently be mentioned here. The first was largely confined to 1549, when activity was languishing somewhat between the now declining output of 4 oz. silver and the rush of 6 oz. issues which was to start later in that year. We may christen this the 'converting testons' operation. The opportunity was taken during this lull to remint some of the base testons into coins of smaller denominations. The operation seems to have been the first part of a plan to bring about a 'two-tier' system of coinage, with shillings and larger silver and gold coins minted to something like the old standard, the base silver being confined to coins of smaller denomination. One of the original reasons given for this plan was to expose the counterfeit testons in circulation.[1] This activity had been authorized by a Commission dated 16 February 1548,[2] but save for a little work at Southwark and at York nothing was done until early 1549, presumably because the Mints had been too busy with their other work.

In all, approaching half a million pounds' worth of 8 oz., 6 oz., and 4 oz. groats and lesser pieces were produced. This is the total for the

[1] See the series of proclamations dealing with the demonetization of testons: Hughes and Larkin, op. cit., nos. 302 (pp. 420–1), 322 (pp. 441–3), 332 (pp. 459–60).

[2] The date and purport of this Commission, which I have not found, are referred to on several of the mint accounts. Cf. the Commission to John Bowes, Under-Treasurer of Durham House, on 29 Jan. 1549: CPR Edward VI, ii. 303–4.

five Mints for which we have accounts over the relevant period. If the two remaining Mints, Durham House and the second Tower establishment, were also engaged on this work—and we know from the Commission which survives amongst the Patent Rolls that Durham House, at least, was authorized to carry it out—this amount would have to be correspondingly increased. One effect of the operation was to affect the distribution of base silver between coins of differing denominations: it was because of it that the base silver recoined by Elizabeth was found to consist chiefly of groats and smaller pieces. In addition, the 'converting testons' operation, like normal mint production, encompassed the reminting of earlier issues into baser coin. It seems likely that of the total value of testons surrendered, which amounted to nearly one-third of a million pounds, some £76,000 worth were 6 oz. testons of the 1545–6 issue. These, of course, had an intrinsic value half as high again as that of the 4 oz., 6 oz., and 8 oz. small coins into which the surrendered testons were transformed, which is one of the reasons why the face value of small coins produced exceeded that of the testons surrendered. The more important reason for this, however, is that in the course of reworking the testons it was necessary, when making 6 oz. or 8 oz. small coins, to add fine silver in order to bring the silver/alloy mix up to the required degree of fineness. (In making 4 oz. small coins it was necessary to add some alloy, the surrendered testons usually including some 1545–6 coins and thus averaging more than 4 oz. fine.) For these reasons the recoining testons operation must be counted as an integral part of the debasement, one which not only altered the composition of the money supply as between various denominations and finenesses, but which also increased the total circulation.[1]

The other aspect of mint activity to which attention is here drawn also involved a change both in the total face value of base silver and in its distribution between the various finenesses. This was the reminting on Government account of quantities of base silver into Irish coinage. This seems to have occurred principally during the reign of Philip and Mary, and especially in 1556–8. The fact that no mint accounts from this period have survived makes it impossible to know just how much of the base silver was disposed of in this way, or *which* of the base issues provided most of the raw material. But surviving

[1] On the recoining of testons, see C. E. Challis, 'The Debasement of the Coinage, 1542–1551', *Economic History Review*, 2nd Series xx, no. 3 (Dec. 1967), 441–66; and below, Appendix E.

Commissions amongst the Patent Rolls make clear that the amounts were not inconsiderable; for the years mentioned together with the first half of 1559 they totalled over £75,000 of base money.[1] In addition, the surviving mint account for 1553–5 shows £6,374 of base silver reminted in this way.[2] At least £80,000, then, has to be allowed for as a so-to-say 'legitimate' disappearance of base coin before the recoinage operation began.

We can now juxtapose and comment on the two sets of figures. First, the 8 oz. silver remaining in 1560 was much less than the output of these coins shown in Table V. Though we cannot be quite sure how, why, and when the bulk of these 8 oz. coins disappeared from circulation, much the most tempting solution is to suggest that they were specially culled—perhaps because they were so much the 'odd man out' amongst the base issues?—for transforming into Irish coin in the manner just described. The fact that, as we shall see, the 8 oz. coins are the only base issue of which the amount remaining at Elizabeth's recoinage was very substantially lower than, or indeed different from, what our reconstruction of the debasement would have led us to expect makes such a solution attractive from more than one point of view. In any event, the amounts involved are trifling by comparison with those of the other base issues.

In the case of the 3 oz. silver a substantial part of the output shown consists of 'estimated' coinage, and here circular reasoning is involved, since the evidence of the recoinage is one of the reasons for setting 'estimated' coinage at the value chosen. But at the same time there is encouragingly little difficulty in explaining the value to which the recoinage points without invoking either substantial loss through export or melting or appreciable augmentation by counterfeit coins. Both the production and the recoinage estimates agree in pointing to a value of some quarter of a million pounds as the total of 3 oz. coins.

The total of 4 oz. silver remaining in 1560–1 is very much what we should have expected. The coinage table suggests a total original output of something over £950,000, which had been slightly reduced by the 'converting testons' operation, which absorbed slightly more 4 oz. testons than it produced of 4 oz. small coins. Allowing for some small addition to this in the last stages of Edward VI's attempts to

[1] Various entries are to be found in CPR Philip and Mary, vols. iii and iv.
[2] A.O. 1/1670/497.

get rid of the base coins, and perhaps a rather larger one from the counterfeiter and from 'unauthorized' coining,[1] and allowing also for a small subtraction during the 1550s for the Irish currency, the recoinage total, equivalent to some £960,000 at original values, seems very much in line. (One implication, incidentally, is to suggest that the quantity of counterfeit and unauthorized 4 oz. coins was not inordinate.)

In the case of the 6 oz. coins of 1549–51, the surviving accounts record the striking, in the course of normal mint activity, of some £508,000 of this coin. The 'converting testons' operation added some £187,000-worth of 6 oz. small coins without, as far as we know, re-absorbing any of the 'normal' production. There was probably a small output at Tower I between November 1550 and March 1551, for which the account is missing, and perhaps also at Tower II. Allowing again for the counterfeiter on the one side and for the Irish coinage on the other, the original total of somewhat less than £700,000 suggested by the recoinage accounts is obviously very much of the right order of magnitude.

As for silver of other mintages, the recoinage accounts confirm the conclusion to which other evidence and deduction from our theory of mint supply combine in pointing, namely, that other base coins—the earlier 6 oz. coins of 1545–6; the 9 oz. coins of 1544–5; and the 10 oz. silver of 1542–4—had to all intents and purposes disappeared, like all pre-1542 issues, before Elizabeth embarked on the recoinage operation.

Thus the evidence of the recoinage of 1560–1 agrees very well with that of the mint accounts extant up to and including 1551. Both similarities and differences between the two can be very satisfactorily accounted for in terms of the theory propounded earlier to explain

[1] As far as the English Mints are concerned, it may be that their chief derelictions of duty lay in producing what H. Symonds cogently argued should be called 'unauthorized' rather than counterfeit coinage. Coins may, that is, have been produced, but not accounted for, which exhibited in all respects the physical characteristics imposed by the mint indentures in question. There was in fact relatively little incentive to produce counterfeit coins falling below authorized standards of purity, for those standards were themselves so low that little gain could be expected. The real incentive lay in the very high rates of seignorage. After April 1549 a gross profit of 38*s*. per pound of 6 oz. silver was available to anyone who could produce 6 oz. coins of the authorized standard and put them into circulation without paying seignorage. It would have been foolishly greedy to seek to increase this already handsome profit by making the coins marginally below their authorized weight or fineness and thus inviting detection.

why and how fluctuations in the level of mint output occurred. This theory, therefore, can legitimately claim support from the first empirical test to which it has been subjected, and confidence in its potential usefulness in other similar contexts can fairly be said to be strengthened.

4

MONEY SUPPLY AND PRICES

IT would be pleasant to follow the chapter on mint output by transforming our estimates into an account of changes in the magnitude of the supply of money, and perhaps by relating this in turn to fluctuations in the levels of economic activity and of prices. Some readers may indeed feel that only such an application of our analysis of mint affairs would justify the effort spent on making it, though the writer prefers to see as its chief gain the clearer understanding which it has provided of determinants of the level of mint activity—an understanding which, systematized into a 'theory' of mint supply, is claimed to offer a useful tool of analysis for the study of monetary questions in other periods before the advent of paper money. There are many difficulties which combine to make it impossible to offer with any real confidence estimates of changes in England's monetary circulation. Chief amongst them is our ignorance of the balance of payments over the period in question. This is a crucial defect, of course, because gold and silver coins, in addition to constituting the greater part of the domestic circulation, were also the ultimate means of settling balance-of-payments residuals. Another deficiency in our knowledge is our uncertainty as to the exact size of the circulation, either at the beginning of the changes in mint regulations in 1542, or, save in so far as the base silver was concerned, in 1560–1, which Elizabeth's recoinage signalized as the end of the period. We thus lack really firm reference-points to which estimates of changes within the period could be linked. There are, of course, gaps too in the mint records which, especially when the activities of the counterfeiters are taken into account, make it impossible for us even to be quite sure of the gross output of new coinage from one period to another.

Yet it is not necessary to inflict total disappointment on the reader who is primarily interested in the supply of money. Our ignorance is far from complete, and reasoned estimates such as those we have made of output where accounts are missing can sometimes fill in gaps in the records. In this chapter, then, an attempt will be made to offer an extremely rough estimate of changes in the supply of money during the debasement period. The reader is asked only to note that at several points the assumptions made have an element of the heroic, and that the author cannot condone or support other scholars who choose to borrow these estimates without hedging them about with the substantial warnings and qualifications which, it is insisted, ought to accompany them.

It is convenient to consider the two metals separately. The silver is the more complicated. Broadly our method is to start from an estimate of the silver circulation in 1542 based upon mint records for the pre-1542 period and to seek to show how the fine silver contained in this coin was subsequently reworked into base issues, and how the fine silver in these issues was reminted in turn into later coinages, exported, or left in circulation in the form of the base silver coins which Elizabeth reminted in 1560–1. Finally, estimates of the supply of money just before the recoinage have been based on the estimates which Stanley, Elizabeth's first Mint Master, made at the time,[1] corrected in the light of the information about the circulation of base silver which can be gleaned from surviving accounts of Elizabeth's recoinage. In this exercise, each of the base-silver issues from 1542 onwards has been considered separately, the attempt being made first to explain where the fine silver contained in it came from, and second to show where it went to. Several constraints have of course operated throughout which in fact have tended to circumscribe the ground open to guesswork more narrowly than the reader might suppose. Evidently the arithmetic has had to add up and subtract correctly. The reminting of older coins, whether on Government or on private account, has had to appear plausible, both in extent and in timing, in the light of the theory of mint supply already presented. The reconstruction of events has had to be consistent with changes in the level of mint activity—to be capable, for example, of explaining the growing scarcity of silver in the Mints in early 1549—and with the occasional literary or numismatic evidence about aspects of the money supply from time to time. And, of course, having reconstructed the adventures of the silver coinage from our starting-point in 1542, we have to be left with the correct amount, and with the correct types of coin, in 1560.

The attempt to reconstruct the course of events to which these requirements have led is shown in the series of diagrams on pages 73–5.

[1] Add. MSS. 40061, fols. 11–12.

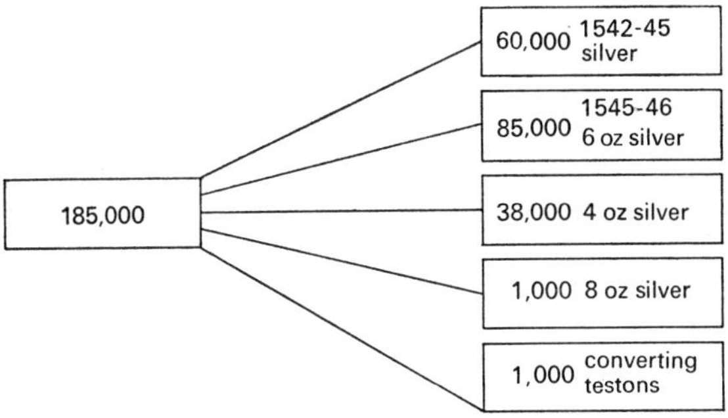

DIAGRAM I. 1542 silver

Note: numbers refer to pounds Troy of fine silver (see text, p. 76)

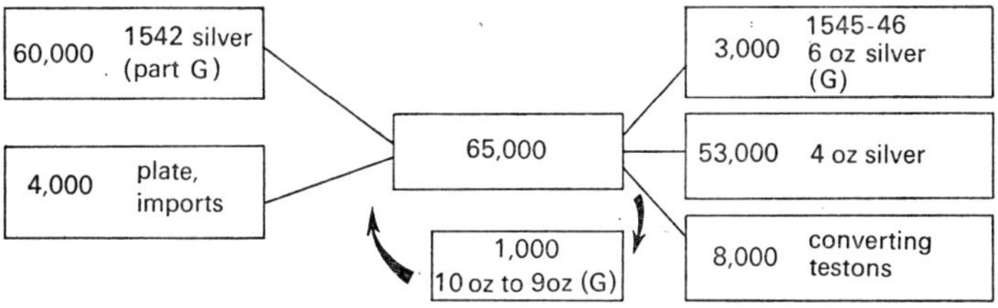

DIAGRAM II. 10 oz., 9 oz. silver (1542–5)

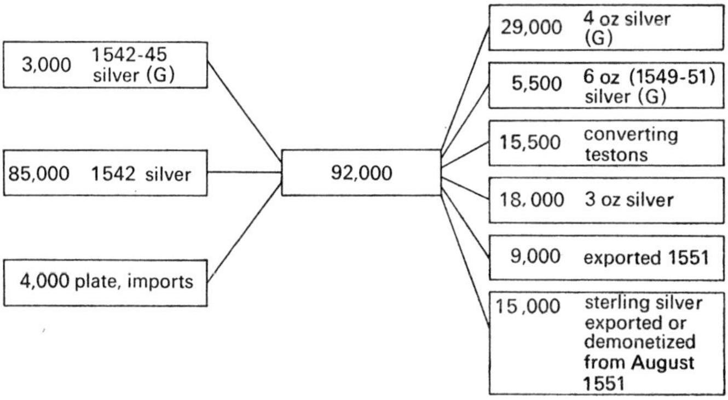

DIAGRAM III. 6 oz. silver (1545–6)

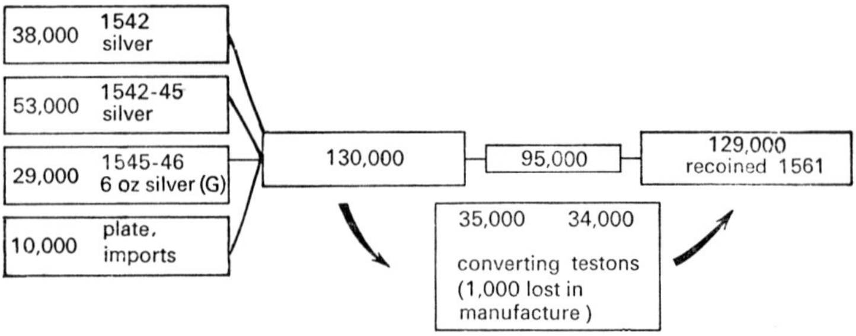

DIAGRAM IV. 4 oz. silver (1546–9)

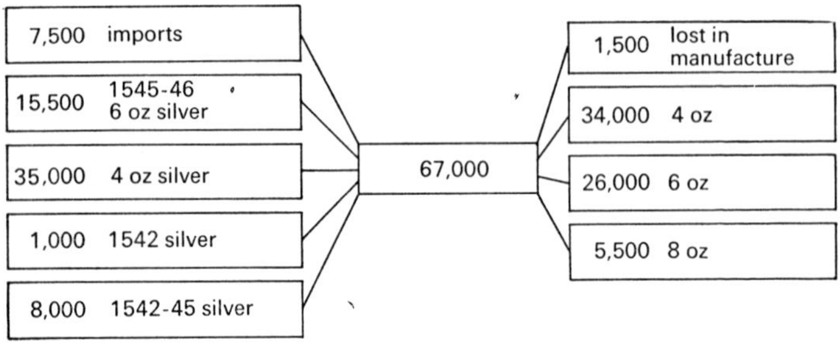

DIAGRAM V. Converting testons (1548–9)

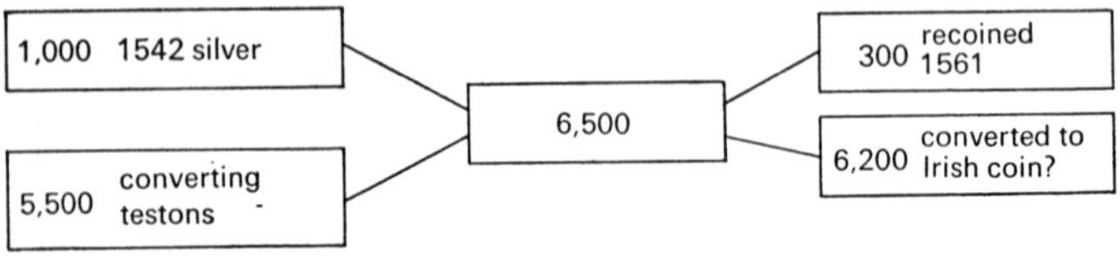

DIAGRAM VI. 8 oz. silver (1549)

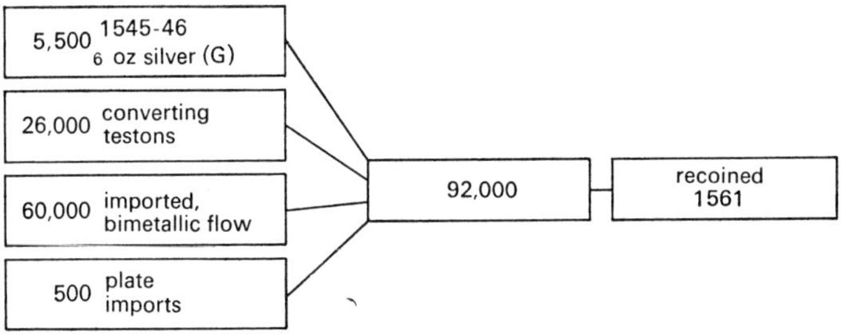

DIAGRAM VII. 6 oz. silver (1549–51)

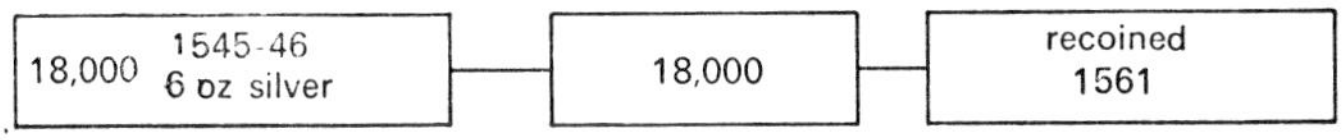

DIAGRAM VIII. 3 oz. silver (1551)

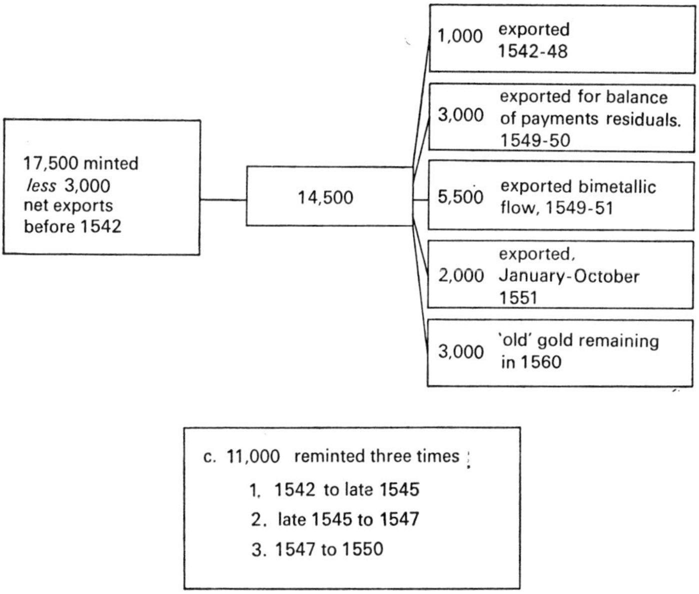

DIAGRAM IX. Gold (1542)

Note: (G) signifies reminting on government account

The numbers refer to pounds Troy of fine silver or gold, the face values of the various issues have all been transformed into fine-silver or fine-gold equivalents primarily to facilitate exposition, though of course the supply of fine silver, given the mint equivalent, was in any event the crucial determinant of the face value of new output. All the values are expressed in round figures to reflect the fact that only a rough approximation is intended or can be hoped for. Counterfeit and unauthorized issues are ignored on the output side; on the other side, and more or less offsetting this, the withdrawal of some base silver for the Irish coinages of the 1550s is also neglected.

The first diagram assumes a silver circulation in 1542 of about £450,000, equivalent to a fine-silver content of about 185,000 pounds Troy. This amount is based on the mint records of bullion coined as presented in the 1929 article by Brooke and Stokes.[1] It is assumed that the increase in mint equivalent implied by the reduction in the weight of the silver coinage in 1526 was large enough to cause virtually all the pre-1526 coins to be reminted in the following years; and further—and heroically—that the export of silver or its demonetization for industrial or artistic uses just about offset the combined effects of the survival of any pre-1526 coins, the slight excess of recorded output from 1526 to 1541 (equivalent to 186,451 pounds of fine silver) over the figure chosen, and the output for the year 1541–2, for which records have not survived. On the right-hand side of Diagram I it is then suggested where and how these 185,000 pounds of fine silver may have disappeared. In Diagrams II to VIII, in turn, the fine-silver equivalent of each successive coinage is shown in the centre box, the source of supply of silver to the mints when striking it on the left, and what subsequently happened to that silver on the right. No diagram is offered for the years following Edward VI's return to sterling silver in October 1551; it is assumed that, as our theory of mint supply would lead us to expect, the gold and sterling silver coins issued between that month and Elizabeth's recoinage were made out of imported gold and silver or of newly monetized gold and silver. The only exception to this is the suggestion that some, at least, of the 15,000 pounds of fine silver in the surviving 1545–6 silver coins was absorbed as raw material for the sterling issues of those years.

It does not seem necessary to justify seriatim every item in these diagrams. The interested reader, equipped with an understanding of

[1] Brooke and Stokes, op. cit.

what has preceded in Chapter 3, will be able to work out most of the reasoning which underlies these diagrams for himself. In general, the only comment called for is perhaps to say that the reconstruction here presented is that which seems to the writer best to meet the various requirements listed above, while at the same time at no point evidently infringing either theoretical probability or what relevant empirical evidence we have. It might be added that some of the more arbitrary decisions made do not in the long run much matter, one way or the other, from our present point of view. For example, we have shown the 6 oz. silver of 1545–6 and the 4 oz. silver of 1546–9 as absorbing, respectively, 3,000 lb. (on Government account) and 53,000 lb. (on Government and private accounts) of 1542–5 silver, and 85,000 lb. and 38,000 lb. of pre-1542 silver. It would be almost equally plausible, in the light of known evidence, to suggest amending these four figures, respectively, to 13,000 lb., 43,000 lb., 75,000 lb., and 48,000 lb. This amendment, however, would matter little to us. Either combination would equally well explain the supply of silver to the Mints in 1545–6 and in 1546–9; either would be consistent with the virtually complete disappearance of pre-1542 silver by late 1547 and of 10 oz. and 9 oz. coins by late 1549; and the adoption of the alternative combination would entail no consequential changes in the remaining diagrams. It would, indeed, call for a modification of the estimate of the money supply for April 1546 which we deduce from these diagrams, but the modification would be of relatively trivial dimensions. Despite such reassurances, it is right to remind the reader once again of the boldness of some of the assumptions underlying these diagrams, and of the highly approximate nature, in consequence, of the estimates of money supply based upon them.

The story of the gold is at once simpler and, regrettably, even more conjectural. Uncertainty strikes us at once as soon as we ask how much gold coin was in circulation in 1542. Partly this is because the mint records as presented by Brooke and Stokes are more incomplete for gold than for silver over the years 1526–42, since as well as 1541–2 the accounts do not record gold output for the Michaelmas years 1530 to 1536. Yet in the four years 1526 to 1530 the annual output was about 1,750 lb. of gold coin, and in the four years 1536 to 1540 about 1,100 lb. It is unlikely, then, that output during the intervening six years was negligible. Arbitrarily I assume an average annual output during those years of 1,200 lb. This give a total output of gold coin 1526 to 1541 of about 19,100 lb., equivalent to a face value of about £480,000 and a fine-gold content of about 17,500 lb.

This, however, is not the end of our difficulties, for, in contrast to the silver, we cannot be sure that all pre-1526 gold coins had disappeared by 1542. In the former year, the mint equivalent of both metals was raised by one-eighth. But whereas for the silver this was achieved by reducing the weight of the coins, in the case of gold it was done by enhancing the fiat value.[1] The former method left the *de facto* mint equivalent of pre-1526 silver coins unaltered; the latter raised that of pre-1526 gold coins just as it did that of coins issued from 1526 onwards. In terms of our theory of mint supply, this implies that pre-1526 silver coins would be reminted, pre-1526 gold coins would not. We do not then know how many such coins may have survived to 1542. However, since the occasion for the 1526 currency alterations was precisely a background of gold export which was supposed to have denuded the realm of much of its gold circulation, probably there was relatively little to survive. On the other hand, we have to reckon on the possibility of a fairly substantial gold export between 1526 and 1542 in connection with the balance of payments and Henry VIII's foreign expenditures. That gold was lost in some way or other seems to be indirectly confirmed by the fact that, when we come to look at the history of gold output *after* 1542, the 17,500 lb. of fine gold already mentioned in connection with that year seem distinctly too much rather than too little. Arbitrarily I assume a *net* gold loss of 3,000 lb. (fine gold) between 1526 and 1542, leaving a gold circulation in the latter year equivalent to 14,500 lb. (equal to about £400,000).

Diagram IX suggests how this gold may have been disposed of. I take from Stanley's 1559 estimate of the circulation that some 3,000 lb. survived until Elizabeth's reign as 'old' gold. The balance was, I suggest, exported at various times (some may in fact have gone into industrial use instead), most of it for balance-of-payments reasons—in this, foreign debt amortization and servicing would bulk large—but the largest single quantity, 5,500 lb., is attributed to the outward side of the bimetallic flow of 1549–51. (The quantity here is of course equivalent, at the international silver/gold ratio of the time, to the silver inflow we have already postulated in treating of the 6 oz. silver coinages of 1549–51.) The assumptions made as to the timing and

[1] Hughes and Larkin, op. cit., no. 112 (pp. 158–63); Harleian MSS. 660, fol. 62.

size of these gold outflows are highly arbitrary; I can only say, conscious of the limitations of this assurance, that they seem to me not implausible in the light of literary evidence and financial history, and that the amounts add up. It is of course true that as the debasement progressed, gold constituted a steadily declining proportion of the circulating medium, so that from the later stages of the debasement onwards any given error in the estimate of gold circulation would represent a relatively much smaller error in the estimate of total circulation.

(This may be the point to mention one intractable problem, namely that of relating balance-of-payments changes—even in so far as we can make any conjectures about them—to the supply of precious metals to the Mints. The first difficulty arises from the fact that over a period of time during which the balance of payments was sometimes positive and sometimes negative, the inflow of bullion to the Mints would be related to the sum of the positive outcomes, not to the net result of positive minus negative outcomes. This is because whereas a surplus was ultimately settled by an inflow of bullion or foreign coin which would normally be sold to the Mints, a deficit was financed by the export of coin whose disappearance had no direct influence on the level of Mint activity. Thus the level of mint supply would reflect cumulative surpluses rather than net surpluses or deficits, while changes in the circulation would reflect the latter. Similarly, since all exchange operations were *not* channelled through one central authority, specie might flow in both directions simultaneously, only the *net* movement corresponding (*ceteris paribus*) to the balance-of-payments residual. Hence there is nothing inherently impossible in showing the Mints receiving a supply of foreign gold or silver during a time of balance-of-payments deficit, or during a time in which there is claimed to have been a simultaneous export of domestic gold or silver.)

To return to Diagram IX, it can be seen that it does not show seriatim the stages of gold coinage during the debasement, as Diagrams II to VIII do for silver. This is because this aspect of the matter appears relatively simple. It seems likely that some 11,000 lb. or so of fine gold—the 14,500 lb. estimated to have been in circulation in 1542 *less* the 3,000 lb. remaining through to the recoinage, and reduced gradually by the net outflow of the later 1540s—may have gone through the Mints three times in separate cycles. It is suggested that about that quantity of fine gold from the pre-1542 issues was reminted between 1542 and late 1545 into 23 carat and then into 22 carat gold; that these issues in turn were reminted between late 1545 and April 1547 into 22 carat and then 20 carat gold; and that these coins were again reminted after April 1547 into 20 carat and perhaps 22 carat gold. Tables V and VI show the inherent plausibility of this reconstruction in terms of our theory of mint supply. The changes in mint price at the beginning of 1546 and in April 1547 occurred at the times which this reconstruction would require, and within each of these periods there was an incentive to remint the issues of the preceding period on private account. Further, roughly the same amount of fine gold passed through the mints within each of these periods, and the reduction of the rate of activity in gold in late 1545 and in the early months of 1547, which the mint accounts reveal, suggests that the end of the first and second cycles had been reached by those dates and that the increases in mint price which followed them were consciously intended to start activity up again and to bring the same gold back for a further round of seignorage.

We have now reached the stage where it is a merely mechanical matter to translate the data into an estimate of the supply of money at any desired point of time. All that is required is to take the quantities of fine gold and silver embodied at that date in the various gold and silver issues then in existence, as nearly as they can be ascertained from our diagrams, to multiply each such quantity by the appropriate *de facto* mint equivalent, and to add the resulting values together. For example, in estimating the supply of money in early 1551, Diagram IX tells us that there were some 5,000 lb. of fine gold embodied in coins which Table III indicates enjoyed a mint equivalent to £37. 1*s.* 10*d.*—a total gold circulation, hence, of £185,460. Diagrams I to VIII show us some 42,000 lb. of fine silver in 6 oz. coins of the 1545–6 issue at a mint equivalent of £4. 16*s.* 0*d.* (£201,600); and 129,000, 6,000, and 92,000 lb. respectively of fine silver in coins of 4 oz., 8 oz., and 6 oz. (1549–51) finenesses, all with the same mint equivalent, £7. 4*s.* 0*d.* (£1,634,400). Hence the total circulation of English coin was a little over two million pounds sterling at this date. (At this as at other dates there was probably a small circulation of foreign gold coins—Stanley put it at £50,000 in 1559—and perhaps a few Irish coins as well as tradesmen's tokens and the like. For lack of information these are excluded throughout.)

In Table VIII estimates of the total face value of the English coinage are presented for a number of dates. The method of working

Table VIII

Estimates of the money supply, 1542–1562

1542

		£
Gold	14,500 lb. @ £27. 8*s*. 2*d*.	397,416
Silver	185,000 lb. @ £2. 8*s*. 8*d*.	450,160
		£847,576

April 1546

Gold	14,000 lb. @ £32. 14*s*. 6½*d*.	458,178
Silver	40,000 lb. Sterling @ £2. 8*s*. 8*d*.	97,332
	14,000 lb. 10 oz. @ £2. 17*s*. 7*d*.	40,306
	47,000 lb. 9 oz. @ £3. 4*s*. 0*d*.	150,400
	92,000 lb. 6 oz. @ £4. 16*s*. 0*d*.	441,600
		£1,187,816

Early 1549

Gold	13,500 lb. @ £36	486,000
Silver	2,000 lb. Sterling @ £2. 8*s*. 8*d*.	4,867
	8,000 lb. 9 oz. @ £3. 4*s*. 0*d*.	25,600
	63,000 lb. 6 oz. @ £4. 16*s*. 0*d*.	302,400
	130,000 lb. 4 oz. @ £7. 4*s*. 0*d*.	936,000
		£1,754,867

Early 1551

Gold	5,000 lb. @ £37. 1*s*. 10*d*.	185,460
Silver	42,000 lb. 6 oz. @ £4. 16*s*. 0*d*.	201,600
	129,000 lb. 4 oz. 6,000 lb. 8 oz. 92,000 lb. 6 oz. } @ £7. 4*s*. 0*d*.	1,634,400
		£2,021,460

7 July 1551

Gold	3,000 lb. @ £68. 7*s*. 0*d*.	205,050
Silver	15,000 lb. 6 oz. @ £4. 16*s*. 0*d*.	72,000
	129,000 lb. 4 oz. 6,000 lb. 8 oz. 92,000 lb. 6 oz. } @ £7. 4*s*. 0*d*.	1,634,400
	18,000 lb. 3 oz. @ £14. 8*s*. 0*d*.	259,200
		£2,170,650

18 August 1551

		£
Gold	3,000 lb. @ £68. 7*s.* 0*d.*	205,050
Silver	15,000 lb. 6 oz. @ £2. 8*s.* 0*d.*	36,000
	129,000 lb. 4 oz. / 6,000 lb. 8 oz. / 92,000 lb. 6 oz. } @ £3. 12*s.* 0*d.*	817,200
	18,000 lb. 3 oz. @ £7. 4*s.* 0*d.*	129,600
		£1,187,850

1560, pre-calling down

Stanley's 1559 estimate of good coins, excluding foreign gold coins	570,000
* Gold struck Jan. 1559–July 1560	25,599
* Silver struck ,, ,,	31,311
† Base silver coins: 8 oz.	1,141
6 oz.	346,073
4 oz.	480,015
3 oz.	126,765
	£1,580,904

1560, post-calling down

Stanley's estimate, 1559	570,000
* Gold struck Jan. 1559–July 1560	25,599
* Silver struck ,, ,,	31,311
‡ Base silver coins: 8 oz.	856
6 oz.	259,555
4 oz.	360,012
3 oz.	47,537
	£1,294,870

1562

Stanley's estimate, 1559	570,000
* Gold struck Jan. 1559–July 1560	25,599
* Silver struck ,, ,,	31,311
* 11 oz. Silver struck by Stanley, 1.10.1560–31.10.1561	22,185
Sterling silver struck during recoinage	742,230
	£1,391,325

NOTES.
* See SP 65/6.
† See Table VII (values shown are half of those in column 8).
‡ See Table VII, column 9.

is identical in each case, though the reader may be reminded that the appropriate multiplier for the various quantities of fine gold and silver is the *de facto* mint equivalent. This is important in view of the reductions in the fiat value of the base silver in 1551 and 1560, and also when estimating the face value of the gold during the summer of 1551.

It can be seen that during the Great Debasement there was an increase in the supply of money, according to these calculations, from some £850,000 in 1542 to a maximum of about £2,170,000 in July 1551. (This month, marking as it did the end of the coining of 3 oz. silver, the nadir of the foreign exchange rate, the maximum expansion of the circulation, and the first of Edward's two proclamations 'calling down' the base silver, can be regarded from every point of view as the climax of the Great Debasement.) In the ensuing six weeks this value was virtually halved by Edward's reduction of the base silver to fifty per cent of its former fiat value. There was then a slow increase again to over one and a half millions on the eve of Elizabeth's recoinage, the result of which was a circulation, in early 1562, of some £1,390,000, or about sixty-four per cent above the 1542 level.

Can anything useful be said regarding changes in the price level in this period and their relationship with the supply of money? Close acquaintance with general price indices, particularly those relating to pre-modern times, tends to generate scepticism as to their validity and usefulness. Those for earlier periods have usually been very heavily weighted with grain prices, and this implies that their value for short-period analysis is greatly reduced by the distorting effect of harvest fluctuations. Three successive good harvests in the later 1540s, for example, completely hide from view in both the Rogers and the Beveridge grain series the inflationary effects of the debasement prior to 1549–50. Similarly the harvest failures of 1555 and 1556 would mislead those who place their trust in index numbers into looking for evidence of monetary instability in the middle of Mary's reign. In addition, the unsuitability for short-term analysis of the contractual origins of some of the price series is well acknowledged. The Phelps Brown–Hopkins index escapes both of these limitations to a greater extent than most and is therefore rather more suitable for our purposes.[1] For the five years centring on 1542 (1540–4) their index averages 169. For 1560, 1561, 1562, 1565, and 1566 (the years

[1] E. H. Phelps-Brown and S. V. Hopkins, 'Seven Centuries of the Prices of Consumables, compared with Builders' Wage-rates', *Economica*, N.S. xxiii (1956), 296–314.

1563 and 1564 were not calculated) the average value is 278, or sixty-four per cent above the 1542 figure. Quantity theorists will doubtless take encouragement from noting that this is exactly the proportion by which, according to my calculations, the money supply in 1562 exceeded that of twenty years earlier.

Closer scrutiny of the Phelps Brown–Hopkins index makes one a little more cautious about claiming this as a signal victory for quantity theory. The behaviour of the index during the intervening twenty years is less easy to link with supposed changes in the money supply. Thus prices by no means increased, in the period up to mid 1551, in the ratio which the two-and-a-half-fold rise in the supply of money from 1542 to that year would have indicated. Still less did they respond, as on the quantity-theory view might have been expected, to the virtual halving of the circulation by Edward's proclamations of July and August of that year. (Their equal failure to decline after 1560 is much less of a problem, notwithstanding the pains which the first editor of the *Discourse of the Common Weal* took to explain it,[1] for, as can be seen from Table VIII, Elizabeth's 'calling down' of the base silver and subsequent recoinage of it had a relatively much smaller effect on the supply of money than the earlier measures of her half-brother and his advisers. From this, as from other points of view, the importance of the year 1551 has in fact been underestimated and that of 1560–1 overestimated by economic historians.) It would still be possible to see a real significance in the similarity in the rise of prices and the increase in the circulating medium from 1542 to 1562, by explaining the intervening discrepancies in terms of 'lag' and 'ratchet' effects—that is, of institutional factors which both retarded the rise of the general price level during the rapid expansion of the supply of money to mid 1551 and prevented its subsequent fall in the face of the drastic contraction in the second half of that year.

But there are other oddities, too. Any residual confidence one might have in the significance of the 'general price level' is further weakened by examination of the far from uniform behaviour of individual commodity prices in this period. It has already been pointed out that the influence of the seasons easily prevailed, in the later 1540s, over that of the increase in the money supply in determining the price of grain. Then, when natural influences combined with monetary ones to turn grain prices sharply upwards in the early 1550s, the price of cloth—so often looked on as a leading influence

[1] Cf. Tawney and Power (eds.), op. cit. iii. 309–10.

on the economy in this period—showed clear signs of having passed its peak and turned downwards. Wool, on the other hand, rose considerably further and fluctuated considerably more than cloth, facts which direct our attention to specific factors affecting its demand and supply, rather than to general monetary influences.[1]

Then there is the question of the effects on prices of uncertainty and expectation, especially in the years when the base silver coinage was 'called down', 1551 and 1560. On both of these occasions the short-term effect of the reduction in the fiat value of the coinage (and, thus, of the contraction of the money supply) was to *raise* prices by inducing a flight from cash and goods hoarding. Thus it was for this reason that Edward VI's advisers, noting that the perverse effect of reducing the base silver to three-quarters of its original fiat value had been to raise prices, brought forward the date of the further reduction to one-half of the original and followed this proclamation by another intended to fix maximum prices for a wide range of victuals.[2] Edward's proclamations lamented the failure of the reduction of the money supply to lead to the hoped-for fall of prices in tones of somewhat bewildered chagrin which it would be entirely proper for the modern quantity theorist to adopt in contemplating the same phenomenon. Even after Edward's second reduction of the base coin, rumours of still another 'crying-down' continued to circulate and to prolong the 'flight from cash'.[3] In the case of Elizabeth's recoinage, too, the trouble did not cease when all the base silver had been safely recoined, for rumours of a 'decrying' of the sterling coin persisted with effects on prices similar to those of 1551.[4] Whether these effects —which, indeed, seem to have arisen chiefly from the precautionary practice of holding assets in goods rather than in money—were merely of a temporary nature, or whether, in conjunction with the 'ratchet' mechanism already noted, prices did not fall back fully as inventories were once more reduced and some longer-term inflationary effect was bequeathed, is uncertain. At all events it seems just a little trusting, in the light of all these discrepancies and perversities, to place any great analytical reliance on the close similarity in the rate of increase of prices and of the money supply over the period 1542 to 1562—especially when the adventurous nature of the estimates of the latter is borne in mind.

[1] See pp. 144 ff. below.

[2] Hughes and Larkin, op. cit., nos. 379 (pp. 529–30) and 380 (pp. 530–3).

[3] APC 1550–2, p. 352.

[4] Steele, op. cit. i, nos. 557, 560.

Discussion of the history of prices during the Great Debasement prompts one further reflection. In an article some years ago I ventured to draw attention to some disadvantages of the widespread practice of converting prices in the currency of the day into 'silver prices' in order to facilitate international and inter-temporal comparisons.[1] I argued, specifically, that to use changes in the mint equivalent of silver as a deflator of current prices was liable to lead to wrong conclusions, because it was not true either that the proportion in which the coinage was debased was invariably reflected by an equiproportional increase in the supply of money, or that the increase in the supply of money necessarily resulted in an equiproportional rise in the price level. The reader who has followed the argument of this book thus far will agree that it appears to confirm the justice of both of these contentions. The case of the second has just been discussed in the preceding pages. As to the first, it suffices to point out that between 1541 and 1551 the mint equivalent of newly coined silver increased nearly six-fold (£2. 8*s.* 8*d.* to £14. 8*s.* 0*d.*), whereas our estimates of the circulation suggest only a two-and-a-half-fold rise. Further objections to using the mint equivalent as a deflator can be added. For one thing, coins of differing *de facto* mint equivalents circulated, as we have seen, at the same fiat value. At no point of time during the debasement period did the mint equivalent of new silver represent the intrinsic value of *all* silver coins actually in circulation; only from the later stages of the 4 oz. coinage until April 1551 did it even correspond with the intrinsic value of the *larger part* of the silver circulation. In such circumstances the very concept of '*the* purchasing power of silver in England' is an elusive one. And if it be argued that the purchasing power of silver in England is best ascertained by measuring what a person importing silver into England could buy with it, it has to be pointed out that, silver bullion and foreign silver coins not being legal tender, it is the mint *price* rather than the mint *equivalent* of the metal which is relevant—and this in turn, of course, leads to the realization that we should then be measuring the changing incidence of seignorage as much as the changing level of prices. All in all, then, it is difficult to see what link there was during the Great Debasement between silver mint equivalent on the one hand and the determinants of price changes on the other which would warrant us in using changes in the former to help us in isolating the various causes of the latter.

[1] Gould, 'The Price Revolution Reconsidered', loc. cit., pp. 256–9.

5

THE EXCHANGE RATE

WE are better informed, statistically speaking, about the behaviour of London's major exchange rate—that with Antwerp—than about any other aspect of the commercial and financial history of the debasement period. We owe this happy circumstance very largely to the industry and skill of Dr. Van der Wee, who in his recent masterly study of the rise of the Antwerp market drew on a large number of sources to provide us with evidence as to the course of the London–Antwerp exchange rate during the years 1515 to 1600.[1] English readers will be particularly grateful that Dr. Van der Wee scrutinized the Antwerp archives in this connection in addition to drawing on English sources.

In his book, however, Dr. Van der Wee presents his information on the exchange-rate only in graphical form (Graph 33). With great generosity he responded to my request for further information by placing the actual figures on which his graph is based at my disposal. I was able, in the event, to add a few quotations which Dr. Van der Wee appeared to have overlooked for those years with which the present study is primarily concerned (1544 to 1562). Some of these additions were taken from that invaluable source, the daybook of Sir Thomas Gresham, most of whose exchange quotations, but not all, had come to the notice of Dr. Van der Wee.[2] I also took a few quotations from Strieder's study of Antwerp notarial records,[3] from Dr. Winchester's thesis on 'the Johnson Letters' (which is particularly valuable for its evidence relating to the 'black' year, 1551),[4] and from a few other sources.

[1] Herman van der Wee, *The Growth of the Antwerp Market and the European Economy* (Martinus Nijhoff, The Hague, 1963).

[2] The daybook is in the possession of the Mercers' Company of London, to whom I am grateful for the opportunity to consult a microfilm copy of this source.

[3] J. Strieder, *Aus Antwerpener Notariatsarchiven* (Deutsche Verlags-Anstalt, Stuttgart, 1930).

[4] Winchester, op. cit.

The exchange quotations thus assembled were marshalled under separate headings, Antwerp to London and London to Antwerp. They were then processed in the following manner. First, quotations in other than 'sight' bills (and bills whose maturity was not known) were adjusted to a 'sight' basis by discounting at 10 per cent. This implied adding 2*d.* in the pound (£$1\times10/100\times1/12$) to the rates mentioned in usance (one month) bills from Antwerp to London, and subtracting at the same rate from those in London to Antwerp bills. Proportionate additions and subtractions were made for periods of maturity other than one month. Secondly, the rates thus adjusted were then grouped month by month. For any month in which one or more quotations in both directions were available, the average sight rate in each direction was calculated. These monthly averages were then summed and averged in order to arrive at the mean monthly difference between London–Antwerp and Antwerp–London (sight) rates. This was found to be $3\frac{1}{2}d.$[1] (Two months were excluded in this calculation, for a reason to be discussed shortly.) $3\frac{1}{2}d.$ was therefore added to all Antwerp–London rates to convert them to a London–Antwerp basis. The resulting figures, together of course with the actual London–Antwerp rates, were then grouped together month by month and an arithmetical average for each month calculated. It is this series which is presented in tabular form in Table IX and, graphically, in Graph A (see end of book).

It is suggested that we can accept the picture of exchange-rate movements which this table and graph present as reasonably accurate and sufficiently detailed for most purposes. True, there are many months during the 1550s and early 1560s for which we do not have even a single quotation; there is even one period of fourteen months (January 1557 to March 1558) during which evidence is lacking. But fortunately this matters less since all the evidence, literary as well as statistical, leads us to believe that the reign of Queen Mary and the early years of Elizabeth I were a period of marked overall stability in exchange rates. The first eight years of our period, by contrast, saw major changes in the exchange rate, and this period is fortunately much better documented—a fact for which, so far as the years 1546–51

[1] The necessity for making this adjustment has, of course, been obvious to other modern scholars and was recognized by contemporaries. See R. de Roover, *Gresham on Foreign Exchange* (Harvard U.P., 1949), p. 143; Thomas Wilson, *A Discourse upon Usury*, ed. R. H. Tawney (London, 1925), pp. 306–7. (Wilson estimated the usual difference as threepence to fourpence, a welcome confirmation of our own estimate.)

Table IX

The London–Antwerp exchange rate, 1544–1563

	s.	d.
1544		
Jan.	26	8
Feb.	27	2
Mar.	26	11
Apr.	26	8
May	26	7½
June	25	9½
July	25	8
Aug.	26	5½
Sept.	26	6½
Oct.	26	9½
Nov.	26	9½
Dec.	25	3½
1545		
Oct.	25	4½
1546		
Apr.	26	3
May	25	5
July	24	6
Sept.	25	0
1547		
Jan.	23	3½
Feb.	23	4½
Mar.	22	0½
Apr.	22	0
May	22	2½
June	22	1
Aug.	22	6
Sept.	22	10
Oct.	22	8½
Nov.	23	0½
Dec.	22	9
1548		
Feb.	22	0½
Mar.	21	10½
June	22	3½
July	22	3
Aug.	22	1
Sept.	22	0
Oct.	22	2
Nov.	22	0½
Dec.	21	3½
1549		
Jan.	21	6
Feb.	21	2½
Mar.	20	2
1549		
Apr.	20	4½
May	20	6
June	20	3½
July	20	4½
Aug.	20	2½
Sept.	20	3½
Oct.	20	1½
Nov.	20	1
Dec.	19	7½
1550		
Apr.	19	4½
May	20	0½
June	19	5½
July	19	6½
Aug.	18	11½
Sept.	18	4½
Oct.	18	0
Nov.	18	0
1551		
Feb.	16	10½
Apr.	15	3
June	13	1½
July	12	9
Aug.	17	10
Sept.	18	7
	15	5*
Oct.	19	2
Nov.	18	8
	16	3½*
Dec.	18	7
1552		
Jan.	17	8
June	17	7
July	19	3½
Aug.	19	6
Dec.	19	5½
1553		
Jan.	19	5½
Feb.	19	11½
Apr.	20	2
Aug.	22	5½
1554		
Jan.	20	11½
Feb.	22	5½
Dec.	21	7½
1555		
July	21	5½
Oct.	21	3½
Dec.	21	9½
1556		
Mar.	21	7½
June	22	6
1557		
Jan.	20	3
1558		
Mar.	21	6½
Apr.	21	8½
June	22	0
Nov.	22	3½
1559		
Mar.	21	10
Sept.	22	3
Oct.	22	3
1560		
Jan.	22	2½
Mar.	22	6
Apr.	23	0½
May	23	2½
July	22	6
Oct.	23	2½
Nov.	23	0
Dec.	22	4
1561		
Jan.	20	6½
Mar.	22	2
Apr.	22	1
May	21	11½
July	23	1
Aug.	22	9
1562		
Feb.	23	5
Mar.	22	7½
Aug.	22	3½
Dec.	22	0
1563		
Jan.	21	10

* Antwerp–London.

are concerned, we are chiefly indebted to the happy preservation by the Mercers' Company of Sir Thomas Gresham's daybook. Only for the years 1551 and, less urgently, 1545 do we find ourselves somewhat embarrassed by lack of evidence; and, so far as 1551 is concerned, it is highly probable that a major reason for the paucity of quotations is that the exchanges were virtually inoperative for a large part of the year. This, as we shall see, is in itself important evidence. For the remainder of our period it seems reasonable to say that what one may hope for from future 'finds' of exchange quotations is that they will fill in the missing detail for the period after 1552 and confirm the trends apparent in the period up to 1552, without in either case necessitating any major revision of the picture painted here.

Before going on to attempt to account for the overall trend of the exchange rate and to discuss its significance in relation to the commercial and monetary changes of the period, a few minor points may be commented on. First, the choice of monthly periods for the computation and presentation of exchange rates was a compromise between two conflicting considerations. On the one hand, there was evident advantage in arranging the data in time-intervals short enough to permit a fairly detailed analysis to be made of the chronology of events. On the other hand, it seemed desirable to achieve some averaging of what are, after all, individual quotations which may in some instances be affected by influences which were not general or widespread at the period to which they relate. A glance at the chart will reveal that only in 1551—when our problem is, in any event, one of inadequate documentation—was the magnitude of changes from one month to the next sufficiently great to make us feel that information about movements of the rate *within* the month could be important.

Secondly, time bills, as we have seen, have been discounted at a rate of ten per cent. The choice of this rate was originally suggested only by conventional notions of the going rate of interest in the period;[1] but it seems to have proved not inappropriate in most cases where bills of different periods of maturity occur in our data in chronologically close company. There are two months, however,

[1] S. T. Bindoff in 'Economic Change' (*New Cambridge Modern History*, ed. G. R. Elton, vol. ii, ch. ii, p. 64) suggests 12 per cent. Van der Wee (op. cit. i, Appendix 45/2) presents evidence of considerable long-term changes in the rate of interest on short-term loans in Antwerp, the later 1540s being characteristically a period of relatively low rates (9–11 per cent).

namely August and September 1549, in regard to which this claim is not justified. In those months the 'spread' between sight and time bills, the former being offered at a little over 20*s*. Flemish to the pound, was of the order of 4*d*. or 4½*d*. for each additional month of maturity. Nearly all of the quotations relating to these months are to be found in the Gresham daybook. It is clear from the number of entries of remittances from London to Antwerp (some of them leaving the rate of exchange unspecified), from the amounts involved, and from the rare appearance of three-months' bills, that there was an unusual pressure at this time to borrow in London for repayment in Antwerp. The consequent pressure on 'deliverers' (that is, buyers of bills) in London presumably enabled them to charge, in effect, a higher rate of interest on time bills—an effective rate of some twenty per cent per annum, rather than ten per cent, is indictated by the 'spread' mentioned. While it would be unwise to read too much into such limited evidence, there does seem to be a useful reminder that in exchange transactions under a system of full-bodied coinage, an unusual shortage of funds might be reflected less in changes in the sight rate of exchange than in a shift from sight to time bills at an abnormally high rate of interest.

It has been mentioned that in computing the average difference between London–Antwerp and Antwerp–London quotations, all months, save two, in which one or more quotations in each direction were available were used. The two exceptions were September and November 1551. In each of these months we have one Antwerp–London and one London–Antwerp rate. The figures are as follows (readers will recall that exchanges on the Low Countries were quoted in shillings Flemish to £1 sterling):

	Antwerp–London	London–Antwerp
September 1551	15*s*. (usance)	18*s*. 8*d*. (half usance)
November 1551	16*s*. (sight?)	19*s*. (double usance)

It can be seen at once that the difference between the London-bound and the Antwerp-bound rates was far greater than was normally the case.

The explanation would seem to lie in the exceptional conditions which affected the money market and exchanges in 1551. The first of these conditions was the confusion over the silver coinage. In the spring this suffered the severest deterioration of the whole debasement period when the minting of coins of only 3 oz. fineness was begun. A few months later this was discontinued.[1] In the meantime, a proclamation had been issued announcing that as from the beginning of September the face value of silver coins in circulation would be reduced by 25 per cent.[2] This gave rise, not surprisingly, to a 'flight from cash' and goods hoarding which raised prices, and the timing of the move was advanced to 8 July.[3] Rumours continued to spread that a further devaluation was contemplated, and despite an official denial of this on 24 July, a further reduction of 33⅓ per cent (i.e. to 50 per cent of the original value) was proclaimed on 16 August.[4] Even this move did not allay suspicion, for a fortnight later we find the Lord Mayor of London being admonished to punish those spreading rumours of a further devaluation of the teston to 4*d.*[5] In the meantime, the foreign exchanges, which had been showing a sharply declining tendency since mid 1550, fell to their lowest level of the whole century. In early June a proclamation was issued rehearsing the statutes against unlicensed exchange and the export of gold and silver.[6] It seems from our data that a few exchange operations continued notwithstanding, but surely *sub rosa.* The Johnson Letters bear witness to the confusion in the City, and their commentator observes that at the end of September the exchanges were operating again, but under cover.[7]

It seems certain that such conditions would tend to put a stop to arbitrage (that is, the buying and selling of foreign exchange with a view to making a profit from differences in quotations—an activity which tended to keep such differences to a minimum). This would allow a 'spread' between the London-bound and the Antwerp-bound rates to emerge. In Antwerp, not unnaturally, the value of the pound remained depressed throughout the second half of 1551, and it could be bought in sight bills for less than 16*s.* Fl. In London, on the other hand, the exchanges recovered better, presumably because those accepting money in London to be repaid in the Low Countries were not exposed to the uncertainties facing those who offered Flemish money in Antwerp on the promise of repayment in London.[8]

[1] APC 1550–2, p. 316.
[2] Hughes and Larkin, op. cit., no. 372 (pp. 518–19).
[3] Ibid., no. 376 (p. 525).
[4] Ibid., nos. 378 (pp. 528–9) and 379 (pp. 529–30).
[5] APC 1550–2, p. 352.
[6] Hughes and Larkin, op. cit., no. 375 (pp. 523–4).
[7] Winchester, op. cit., i. 403–4.
[8] This may not be the only reason for the divergence of the London–Antwerp and Antwerp–London rates: see p. 105 below.

While the resultant spread between the rates in London and in Antwerp was particularly marked in late 1551, the figures for July and August 1552 (which we *have* used in the computation referred to earlier) reveal that the London–Antwerp rate still exceeded that in the opposite direction by a substantial margin. Indeed, these months exhibit the largest margin of London–Antwerp over Antwerp–London rates in the whole period, excepting only the excluded months of September and November 1551. Since there are no months between November 1551 and July 1552 for which we have rates in both directions, nor do we have them for October 1551, it may well be that there was a 'spread' between rates in the two centres throughout the whole period September 1551 to August 1552, or even longer (though if so, the magnitude of this spread almost certainly declined after the later months of 1551). This possibility is reflected in the graph by the drawing of *two* lines representing, respectively, London–Antwerp and Antwerp–London rates over the period in question.

We now turn to comment generally on the causes and effects of changes in the exchange rate. The former have commonly been explained by modern writers in terms of the debasement of the coinage. Thus, for example, Unwin stated confidently that 'the broad movements . . . can be accounted for by simple mechanical causes, and require no great subtlety of economic science to explain them'.[1] Unwin preceded this conclusion by drawing attention to the reduction in fineness of the silver coinage by successive stages from 11 oz. about 1520 to 3 oz. under Edward VI, and to the fall in the exchanges from 32*s*. Fl. in the former year to 13*s*. 4*d*. in 1550 ([*sic*]: Unwin was a year out here). He further attributed the recovery of the exchanges in the second half of 1551 to the 'reduction' of the silver coinage in August of that year to half its previous value.

It can be seen that this view of the matter is founded upon the following implicit assumptions: (*a*) that the par rate was determined by the relative precious-metal contents of the currencies of the countries concerned; (*b*) that in this respect it was the intrinsic value of the *silver* coinage which was relevant; (*c*) that actual exchange rates diverged from the par rate only within the (fairly narrow) limits of the specie import and export points. Unwin has been followed in this interpretation by other modern writers.

Yet that Unwin himself felt a certain unease regarding this explanation is suggested by the choice of the adjective 'broad' at the

[1] Unwin, op. cit., p. 155.

beginning of the above quotation. It is as though he realized that the correspondence between changes in silver content and changes in the exchange rate was only approximate—as well he might, for on the figures he himself gave the exchanges should have fallen in 1551 to about 8*s*. 8½*d*. (i.e. (32 × 3/11)*s*.), rather than 13*s*. 4*d*. Moreover, Unwin in fact erred in his data; had he taken the correct figures, they would have led to an expectation as to the fall of the exchanges even more at variance with the facts. Thus, he assumed the fineness of the traditional sterling-silver coinage to be 11 oz., whereas in fact it was 11 oz. 2 dwt. (i.e. $11\frac{1}{10}$ oz.). Second, and much more important, he noted only the reduction in the *fineness* of the coinage, overlooking that its weight had also been reduced. Allowing for these facts, and assuming that the exchange rate should have declined in the same measure as the fine-silver content of the newly minted English silver coinage, one would have looked for a Flemish equivalent of the pound sterling in mid 1551 of no more than about 4*s*. 10*d*.[1]

The unsatisfactory correspondence between the two series is also apparent when we look at events in closer detail. Thus, for example, the exchanges had largely stabilized during 1549 at around 20*s*. Fl., or little more than one-fifth below the pre-debasement level. Yet by that year the fine-silver content of newly minted silver coins had already been reduced to a mere two-fifths of the 1542 level. Then, in mid 1550, the exchanges entered on a long and pronounced decline for which, until the spring of 1551, no warrant was afforded by any further change in the intrinsic value of newly minted silver coinage. Finally, the possibility of a sharp divergence between the silver coinage and the exchanges was again demonstrated by the experience of 1560, when Elizabeth prepared the way for the restoration of the coinage by 'calling down' the silver coinage to three-quarters (in the case of the 3 oz. issue of 1551, three-eighths) of its former value. This event caused no more than a barely perceptible ripple in the movement of the exchanges.

The view that changes in the exchange rate during this period can be adequately explained by changes in the intrinsic value of the silver currency cannot, therefore, be sustained. What, if any, alternative or additional explanations can be propounded?

First, it will be useful to remember that it is more hazardous today than it was for the economists of Unwin's day to propose to account

[1] Most easily calculated by using silver mint equivalents $\left(\text{i.e. } 32s. \times \frac{£2.\ 3s.\ 3d.}{£14.\ 8s.\ 0d.}\right)$.

for economic data in terms of 'simple mechanical causes'. (Is there not a curiously unemphasized but still real tension between the recent increase in mathematical sophistication in economic explanation, on the one hand, and the fairly general retreat, on the other, from the belief that economic systems function in a mechanistic way?) The exchange quotations from which the graph (see end of book) has been constructed were contained, for the most part, in exchange contracts drawn up by private individuals; the rates agreed on represented the decisions of human beings, not the inevitable working-out of blind mechanical forces.

This raises the question, in the first place, whether some degree of caution might be appropriate in accepting the evidence on which the graph is based. A high proportion of the quotations for the later 1540s are from one source—Thomas Gresham's daybook—and it could well be that elements of conventionality, or circumstances peculiar to this particular firm, may have influenced the rates agreed upon by Gresham's agents and those with whom they did business. Indeed, it may be that the concept of '*the* exchange rate'—meaning a unique price, in a given time and place, for the purchase and sale of claims on a foreign currency—is somewhat premature, much as it is misleading, even today, to speak of '*the* rate of interest'. Yet the need for such caution should not be pressed too hard. There are, after all, a good many quotations amongst those which Dr. Van der Wee has assembled from sources other than the Gresham account, which in any event covers only the years 1546 to 1551. This other evidence undoubtedly supports, in general, the trend of the exchange rate which the Gresham account suggests; and, moreover, that trend is one which appears to have a reassuring internal consistency and to be amenable (as we shall see) to rational explanation. The writer, at least, is convinced that, save perhaps during the confusion of 1551, the empirical evidence of exchange movements here presented is sufficiently reliable and general for the purpose for which we require it.

More important is the reflection that since exchange rates were determined by human beings, not by mechanical forces, the state of mind, of knowledge, of those individuals was vitally important. Slowness of communication, the incomplete integration of markets, and uncertainty regarding vital elements in the situation—the Government, as we have seen, had a definite incentive to conceal information regarding the coinage during the debasement—would be expected to lead at times to exchange prices for which it is difficult for one possessing hindsight to find objective justification. Generally, perhaps, we should expect a lag of exchange movements behind changes in the conditions which influenced them: for example, we might expect the rate, during its long secular decline in the later 1540s and early 1550s, to have been somewhat higher at any one time than that which the state of the currency and of the balance of payments justified. It is barely possible to see some support for this expectation in the fact that the exchanges do seem during that period to have been generally closer to the specie import point (the higher value) than to the specie export point. But ignorance could at times work the other way: in conditions of particularly rapid change and uncertainty one might look for evidence of hedging, of prudential marking down below levels which objective conditions warranted. There is ample evidence, for example, in the *Letters and Papers* of Henry VIII of the confusion and distrust caused in the Low Countries by the early stages of the debasement and of the fact that this led to a refusal to accept English coins even at that valuation which their intrinsic goodness would have warranted.[1] Probably, again, something of the same sort influenced the exchanges in the confused summer months of 1551. At all events fairly substantial divergences from values to which technical data point are only to be expected. A recent study has shown that even in the nineteenth century the Anglo-American exchange often strayed before the advent of the transatlantic cable, and surprisingly often even after it, outside the specie export and import points.[2] Yet it frequently took men, money, and information longer to get from London to Antwerp in the 1540s than to get from England to America in the 1840s; and there were probably several elements in the domestic economies too which were more prone to lead to imperfections and irrationalities in the earlier period than in the later. A theory which finds explanations of every minor shift in the sixteenth-century exchanges in terms of 'simple mechanical causes' is a theory we should do well to view with a highly critical eye.

Yet, in any event, it is not really a case of merely noting and explaining divergences of the actual exchange rate from the 'mint par'. For the view which Unwin and most of his followers implicitly

[1] Several of Norfolk's dispatches and Vaughan's letters in the second half of 1544 testify on this point: *L and P* xix, parts 1 and 2, *passim*.

[2] L. E. Davis and J. R. T. Hughes, 'A Dollar–Sterling Exchange, 1803–1895', *Economic History Review*, 2nd Series xiii, no. 1 (August 1960), 62–4.

adopted, that in the mid sixteenth century the exchange rate was determined by the relative intrinsic values of newly minted silver coins—by the reciprocals of what I have christened the mint equivalent—is simply incorrect. As I have already shown, the divergence between the actual course of the London–Antwerp exchange and the course one would have predicted on the basis of changing silver mint equivalents was far too large and indeed consistent to be accounted for merely in terms of market imperfections.

The view that the exchange rate is determined by the relationship between mint equivalents in the two countries concerned is predicated on the correct assumption that transporting specie is an alternative way of transferring financial claims from one currency area to another. But, in the first place, this transfer is not costless; and in the sixteenth century, specifically, the normal costs of moving specie were augmented by the exceptional hazards of war and of piracy and in some countries, including England, by the laws against the export of precious metals. Hence the specie import and export points—the margins above and below mint par at which it became profitable to import or export specie rather than transfer money by exchange—were correspondingly further apart. Moreover, the exaction of seignorage had the effect of widening the gap between the specie points still further. Suppose that the rate on London in Antwerp rose above the critical level, and that the alternative method of transferring funds to England was to export silver there. Neither silver bullion nor foreign silver coins were legal tender in England (though certain foreign gold coins were). Such silver, then, to command general purchasing power, would have to be sold either on the open market or to the Mints. If the Mints were receiving an adequate supply of silver (other than in the form of 'compulsory deliveries') this would signify that the open market price for silver was not appreciably above the mint price, while of course if it was appreciably below, the holders of bullion would sell to the Mints anyway. Thus the specie import point would be fixed by reference, not to the mint *equivalent* of newly-minted silver coins, but to their mint *price*. This argument has to be modified in the case of those foreign coins which *were* legal tender, for here the exaction of seignorage could be avoided simply by importing such coins instead. But these coins, generally gold, were usually rated in England at fairly unrealistically low rates; they were mostly part of that stock of 'valued gold' coins which, in the Low Countries, could be bought with coins of less certain value only at premiums of half to two per cent—premiums which, in the event of an abnormal demand for these coins for export, could rise to higher levels, if indeed such coins did not become quite unobtainable.[1] During the later stages of the debasement, moreover, the silver/gold ratio fell as we have seen to unrealistically low levels, and in doing so made the import of gold virtually impossible. In any event, rates of seignorage on gold were always, percentagewise, substantially below those on silver; during the debasement period the highest value of seignorage as a percentage of face value per pound of gold struck was reached in April 1546, when for a time £4. 10*s*. 0*d*. was exacted out of a face value of £30 (15 per cent). From April 1547, seignorage never exceeded £1 out of £30, or 3⅓ per cent. By contrast, in 1546–7, 29*s*. 4*d*. was retained out of each 48*s*. of 4 oz. silver (61·1 per cent); and from April 1545 onwards, silver seignorage was never less than 40 per cent of mint equivalent. Hence the qualification implied by the fact that certain foreign gold coins were legal tender was of relatively small importance.

The facts just rehearsed do, however, bring into prominence the question: was silver, as so many writers have assumed, the metal which dominated international commerce and ruled the foreign exchanges? Or did gold have an equal or, perhaps, more important role to play? Many economic historians seem to have assumed rather vaguely that silver ruled the roost throughout the medieval and early modern periods. Certainly by the early seventeenth century this was the view of knowledgeable contemporaries, too: Malynes said that silver coins 'rule the market in all places', outnumbering gold by 500 to 1.[2] This was an exaggeration even when he wrote; but for the mid sixteenth century it would have been not so much an exaggeration as a complete misrepresentation of the basis of international financial transactions. The truth is that with the rise of commerce and of prices in the early sixteenth century, at a time when silver was in relatively short supply and was chiefly minted into coins of small denomination, gold coins came to play a vital role in trade, particularly in international trade. As a recent historian of Antwerp's economy has written, in the first half of the sixteenth century gold acquired a 'very important and possibly dominant position' in the money supply of

[1] H. Buckley, 'Sir Thomas Gresham and the Foreign Exchanges', *Economic Journal* xxxiv (1924), 590.

[2] Quoted by B. E. Supple in *Commercial Crisis and Change in England 1600–1642* (Cambridge U.P., 1959), p. 173.

the Netherlands.[1] Only in the later sixteenth century did the flood of New World silver, which had barely begun to make itself felt in the years covered by this study, and the minting of silver coins of large enough denomination in large enough quantities to remove the inconvenience of using silver as a basis for international trade, gradually lead to a return to the hegemony of silver and to a state of affairs which substantially, if not entirely, corresponded with the assumptions of analysts of the exchanges from Malynes onwards.

It is difficult, of course, to know just how important, relatively, gold and silver were under what seems to have been the genuinely bimetallic regime of the mid sixteenth century. Not only is the evidence inadequate; it is not obvious, in any event, what would constitute an appropriate measure of relative importance. There was ample scope, under a bimetallic system, for the roles of the two metals to vary from context to context. Certainly, in general, silver was relatively more important in domestic and gold in international trade. Certainly, too, the debasement of the English coinage, so much more severe in regard to the silver than to the gold, generated in Antwerp a distrust of English silver which added to the difficulties of England's financial agents there and probably drove England's international financial dealings more completely on to a gold basis than at any other time. But it was still possible for the method of settling international debts to vary, say, from one firm to another.

The usual wording of the mid sixteenth-century bill of exchange was noncommittal and uninformative. The drawee was generally required to satisfy the taker's debt 'in current money', as the Gresham daybook usually says, or 'mit gelde (das) in gemeiner kuyffmanschafft gangbaer ist', or 'mit ghelde so in kopenschap gancbaer is'.[2] It seems fairly clear, however, that this apparently loose requirement often implied in practice a range of coins much more restricted than those endowed with the attribute of legal tender. In particular, most English coins seem to have been looked on very unfavourably in the Low Countries during the debasement period; only angels, the best-known of the older gold coins, seem to have retained easy acceptability more or less throughout. Generally, Dr. Van der Wee suggests, gold was in this period the most usual means of settling foreign debts. This convention was indeed embodied in legislative form in the Low Countries when in 1541 the Government decreed that bills of exchange and bonds should be settled as to a minimum of two-thirds

[1] Van der Wee, op. cit. i. 110.

[2] Strieder, op. cit., pp. 144, 165.

in recognized gold specie.[1] De Smedt appears to take the view that this was intended to apply only to the repayment of loans, not to exchange transactions arising out of commodity trade.[2] It is difficult, however, to believe that the banking community could or would observe such a distinction; and the dispatches, for example, of Stephen Vaughan, Henry VIII's financial agent in Antwerp, seem to confirm that this was the normal way of settling all exchange transactions.[3] Even on De Smedt's view the considerable importance towards the end of Henry VIII's reign and in that of his successor of loan repayments as compared with balance-of-trade residuals would have meant that at this particular period gold was of major importance in determining the level of England's exchanges.

It seems to be clear, therefore, that a theory which purports to explain changes in the exchange rate exclusively by reference to changes in the mint equivalent of silver coins is awry on at least two major counts: it overlooks the significance of seignorage, and it unjustifiably discounts, by implication, any possibility of effecting international settlements in gold. Having disarmed the orthodox explanation of sixteenth-century exchange movements, we shall now try to offer more appropriate formulae for calculating, respectively, the specie import point and the specie export point.

I assume that inward balance-of-payments residuals would be settled, once the exchange rate in shillings Flemish to the pound sterling stood higher than the specie import level, by the import of whichever metal promised the lower real cost to the importer of making the settlement. It is assumed that subject to the minor qualification discussed above regarding foreign gold coins which were legal tender in England, gold or silver so imported would have to be sold to the Mints or on the open market at something very close to the ruling mint price. *Which* metal was imported, then, would depend on the relative magnitudes of the ratio of mint price of gold to mint price of silver in England, on the one hand, and of the silver/gold ratio prevailing among England's trading partners on the other. If the former (which may be christened the mint price ratio) exceeded the latter, gold would be imported to settle balance-of-payments residuals; if the latter exceeded the former, silver. It seems likely, however, that a relatively small difference between the two ratios

[1] Van der Wee, op. cit. i. 120; ii. 203.

[2] O. de Smedt, *De Engelse natie te Antwerpen* (Antwerp, 1954) ii. 501.

[3] *L and P* xix, part 2, no. 66.

would not suffice to tip the scales decisively in favour of one or the other metal. This seems probable, partly because the continual changes in mint price of one or the other metal during the debasement period implied a margin of uncertainty in either direction; partly because the actual fine-gold or silver content even of the best coins was rarely known with certainty or identical from one piece to another; and partly because the prevailing silver/gold ratio was never exactly the same at any one time in all currency areas. I assume, therefore, that there was a band of values of the mint price ratio in England within which gold or silver might both be imported; that at mint price ratios above the upper limit of this band, only gold would be imported; and at ratios below its lower limit, only silver. Somewhat arbitrarily, but I hope not unreasonably, I assign to this band the range of values above 10·5 and below 11·5 to 1.[1]

TABLE X

Specie import point, 1542–1559

	(1)	(2)	(3)	(4)	(5)	(6)	(7)
	Mint price of				*Mint price of imported*		
	gold	*silver*	(2) × 11	(1)/(2)	*coin*	*Index*	*Value*
							s. d.
1542	*28·8*	2·4	26·4	12·0	28·8	100·0	28 2½
1544	*28·8*	2·621	*28·8*	11·0	28·8	100·0	28 2½
1545	*30·0*	2·8	*30·8*	10·7	30·4	94·7	26 8½
1546 (Jan.)	*30·6*	2·8	*30·8*	10·9	30·7	93·8	26 5½
1547	*34·8*	3·2	*35·2*	10·9	35·0	82·3	23 2½
1548 (Oct.)	34·8	3·4	*37·4*	10·2	37·4	77·0	21 9
1549	36·0	3·6	*39·3*	10·0	39·3	73·3	20 8½
1550 (July)	36·0	4·0	*44·0*	9·0	44·0	65·5	18 6
1550 (Sept.)	36·0	3·9	*42·3*	9·2	42·3	68·1	19 2½
1551 (Apr.)	36·0	6·0	*66·0*	6·0	66·0	43·6	12 3½
1551 (late)	*35·838*	3·204	*35·2*	11·2	35·5	81·1	22 10½
1553 (Mar.)		$\left(22s.\ 10\tfrac{1}{2}d. \times \frac{16}{15}\right)$					24 4½
1553 (Aug.)	*35·9875*	3·192	*35·1*	11·3	35·55	81·0	24 4½(3)
1559		$\left(24s.\ 4\tfrac{1}{2}d. \times \frac{10}{9}\right)$					27 1

NOTES.

(1) For explanation of columns and working, see text, pp. 102, 107–9.

(2) Italic type in columns (1) and (3) denotes the metal or metals favoured for import.

(3) Multiplier of $\frac{16}{15}$ applied.

Cf. W. G. Shaw, *The History of Currency* (2nd edn., London, 1896), pp. 67 ff.

The effect of making this assumption is shown in Table X. Columns (1) and (2) show the mint prices in pounds sterling, respectively, of gold and of silver. Column (3) is column (2) multiplied by 11, and thus represents the purchasing power which could be commanded in England by selling to the Mint eleven pounds of fine silver (assumed to have been worth on average the same in the exporting countries as one pound of fine gold). Column (4) is the mint price ratio (that is, column (1) divided by column (2)). It can be seen that, according to the preceding argument, gold alone would have been imported to settle balance-of-payments residuals in 1542; silver alone from 1548 to mid 1551; and gold or silver indifferently at all other times. The appropriate values are then transferred to column (5)—that is, for 1542 from column (1); for 1548 to 1551 from column (3); while for other years the means of columns (1) and (3) are taken. In column (6), column (5) is transformed into an index of the values of the specie import point, with 1542 = 100, by calculating the value of

$$\frac{28{\cdot}8\times 100}{\text{column (5)}}.$$

Now as to the specie export point. Here it is clearly the mint equivalent rather than the mint price which was relevant, for what was in question was the value of English coins abroad, and this depended on their intrinsic value. But of which coins? For as we have seen it was characteristic of the period covered by this study that in the case both of gold and of silver, coins minted to different standards (that is, having different mint equivalents) circulated side by side at the same time.

There are two limiting cases to consider. First, coins might differ in intrinsic values yet pass current at the same fiat value. In this event, clearly the best coins (that is, those with the lowest *de facto* mint equivalents) would be culled for export, for their purchasing power abroad (where they would be valued on the basis of their fine-metal content) would be higher than that of other coins of the same fiat value, whereas at home it was not. In the second case, coins of different intrinsic values, though supposed to circulate at the same fiat values, might actually change hands at differing values proportionate to their intrinsic values. In this case, the *de facto* mint equivalents of all such coins would be equal, and there would be no temptation to cull any particular variety for export unless familiarity with them (as with the English angel) or some similar attribute particularly recommended them abroad. One can conceive, too, an intermediate case in which the better coins circulated at a face value above their fiat value but below their intrinsic value; this case would resemble the first save that the temptation to cull them would be reduced to the extent that their *de facto* face value was above their fiat value. It will be seen, on reflection, that the appropriate figure to use in *all* of these cases, when calculating the export value of these coins, is the *de facto mint equivalent of the best coins*. This might be equal to (in the second case) or lower than (in the first and third cases) that of other coins of the same metal in circulation, but would in all cases identify the intrinsic quality of those coins actually liable to be exported. (Note (2) to Table XI makes it clear that I have infringed the rule advocated in this paragraph in respect of gold in 1542, by choosing the *de facto* mint equivalent of angel gold rather than of crown gold. I argue that the slightly lower mint equivalent of the latter was inadequate to offset the superior acceptability and familiarity of angel gold in the Low Countries. The 'mint equivalent ratio' was in any event at or very close to that value which threw the burden of determining the specie export point on silver rather than on gold.)

The question remains, then, under what conditions gold coins, and under what conditions silver, would be used to finance outward balance-of-payments residuals. It seems that we need yet a third variant of the silver/gold ratio to answer this question, that is, the ratio of the *de facto* mint equivalent of the best gold coins to that of the best silver. This ratio, as before, can then be compared with the silver/gold ratio prevailing in trading-partner economies. If lower than the latter, gold would be exported; if higher, silver. As before, we assume an average silver/gold ratio abroad of 11 to 1 and a range of $> 10{\cdot}5 < 11{\cdot}5$ to 1 in which either gold or silver might be exported. The relevant data are presented in Table XI. From this we see that gold was favoured for export in 1547, 1549, 1550, and early 1551, silver in 1542, 1544, 1545, 1546, and the second half of 1551, and silver and gold equally at other dates. On this basis, values are transferred from columns (1) and (3) to column (5), and, as before, column (5) is then transformed into an index of the specie export point with 1542 = 100.

A special difficulty attaches to late 1551. It has been argued earlier that some of the 6 oz. silver coins of the 1545–6 issue still survived at that date, though disappearing between then and Elizabeth's coinage, being either exported or reminted. These coins, like all the other base silver, were called down by Edward VI in the summer of 1551, in two

TABLE XI

Specie export point, 1542–1559

	(1)	(2)	(3)	(4)	(5)	(6)	(7)
	Mint equivalent of best				*Mint equivalent of exportable*		
	gold	*silver*	(2) × 11	$\frac{(1)}{(2)}$	*coin*	*Index*	*Value*
							s. d.
1542	27·979	2·433	*26·8*	11·5	26·8	100·0	25 1½
1544	29·675	2·433	*26·8*	12·2	26·8	100·0	25 1½
1545	30·9125	2·433	*26·8*	12·7	26·8	100·0	25 1½
1546	32·15	2·433	*26·8*	13·2	26·8	100·0	25 1½
1547	*33·3875*	3·2	35·2	10·4	33·4	80·2	20 2
1548	*34·625*	3·2	*35·2*	10·8	34·9	76·8	19 3½
1549	*35·858*	4·8	52·8	7·5	35·9	74·7	18 9
1550	*37·092*	4·8	52·8	7·7	37·1	72·2	18 2
1551 (Jan.)	*37·092*	4·8	52·8	7·7	37·1	72·2	18 2
1551 (July)	68·35	4·8	*52·8*	14·2	52·8	50·8	12 10
1551 (late)	36·0	2·4	*26·4*	15·0	26·4	101·5	25 6
1552 (Mar.)	*36·0*	3·258	*35·8*	11·0	35·9	74·7	18 9
1553 (Mar.)		$\left(18s.\ 9d. \times \frac{16}{15}\right)$					20 0
1553 (Aug.)	*36·1875*	3·258	*35·8*	11·1	36·0	74·4	19 11½
1559		$\left(19s.\ 11\tfrac{1}{2}d. \times \frac{10}{9}\right)$					22 2

NOTES.

(1) For explanation of columns and working, see text, pp. 102–9.

(2) For 1542 I have assumed that angel (23 c. 3½ gr.) gold was favoured for export, despite its rather higher mint equivalent as compared with crown (22 c.) gold. (In the following years, angel gold generally had the lowest mint equivalent, so that no such difficulty occurs.) I have further assumed that from June 1542 the *de facto* mint equivalent of angel gold began to rise in a linear trend towards the value of £29. 13*s.* 6*d.* which it attained in May 1544 (see Table III, col. 4, p. 26), and the value shown for 1542 is the average *de facto* mint equivalent for that year calculated on this assumption.

(3) Italic type in columns (1) and (3) denotes the metal or metals favoured for export.

stages, to half of their previous fiat value. After the second reduction, the *de facto* mint equivalent of these coins was but £2. 8*s.* 0*d.* This was substantially less than that of the fine silver which Edward then authorized (in other words, the 1545–6 coins, at their new fiat value, were the finest silver in existence). This would imply a temptation not only to remint them but to export them. For one thing, the *de facto* mint equivalents attributed to them and to gold for late 1551, in Table XI, yield a ratio which clearly points to these 6 oz. silver coins as the obvious means of settling outwards balance-of-payments residuals. But, equally, to use the same value, in conjunction with the mint price of gold, yields a silver/gold ratio which points unequivocally to the profitability of a bimetallic flow in which this silver might be exported to finance an import of gold.[1] Actually, the potential margin of profit from exporting these coins was probably slightly larger than that from reminting them.

The values in columns (5) and (6) which result from placing £2. 8*s*. 0*d*. as the *de facto* mint equivalent of these coins in column (2) are certainly striking and result in a specie export point higher than the specie import point. Is this possible? There seems in fact to be no logical contradiction in asserting that it was profitable to export certain coins which were no longer being minted at an exchange rate at which it was also profitable to import specie for minting at a new, and higher, mint price. It may indeed be easier in the light of this situation to account for the unusually wide 'spread', already discussed, which developed at this time between the London–Antwerp and Antwerp–London exchange rates, the former tending to follow the specie export point and the latter the specie import point. But a number of uncertainties have to be mentioned in regard to this particular calculation. We are not quite sure how much of this 1545–6 silver issue remained in circulation in September 1551, nor how long it lasted as a reserve to finance balance-of-payments residuals and thus sustain a high specie export point. In any event, it may well be unrealistic to attribute to it, as we have done, a *de facto* mint equivalent based on the assumption that its value in circulation remained fixed at the level established for all base silver by Edward's two 'calling-down' proclamations. In view of the strong demand which their profitability for reminting and for export exerted on these coins, and also of the fact that they can have constituted only a small fraction of the total circulation, it would be plausible to expect that their face value should have 'broken loose' from the fiat value allotted to them, and that they should have come to command a substantial premium. In this event, of course, their *de facto* mint equivalent would have been correspondingly higher, and the specie export point correspondingly lower. It is tempting, too, to suspect that their intrinsic value may have been discounted abroad because of the general disrepute in which all the base silver coins were held, and because of the fact that even the largest of them were now worth only sixpence. It is possible to see some support for the view that these last points were the crucial ones in the facts that the mint accounts for

[1] See Table IV, p. 31.

the period October 1551 to March 1552 reveal no evidence of a bimetallic flow, whereas there was a considerable output of sterling-silver coin in this period, the raw material for which may well have come from the melting down of coins of the 1545–6 issue.[1] At the same time, the continued downward trend in the volume and perhaps even more in the value of cloth exports entitles us to suspect a balance-of-payments deficit, the settlement of which may nevertheless partly account for the rapid disappearance of the remaining coins of the earlier 6 oz. issue. On balance, it might seem preferable to reject the *de facto* mint equivalent attributed to silver in late 1551 and to revise downwards the specie export level shown for that period—or, at the least, to regard it as of very short duration. One is encouraged in this interpretation by noting that from late 1550 to August 1551 the actual London–Antwerp rate 'hugs' the specie export line very closely, as one would expect during a period of balance-of-payments deficit. Unless this close agreement ceased soon after August 1551 the specie export point for the following October must be substantially too high.

It should of course be pointed out that calculating the specie export point is a more hazardous undertaking anyway than calculating the specie import point. This is because the latter depends primarily on current mint prices for gold and silver, which are known with certainty, whereas the former depends primarily on the *de facto* mint equivalents of the best coins of each metal, which are not. These are *not* known with certainty both because we cannot always be sure how long older and better coins remained in circulation, and because evidence is not always forthcoming as to the extent to which their *de facto* face value diverged from the fiat value at which the coins had been originally issued. In Table XI I have made assumptions on these matters which came to seem reasonable in the course of the calculations which underlie the earlier chapters of this book; to some extent, the reasoning which lies behind the values shown in columns (1) and (2) of Table XI has in fact been made explicit, rather sporadically, in the preceding pages.[2] It does not seem necessary to attempt here a systematic and detailed justification of the choice of these particular values, but the reader who chooses to be sceptical about them deserves sympathy. Only two reassurances, beyond the general one arising

[1] A *de facto* mint equivalent below the mint price for new silver generated an incentive not only to remint or export the 6 oz. coins, but to melt them for industrial use. Cf. Hughes and Larkin, op. cit., no. 381 (pp. 534–5).

[2] See, especially, pp. 17–18, 22–6, 52–3.

from the objective and fairly thorough consideration of the matter which the writer hopes he may claim to have made, will be offered. One is that some of the small miscalculations which may have occurred may have made no difference to the result. For example, the *de facto* mint equivalent for gold written into column (1) for 1551 (July) is based upon the assertion in the Johnson Letters, dated the 8th of that month, that angels could not be bought for 18*s*. 4*d*., whereas a few days earlier those selling them had been glad to take 17*s*. for some 'old and very good' ones.[1] It is the valuation of angels at 18*s*. 4*d*. which has been used to calculate the value for 1551 (July) written into column (1), and it can be seen that the evidence in favour of this is limited and that, in any event, the value may have held for only a short period of time, for everything points to early July as the most critical period in financial and exchange business. Nevertheless, even a substantially lower *de facto* face value for these gold coins would still have sufficed to throw the burden of fixing the specie export point on the *silver* coinage, so that the same value, £53. 8*s*., would in any event still have appeared in column (5) for that date, and the index number in column (6) would still be the same.

The other and greater source of reassurance arises simply from the explanatory power which the theory here put forward appears to confer on the analyst of exchange-rate movements. It will be seen from Graph A that our arguments and calculations yield values for the specie points which fit remarkably well the actual course of the exchange rate. That they do so far better than the simple explanation in terms of a mint par reflecting the current mint price for silver is shown by the line also included in the graph, showing the par rate of exchange which would have obtained had this changed from time to time, as for example Unwin supposed, solely in response to the changing intrinsic values of new silver issues. Before commenting further on the outcome of these calculations, however, the final steps by which the data have been transformed into the values plotted as the specie import and export points remain to be explained.

First, adjustments become necessary when we take into account, as we should, changes in currency arrangements amongst England's trading partners, and specifically in the Low Countries. Such adjustments would ideally call for an examination of financial and mint arrangements there, at least as thorough as that undertaken in this study with regard to England. This examination has frankly surpassed

[1] Winchester, op. cit., letter no. 700.

the time and knowledge which the present writer could command. However, it is easy to identify the changes which had the most direct and greatest significance in this period for the level of the London–Antwerp exchange. They were the two reductions in the fine-silver contest of the Brabant groat which occurred in 1553 and in 1559.[1] The first reduction, on 23 March 1553, was from 0·32 grammes to 0·30 grammes; the second, on 24 October 1559, from 0·30 grammes to 0·27 grammes. As Dr. Van der Wee has shown, the Flemish and Brabant groats, linked together in the ratio 2:3, formed the basis, the 'link money' as it was called, on which the whole system of money of account in the Low Countries rested.[2] A reduction in the actual fine-silver content of this 'link money' implied, sooner or later, a proportionate decrease in the value of the money of account, which of course would imply *inter alia* a corresponding decrease in its external exchange value. Hence the reduction in the silver content of the groat brought about, indirectly, a strengthening of the London–Antwerp exchange in England's favour.

Columns (6) of Tables X and XI have, then, been transformed into actual exchange quotations in Flemish shillings to the pound sterling by multiplying the chosen 1542 values for the specie import and export points by the appropriate index number for each point of time and dividing by 100. From 23.3.1553 and 24.10.1559 onwards further multipliers of $\frac{16}{15}$ and $\frac{10}{9}$, respectively, have been applied to allow for the effect on the exchange rate after those dates of the reductions of the fine-silver content of the 'link money' in the Low Countries. The question, then, only remains of the starting values (that is, for 1542) to which these multipliers were applied. This question, however, is not so easily resolved as might appear. There is no difficulty, thanks to Dr. Van der Wee, in knowing what the exchange rate was in 1542. But in the first place, we do not know whether the actual rate in that year lay closer to the specie import or to the specie export point, or even indeed outside one of them. Nor is it easy to be sure how far apart the points were at that time. On this specific point, as indeed more generally, a calculation of the specie points based *inter alia* on a detailed examination of the intrinsic values of the multiplicity of coins circulating in Antwerp would provide a surer basis. However, our rough and ready route to estimating the import and export points does not fail, in this last stage of the journey, to offer an acceptable 'short cut'.

[1] Van der Wee, op. cit. i. 128. [2] Ibid. i. 107 ff.

We note that—ignoring for the moment transport costs—the specie import point in 1542 was that exchange rate at which the amount of Flemish money equivalent to one pound of gold equalled £28. 16*s*. (st.), for at any higher rate transmitting from Antwerp to London by exchange would yield less sterling than the £28. 16*s*. which could be had by importing the gold and selling it to the Mint. Similarly, the specie export point in 1542 was that exchange rate at which the amount of Flemish money equivalent to eleven pounds of silver equalled £26. 16*s*. (st.), for at any lower rate the eleven pounds of silver contained in £26. 16*s*. of English silver coins would yield more Flemish money than transmitting the same sum by exchange. Since, by our assumption, the same sum in the Low Countries was equivalent *both* to one pound of gold and to eleven pounds of silver, the ratio of the specie import point to the specie export point was $\frac{£28.\ 16s.}{£26.\ 16s.}$, or 1·075 to 1. In other words, the former was about 7½ per cent above the latter. Now introduce transport costs. I assume these, allowing for interest forgone during the time of shipping and for an appreciable risk premium, to have been of the order of 2 to 2½ per cent in either direction. Adding twice this value to the 7½ per cent we have a total gap of about 12 per cent (of the lower value). I now assume that the average sight rate for 1542, which was 26*s*. 9*d*., was about midway between the specie import and export points, and thus set these respectively at 105½ and 94 per cent of the sight rate, or 28*s*. 2½*d*. and 25*s*. 1½*d*. It is these sums which, in turn, we take as = 100 and to which we apply the multipliers already explained. The resulting values for the dates calculated in Tables X and XI are then plotted on Graph A and connected up, respectively, as the specie import and export points. Specie import points are connected stepwise, since the adoption of the new mint prices which determine them occurred on specific dates. Specie export points, on the other hand, are connected by straight lines appropriate to the assumption of a gradual increase in *de facto* mint equivalents.

The graph seems to confirm in an encouraging way the general rightness of the analysis of the determinants of the specie points made in the preceding pages. It can be seen that only briefly does the actual rate stray a little outside them. It may of course be that this encouraging result is to some extent spurious, and springs from having set the starting values (for 1542) rather too far apart, so that there is a correspondingly wide path along which the actual rate can meander.

But this could be true only in a minor way, in so far as the assumptions on costs of transporting specie are too generous. It may on the other hand be that the assumption that the actual rate in 1542 was midway between the specie import and export points is mistaken. Perhaps it was in reality closer to the export point; were this so, both the import and export points should be correspondingly higher throughout. This could explain the tendency on the graph for the actual rate to lie generally closer to the import than to the export point in the later 1540s. On the other hand, the fact that our calculated values for 1553 to 1559 lie for the most part so encouragingly in the middle of the range tells in the opposite direction. It may be that the explanation tentatively put forward earlier is the correct one: namely, that knowledge of the deterioration of the English currency generally lagged somewhat behind events, so that at any one time the actual rate, during its continued decline from 1546 to 1551, remained a little higher than circumstances objectively justified.

On the other hand, the explanation may be quite different. The general theory of exchange determination which we have embraced assumes, of course, that the actual rate is free to move *within* the specie points in accordance with changes in the size and direction of balance-of-payments residuals. The most natural way to account for an actual rate close to the specie import point is, therefore, by reference to an active balance of payments. Most regrettably we neither have nor seem justified in hoping for anything like satisfactory information regarding the balance of payments in this period. But it does not seem prima facie at all difficult to envisage an explanation of rates which, in the late 1540s, lay close to the import point, in terms of the cloth export boom of those years. Nor is there anything apparently inconsistent between rates at or near the export point and the export slump which followed the boom in the early 1550s. Mention of such possibilities invokes the whole question of shorter-term movements of the exchanges within the export points and their relation to commercial and financial conditions. Regrettably, our knowledge is simply not complete or detailed enough to permit a study such as this question deserves. Even our knowledge of the volume of cloth exports, as will be seen in the following chapter, admits to serious gaps, and no satisfactory attempt has yet been made to transform volumes into values, as would be necessary for the purpose in hand. On the import side our knowledge is even more exiguous; the more heterogeneous nature of imports has so far discouraged scholars from attempting anything in the nature of an index of import volumes or values. Finally, of course, there is reason to suppose that capital transfers were more than usually important for at least the first part of our period, and if so they would certainly have to form part of a complete explanation of short-term movements of the exchanges. Yet their intricacies have so far resisted, it seems, not only my own ignorant attempts to impose some rough order on them, but also those of much more knowledgeable scholars.

It is worth notice in passing that this lack of information about the balance of payments did not deter Unwin from making firm pronouncements about the behaviour of the exchange rate within the specie points. Thus he asserted that the normal experience in the mid sixteenth century was a 'favourable' exchange (that is, a rate closer to the specie import than to the export point) because of the flow of New World silver to England through Antwerp. During the debasement, however, an outflow of good money reversed this situation and led to an unfavourable rate (that is, closer to the specie export point). Finally, once base coin was no longer being minted, the resumed inflow of silver brought a return to favourable—indeed, for a time, exceptionally favourable—rates.[1] There are a number of comments to be made on this. One is that Unwin offered no evidence either for the *explicandum* or for the 'facts' proffered as elements in his explanation. A second is to express surprise that Unwin could speak of a 'normal' inflow of Spanish silver and of a temporary outflow of good money during the debasement without perceiving the need to relate either of these alleged flows to the balance of payments at the time. Finally, so far as the evidence of our reconstruction of the exchanges permits any judgement, it is that the facts were the reverse of those postulated by Unwin. England's exchange rate with the Low Countries seems to have lain generally closer to the import point during the debasement and to the export point during the 1550s.

If commentary on short-term movements of the exchange *within* the specie points is still by and large beyond our capabilities, there are yet lessons to be drawn from their broader conformity to the path charted for them by the values of the specie import and export points calculated as described in the foregoing pages. The most general one is that already mentioned: that the 'theory' underlying these calculations receives an encouraging degree of support when they are

[1] Unwin, op. cit., pp. 156–7.

brought face to face with fact. But the implications of this have yet to be spelled out. In the first place, it seems to follow that the mid sixteenth-century exchanges represented a sector of the economy which functioned, to a considerable degree, in a rational and mechanistic fashion. The warning given earlier against underestimating subjective elements and embracing oversimplified 'mechanistic' theories of the sixteenth-century economy is not otiose; there were certainly occasions, as in the movement of the exchanges in 1551 or in England's capital borrowings in Antwerp in the 1540s, when subjective factors played a significant role. But that this limitation on the automaticity of the exchange market was not too severe seems to be fairly implied by Graph A and the preceding analysis. It is not clear, for example, on what grounds we could deny to the London–Antwerp exchanges in the mid sixteenth century at least as smooth and well-integrated a mechanism as characterized those between London and New York in the early nineteenth.[1] This conclusion in turn seems to imply a degree of sophistication in the institutional structure of mid sixteenth-century finance which modern scholars have not always been prepared to concede. It also casts doubt on the allegations of 'exchange-rigging' which are so familiar a theme of pamphleteers in the early modern period. I doubt, for example, whether I should now be prepared myself to argue as readily as once I did against dismissing as self-evidently absurd the contentions on this score of Gerard Malynes.

A further implication of the apparent adequacy of our 'theory' of exchange movements is that the technical assumptions underlying it cannot be too far from the truth. Perhaps the most important of these is the assumption that the international currency system of the mid sixteenth century was truly bimetallic; that gold played an equal and indeed at times and in some respects a preponderant role in the conduct of international trade and financial relations and in determining its technical coefficients.

A final reflection when reviewing the argument and conclusions of this chapter concerns the adequacy of the statistical data relating to the coinage and to the external sector. The many deficiencies of these

[1] Of course, the early nineteenth-century transatlantic exchange rate fluctuated in part precisely because of bank payments suspensions (which in effect revoked the gold standard for the time being) in times of financial crisis. On this ground we are entitled to expect greater exchange stability in a monetary system of full-bodied coins, which is more irrevocably tied to a gold and/or silver standard.

have been referred to candidly and in firm language. But the surviving evidence has seemed adequate to support a distinctly more rigorous quantitative analysis of the currency and the foreign exchanges in the middle decades of the century than they have commonly received, and that despite the fact that as far as the survival of evidence is concerned these decades have generally been rather less fortunate than either the preceding or the following period. In encountering the frequently heard assertion that sixteenth-century economic history is doomed to 'qualitative' treatment because of the absence or frailty of evidence capable of yielding statistical data, one finds oneself sometimes wondering whether this judgement is less the result of the character of its historical records than of the inclinations and qualifications of its historians. It is not for example clear how far one could sustain the belief that the eighteenth century is on balance better furnished in this respect than the sixteenth; and one wonders how long it will be before the analytical techniques of econometric history begin to infiltrate some of the hitherto obscure recesses of the Tudor economy.

6

EXPORTS AND THE DEBASEMENT

1. The Problem of Interpretation

WE have seen already that economic historians, though generally imputing to the debasement of the coinage a considerable influence on overseas trade, are not agreed what that influence was. Unwin wrote that confusion and loss of confidence generated by the debasement 'completely demoralized' trade and 'entirely dislocated' commercial and financial relations with foreign countries.[1] The more typical modern view is that brilliantly urged by Professor Fisher, who in his seminal 1940 article 'Commercial Trends and Policy in Sixteenth-Century England'[2] argued that debasement acted in essentially the same way as a modern devaluation, stimulating exports (and discouraging imports, though this aspect was not considered at great length in Fisher's article) by bringing about a more rapid fall of the foreign exchanges than rise of domestic prices and incomes. This, of course, would reduce the prices of domestic goods in terms of foreign currencies and increase those of foreign commodities in terms of the domestic currency. In his important critique of Fisher's argument, Professor Stone first queried the reality, or at least the magnitude, of the expansion of exports on the assumption of which Fisher's whole case was predicated.[3] He then suggested that thc timing of this expansion was such as to cast doubt on Fisher's explanation of it, since the exchanges, Stone claimed, did not weaken appreciably until 1547, by when the expansionary trend had largely run its course. Stone was aware that higher export volumes were occasionally recorded *after* 1547 than in any preceding year, but seems to take the view that these were interspersed with and balanced by correspondingly severe slumps, and cannot therefore legitimately be interpreted as a continuation of the upward trend of the period since about 1535. At

[1] Unwin, op. cit., p. 149.

[2] Fisher, 'Commercial Trends', op. cit., p. 99.

[3] L. Stone, 'State Control in Sixteenth-Century England', *Economic History Review* xvii (1947), 104 ff.

least one more recent writer, noting these discrepancies, has adopted caution as his watchword. In his valuable monograph on the wool trade, Dr. Bowden writes of the export expansion of the 1540s: 'In its final stages, this boom was probably stimulated by exchange depreciation consequent upon currency debasement.'[1] Dr. Bowden's caution, regrettably, has not been emulated either by textbook writers or, in the writer's experience at least, by most university students.

The differences of opinion just summarized arise from a number of causes. To some extent they reflect varying interpretations of, and deficiencies in, the statistical evidence. Stone's critique of Fisher was founded on the contention that by concentrating on *broad cloth* exports (to the neglect of wool and of worsted cloth), and on *London's* exports (to the neglect of those of the outports), Fisher had painted a very unbalanced picture of the over-all trend of *English* exports in the early sixteenth century. The analyses both of Fisher and Stone, and indeed of all other writers, have moreover suffered from the paucity of evidence regarding exports in the debasement period itself. It is indeed regrettable that the magnificent series of Enrolled Customs Accounts, the data from which relating to wool and cloth exports have been so valuably made available in published form by Professor Carus-Wilson and Miss Coleman,[2] should peter out shortly before the end of Henry VIII's reign, leaving us without their systematic evidence just over the very period for which it is, for our purposes, most vital. It will be amongst the objects of this chapter and of Appendix C (which gives details of the sources and methods used to construct the tables presented here relating to the export trade) to reconsider export trends in the early sixteenth century in the light of the Carus-Wilson–Coleman publication, and to assemble the scattered but not negligible evidence available, in the Particular Accounts and elsewhere, as to the course of exports in the 1540s and 1550s.

There is, however, another and very different type of reason for the conflict of interpretation referred to. This arises from the nature of causal analysis in the social sciences. In the first place, it need hardly be said that the mere temporal juxtaposition of two historical events does not in itself prove any causal connection between them. If

[1] P. J. Bowden, *The Wool Trade in Tudor and Stuart England* (Macmillan, 1962), p. 112.

[2] Carus-Wilson and Coleman, op. cit.

exports were rising during the same period that the coinage was being progressively debased, this does not mean that the second was necessarily either the cause or the result of the first. An immediate reaction to the allegation of such a causal link might be to inquire whether exports had been similarly rising before the coinage began to be debased; if we find that they had, the hypothesis of a causal link has on this evidence little to commend it. It is partly for this reason that we propose, in fact, to re-examine export trends in the first four decades of the sixteenth century, as well as in the debasement and immediate post-debasement years. The presumption that a causal connection exists between two variables becomes stronger the closer the similarity between their movements. A so-to-say fine-grained correlation between changes in mint price and the rises and falls of England's overseas trade would create a presumption of a causal link between them. Unfortunately, the gaps in the evidence relating to exports during the debasement period, and the fact that in any event they can only be estimated on an annual basis, make it impossible to attempt as detailed a chronological comparison as we should wish between the courses of debasement and of exports.

In such circumstances we are forced to rely even more heavily that usual on direct appraisal of the causal links suggested by some writers. This, of course, is in any event inescapable. The most perfect correlation between two variables, A and B, does no more than prove the existence of *some* causal connection between them. It remains equally possible (*a*) that A is the cause of B, (*b*) that B is the cause of A, or (*c*) that A and B are both results of X. And, of course, even if we can choose between these three possibilities, it still remains to investigate the *nature* of the causal mechanism. There are many well-attested statistical regularities in the natural universe (for example, in medicine) for which no causal explanation has been propounded even after years of intensive research.

In the present case, we have little difficulty in recognizing in which direction the causal effect, if there was one, must have been exerted. It seems perfectly clear that the 'cause' of debasement lay in decisions to alter mint prices and seignorage taken by Henry VIII or his advisers and by the advisers of Edward VI, decisions generated primarily by the pressing need for revenue. We cannot then believe that changes in export volumes were the 'cause' of debasement. Nor can we believe that Henry or Edward or their advisers merely 'willed', as it were, increases or decreases in exports, so that in this instance A and B were not the joint results of X. If then statistical analysis could demonstrate beyond doubt the existence of a causal link between debasement and a rise in exports, we could scarcely doubt that it was the former which 'caused' the second. But in the absence of unequivocal statistical proof of a causal link we are driven to rely on a more direct assessment of the validity of the suggested causal mechanism. It is here that room for differences of opinion as to the net effect of debasement on exports exists; for it may well be that we shall adjudge to be equally plausible two possible influences which work, so to say, in opposite directions. It might be found quite plausible, on closer empirical inquiry, to assert with Fisher that debasement tended to stimulate exports, like a modern devaluation, by reducing the price of domestic exports in terms of foreign currencies. But it might seem equally plausible to assert with Unwin that debasement tended to 'demoralize' and 'dislocate' trade by engendering confusion and loss of confidence in the money and foreign-exchange markets. The puzzle would then be to know whether the first (favourable) effect outweighed the second, or the second the first, or whether the two neatly cancelled each other out.

Such a problem would not necessarily be beyond the reach of human ingenuity. For example, we might argue that the 'Fisher effect', as formulated above, would tend to increase exports but to decrease imports, whereas the 'Unwin effect' would tend to decrease both. A parallel movement of both exports and imports would therefore tend to favour the Unwin view, a divergent movement—exports rising more than or falling less than imports—the Fisher one. There is, however, the further difficulty of disentangling the effect of the debasement from that of other influences on the level of imports and exports. Fisher states, quite rightly, that 'the relevant statistics are too imperfect *and the intrusion of other factors is too great* for any exact correlation to be possible'[1] (my italics). One could not therefore be sure, even were the statistics better than they are, how much of the observed movements of exports and of imports should be ascribed to the effect of the debasement and how much to other causes, unless some way were discovered not merely of identifying but of quantifying the effects both of the debasement *and* of other influences on trade.

It has to be said at once that the present chapter is very far indeed from attempting even as full an exploration of these problems as the

[1] Fisher, 'Commercial Trends', p. 99.

surviving evidence would permit. In particular, two major shortcomings must be identified. First, limitations of the author's knowledge have prevented him from assessing, in any detailed way, the impact on trade of influences other than the debasement of the coinage. And second, the limited time which it was possible to devote in London to the study of original sources did not suffice to enable the writer to attempt any calculation of the course of the volume of imports. In this respect, of course, I found relatively little help in previous work. The more heterogeneous nature of imports in the Tudor period renders the compilation of an import index conceptually more hazardous and statistically more complex than that of an export index. Yet without such a tool the analyst of sixteenth-century trade is like a boxer with one hand tied behind his back. The scholar who attempts the tiresome but surely feasible task of constructing some sort of index of English imports in the Tudor period will indeed earn the gratitude of historians of that age.

The aims of the present chapter in regard to the debasement period are more modest: they are to assemble and present the evidence on exports of cloth and wool for the debasement period, and to draw the reader's attention to such light as the facts and arguments put forward in the preceding chapters of this monograph seem able to throw on the effect of the debasement on the volume of those exports.

2. Export Trends in the Early Sixteenth Century

Before going on to consider exports during the debasement and immediate post-debasement years, however, we shall devote a little time to re-examining export trends in the decades prior to the Great Debasement. This is easily possible thanks to the publication by Carus-Wilson and Coleman of the cloth and wool export figures contained in the Enrolled Customs Accounts. It is desirable for two reasons. First, as already suggested, the most obvious statistical step is to examine whether a marked break in export trends occurred at about the time debasement began; if it did, the assertion of a causal influence is made to appear prima facie plausible, though no more than that; if it did not, the task of the advocate of such a link becomes that much harder. Secondly, Professor Fisher in the article referred to imputed some expansionary influence on exports to the earlier raising of the English mint price in 1526, and the plausibility of such an interpretation is naturally of some passing interest to us. Accordingly we present in Table XII a summary of the course of England's cloth and wool exports from the later fifteenth century to the eve of the Great Debasement, compiled from the Carus-Wilson–Coleman publication.

Professor Carus-Wilson and Miss Coleman have reproduced in their volume the figures of cloth and of wool exports for each port and for each year—the Exchequer year ran from Michaelmas to Michaelmas (29 September)—further subdividing to show exports of denizen, Hanseatic, and other alien merchants separately. For the most part this last distinction does not concern us and has been eliminated in our own summary of the Carus-Wilson–Coleman figures. Nor are we interested, again for the most part, in tracing the fortunes of individual outports, so that outport exports have been aggregated. Total outport exports are, however, shown separately from the London totals, since the changing distribution of exports as between London and the outports is an important reason for the disagreements as to the course of exports in the early sixteenth century. There are a few gaps in the Enrolled Accounts, but over the period with which we are concerned at present the gaps only deprive us of occasional outport figures, and for the most part, happily, of relatively unimportant outports at that. Only for one of the years, 1528–9, is the London account incomplete. Where accounts are missing or—as sometimes happens—cover only a part of the twelve-month period, the gap has been filled by interpolating a figure calculated according to the conventions described in the note to Table XII. It should be stressed that for twenty-eight of the fifty years for which cloth exports are shown in Table XII the accounts are complete, while for only a few of the remaining years is there any chance, in the writer's view, that the error introduced by the interpolation referred to should have exceeded one per cent of the total. The wool figures are even better, the accounts being complete for thirty-two of the forty-nine years presented. (No wool estimate is offered for 1543/4 owing to the absence of the London account for that year. The view has been taken that London normally exported so high a proportion of the total that it would be impermissible to interpolate a figure for it.) As to the overall reliability of the Accounts, the reader is referred to the admirable discussions by Carus-Wilson and Coleman in the volume referred to.[1] There remains the problem of converting exports of wool and of cloth to some common basis to permit of aggregating them. Money value is the obvious one but has not been adopted for lack of evidence. Instead, wool has been converted to a 'cloth equivalents'

[1] Carus-Wilson and Coleman, op. cit., pp. 18–33.

TABLE XII

Woollen exports, 1488/9–1543/4

Year	Total	Cloth		Wool		London		Outports	
		Number	%	Cloth equiv.	%	Cloth equiv.	%	Cloth equiv.	%
	(1)	(2)	(3)	(4)	(5)	(6)	(7)	(8)	(9)
1488/9	95,358	53,505	56·1	41,853	43·9	59,556	62·5	35,802	37·5
1489/90	102,786	58,310	56·7	44,476	43·3	64,519	62·8	38,267	37·2
1490/1	70,910	56,184	79·2	14,726	20·8	43,035	60·7	27,875	39·3
1491/2	74,291	54,724	73·7	19,567	26·3	44,278	59·6	30,013	40·4
1492/3	86,435	55,325	64·0	31,110	36·0	47,812	55·3	38,623	44·7
1488/9–1492/3/ (ann. ave.)	85,956	55,610	64·7	30,346	35·3	51,840	60·3	34,116	39·7
1499/1500	106,724	75,262	70·5	31,462	29·5	67,907	63·6	38,817	36·4
1500/1	109,092	79,321	72·7	29,771	27·3	62,018	56·8	47,074	43·2
1501/2	126,668	86,420	68·2	40,248	31·8	70,481	55·6	56,187	44·4
1502/3	113,999	76,182	66·8	37,817	33·2	66,725	58·5	47,274	41·5
1503/4	101,020	75,240	74·5	25,780	25·5	55,244	54·7	45,776	45·3
1504/5	100,000	68,299	68·3	31,701	31·7	53,616	53·6	46,384	46·4
1505/6	98,143	77,998	79·5	20,145	20·5	54,867	55·9	43,276	44·1
1506/7	113,395	83,386	73·5	30,009	26·5	70,499	62·2	42,896	37·8
1507/8	130,236	93,783	72·0	36,453	28·0	73,111	56·1	57,125	43·9
1508/9	125,893	92,526	73·5	33,367	26·5	79,605	63·2	46,288	36·8
1509/10	112,219	76,460	68·1	35,759	31·9	73,238	65·3	38,981	34·7
1510/11	123,451	86,315	69·9	37,136	30·1	89,849	72·8	33,602	27·2
1511/12	104,344	77,115	73·9	27,229	26·1	75,817	72·7	28,527	27·3
1512/13	111,954	86,641	77·4	25,313	22·6	75,529	67·5	36,425	32·5
1513/14	125,155	92,524	73·9	32,631	26·1	88,681	70·9	36,474	29·1
1514/15	122,796	93,412	76·1	29,384	23·9	80,819	65·8	41,977	34·2
1515/16	114,092	82,106	72·0	31,986	28·0	81,097	71·1	32,995	28·9
1516/17	117,329	87,290	74·4	30,039	25·6	78,188	66·6	39,141	33·4
1517/18	120,146	91,765	76·4	28,381	23·6	81,834	68·1	38,312	31·9
1518/19	134,371	91,153	67·8	43,218	32·2	90,707	67·5	43,664	32·5
1519/20	138,876	98,267	70·8	40,609	29·2	89,063	64·1	49,813	35·9
1520/1	108,864	75,893	69·7	32,971	30·3	71,962	66·1	36,902	33·9
1521/2	82,312	61,827	75·1	20,485	24·9	63,670	77·4	18,642	22·6
1522/3	107,374	86,061	80·2	21,313	19·8	65,853	61·3	41,521	38·7
1523/4	109,984	90,294	82·1	19,690	17·9	82,748	75·2	27,236	24·8
1524/5	110,817	96,231	86·8	14,586	13·2	88,334	79·7	22,483	20·3
1525/6	110,996	91,391	82·3	19,605	17·7	82,708	74·5	28,288	25·5
1526/7	119,968	91,140	76·0	28,828	24·0	89,713	74·8	30,255	25·2
1527/8	121,857	99,646	81·8	22,211	18·2	96,901	79·5	24,956	20·5
1528/9	109,988	96,877	88·1	13,111	11·9	83,510	75·9	26,478	24·1
1529/30	109,657	90,672	82·7	18,985	17·3	85,044	77·6	24,613	22·4
1530/1	98,332	86,661	88·1	11,671	11·9	73,173	74·4	25,159	25·6
1531/2	94,423	81,818	86·7	12,605	13·3	69,884	74·0	24,539	26·0
1532/3	108,744	100,104	92·1	8,640	7·9	88,770	81·6	19,974	18·4
1533/4	125,509	110,124	87·7	15,385	12·3	94,788	75·5	30,721	24·5
1534/5	107,190	91,631	85·5	15,559	14·5	88,995	83·0	18,195	17·0
1535/6	127,994	108,308	84·6	19,686	15·4	103,135	80·6	24,859	19·4
1536/7	117,054	103,050	88·0	14,004	12·0	95,800	81·8	21,254	18·2
1537/8	116,219	103,754	89·3	12,465	10·7	93,340	80·3	22,879	19·7
1538/9	131,567	113,883	86·6	17,684	13·4	109,851	83·5	21,716	16·5
1539/40	137,593	117,465	85·4	20,128	14·6	115,606	84·0	21,987	16·0
1540/1	150,458	130,938	87·0	19,520	13·0	125,557	83·4	24,901	16·6
1541/2	134,878	111,941	83·0	22,937	17·0	114,683	85·0	20,195	15·0
1542/3	105,015	89,128	84·9	15,887	15·1	84,167	80·1	20,848	19·9
1543/4	—	137,282	—	—	—	—	—	—	—

For note to Table XII see opposite page.

basis by assessing the raw-material content of four and a quarter cloths of assize as equivalent to one sack of wool. (The figure is an approximate average of the closely agreeing values chosen by other scholars or mentioned by contemporaries.) Thus in Table XII wool exports are expressed in 'cloth equivalents', not in sacks. Carus-Wilson and Coleman converted wool-fells to sacks at the customs rate of 240 fells = 1 sack; I have adopted the same practice myself in my own estimates of exports for the debasement years.

Table XII, then, presents annual volumes of cloth and wool ('cloth equivalents') exports for the years 1488/9 to 1542/3 (1543/4 for cloth only) as computed from the published figures of Carus-Wilson and Coleman. For each year the total volume is broken down two ways, London/Outports and cloth/wool, each of these subtotals being shown both in absolute values and as a percentage of the total. The main concern is, of course, with the sixteenth century, but the five years 1488/9–1492/3 have been included so as to demonstrate the very important expansion which occurred in the reign of Henry VII. The Michaelmas year used by the Exchequer has been retained here despite the expository clumsiness which it entails, for lack of consistency in transforming Michaelmas years into calendar years has been a minor source of interpretative confusion amongst the historians of the period.

What, in broad terms, does Table XII show? Does it, first of all, support Fisher in his contention that there was a very marked expansion of exports in the first half of the sixteenth century, or Stone in his argument that Fisher misrepresented the truth by disregarding all wool exports on one side and outport cloth exports on the other? The answer to this question is abundantly clear. Fisher's table of

---

NOTE. Where, for any given port, the account is missing or covers a period other than the Michaelmas year, a figure has been interpolated according to the following conventions:

(1) if there is no record at all, the figure has been taken as equal to that for the chronologically nearest year, earlier or later, or for the average of the two nearest years, if equidistant;

(2) where the account or accounts cover a period of two adjoining years, but are not divided into 12-monthly periods, the figure for each year has been taken as equivalent to half the value for the two years combined;

(3) where the account covers a period of *n* months, *n* being less than 12 but more than 3, the figure given has been multiplied by 12/*n* to give a value for the full year;

(4) where the account covers *n* months, *n* being less than three, the procedure described in (1) above has been adopted.

London shortcloth exports (presented in calendar years) shows an annual average value for 1539–44 inclusive some 105 per cent above that for 1500–2. Our total of cloth plus wool exports (which we shall call woollen exports) yields an annual average for 1539/40–1542/3 only some 13 per cent above that for 1500/1–1502/3. Stone's contention that London cloth exports are a misleading guide to England's woollen exports, since they overlook the growth of cloth at the expense of wool and of London at the expense of the outports, is richly vindicated.

It might of course be contended that this measure of exports, that is in terms of raw-material content, is inappropriate; that by transforming the wool and cloth exports on a raw-material basis into export values, even in constant prices, a more rapid rise would ensue. This is true, since four and a quarter cloths of assize were naturally worth more than the sack of wool which we have assumed to be their raw material content, and the export of cloth was growing while that of wool was declining. Which measure is the more 'appropriate' depends on the purpose we have in mind. If the intention is to assess the impact of the cloth industry on enclosures and conversion—and Fisher's figures have often been pressed into such a service—then evidently the raw-material basis is the appropriate one. If our interest is in the balance of payments, a value series would be more useful. But it may be suggested that in any event translation of our raw-material figures into value terms would still not yield a rate of increase comparable with that which the London shortcloth figures alone seem to suggest. Needless to say, we do not have figures of the value of woollen exports. Nor do we know for all relevant periods the prices of the various types of cloth and of wool which were exported, nor the actual composition of cloth exports in which the various individual types were translated conventionally into 'cloth of assize'. But a very rough estimate of the increase in the value of England's woollen exports at constant prices can be made by assuming a constant ratio between the values of wool exported in its raw and its manufactured state. Stone, in the article referred to, equates the value of one sack of wool with two cloths (basing this on the figures and arguments of Schanz).[1] At the rate of 4·25 cloths to one sack of wool (raw-material content) this would make wool 2·125 times more

[1] Stone, 'State Control', p. 105, fn. 3; G. Schanz, *Englische Handelspolitik gegen Ende des Mittelalters* (Leipzig, 1881) ii. 31–3. Cf. P. Ramsey, 'Overseas Trade in the Reign of Henry VII: the Evidence of Customs Accounts', *Economic History Review*, 2nd Series vi, no. 2 (Dec. 1953), 179, fn. 4.

valuable in its manufactured form. On the other hand, the average price of wool bought by the Staplers for export, according to a document probably dating from late 1547,[1] was about £7. 10*s*. 0*d*. a sack, and combining this with the £5 or £6 which Gresham was paying for 'Castlecombes' about that time, we get a manufactured to raw ratio of rather less or more than 3:1. The discrepancy between the two ratios does not prove that either is inaccurate, bearing in mind the difference of date and the wide range of prices at any one time for different varieties both of wool and of cloth. Still, let us take the higher ratio, which prejudices our own case (for a relatively slow rise of export values) and favours Fisher's, by attaching a relatively large weight to the expanding export and a low weight to the contracting one. Then the average annual value of woollen exports in 1500/1 to 1502/3 was

$$\pounds(3\times 80{,}641)x+(35{,}945)x = \pounds(277{,}868)x,$$

where $x =$ the value of the sack of wool in pounds sterling in the base year, and in 1539/40 to 1542/3 was

$$\pounds(3\times 112{,}368)x+(19{,}618)x = \pounds(356{,}722)x;$$

so that the value of woollen exports for the later years as a percentage of that for the earlier was

$$\frac{(356{,}722)x\times 100}{(277{,}868)x},$$

or a little over 128 per cent. Thus even on assumptions as favourable as possible to the hypothesis of a rapid rise, the value of woollen exports at constant prices seems to have risen during the first four decades of the century by not much more than a quarter.

There is another consideration which further strengthens the present argument, and that is that we have so far taken no account of 'worsteds' in our calculations. 'Worsted' cloths were separately recorded in the Customs Accounts, since they paid a much lower rate of duty. The significance of their omission from the present standpoint is that worsted exports, like exports of wool, declined considerably in the first half of the sixteenth century. Taking them into account would therefore depress still further the rate of growth of woollen exports, which we have already shown to have been seriously overestimated. Worsteds have been omitted chiefly because it is difficult to know at what rate it would be appropriate to transform them into 'cloth equivalents' for purposes of aggregation. But it can be said

[1] SP 10/2, fols. 56 ff.

with confidence that the ratio 14 single worsteds = 1 broadcloth, adopted by Carus-Wilson and Coleman in their book,[1] greatly understates the importance of worsted cloth either in value terms or in terms of raw-material equivalent. Their ratio of 14:1 reflects only the difference between rates of duty paid by denizen merchants for broadcloth and for worsted (1*s*. 2*d*. and 1*d*. respectively). It is quite certain, notwithstanding the vagueness of the terminology and the wide variety of cloths subsumed both under 'cloth of assize' and under 'worsted', that on average cloths entered as worsteds would be worth much more than one-fourteenth of those entered as cloths of assize, and would contain much more than one-fourteenth of the raw material. Stone, again basing himself on Schanz, assumes the worsted to have been worth on average two-thirds of the cloth of assize,[2] but from merchants' accounts one might think this rather overestimates worsteds. Take the ratio of average prices, for argument's sake, as 1:2. In the early years of Henry VIII's reign, according to Schanz's tables, nearly 6,000 worsteds a year were exported on average. At the same time annual woollen exports (on our definition) were about 115,000 cloth equivalents, of which cloth accounted for rather less than 85,000 and wool for rather more than 30,000. A little calculation then suggests that to include worsteds along with other woollen exports would raise the aggregate value by nearly 3 per cent. By the early 1540s, on the other hand, only about 1,580 worsteds were exported annually in comparison with woollen exports of about 130,000; the surviving evidence in the Particular Accounts suggests that there was a further sharp fall, both relative and absolute, in worsted exports during the reign of Edward VI and Mary, by when worsted exports were probably worth less than one half of one per cent of the total. Clearly, then, to include worsteds, as is ideally desirable, would further weaken the case for a rapid rise of exports in the first half of the century.

It is as well to be clear that in impugning the validity of the thesis of a rapid rise in woollen exports in the first half of the sixteenth century, there is no intention to suggest that Professor Fisher, the most influential exponent of this thesis, consciously misled his readers. His widely quoted table on which so impressive a structure of interpretation has been reared is clearly headed *Triennial Averages of Shortcloths Exported from London*. Yet it is fair to say that the com-

[1] Carus-Wilson and Coleman, op. cit., p. 199, fn. 5.
[2] Stone, 'State Control', loc. cit.; Schanz, loc. cit.

ments in the text do not warn the unwary reader as clearly as they might of the limitations of this evidence. Thus we read that 'a reasonable guide to the main commercial trends of the time is to be found in the figures of shortcloths exported from London, for throughout the sixteenth century cloth was by far the most important commodity exported and by far the greater proportion of English cloth went out through London'.[1] The truth is that whereas at the beginning of the Great Debasement, in 1544/5, exports of cloth through London were indeed some 86 per cent of the national total of woollen exports as here computed, in the first five years of the sixteenth century they had averaged only 43 per cent of it. Fisher's table reveals the relative growth of London's cloth exports much more than it testifies to a growth in national exports of woollens. Again, we read a few lines later that 'the vital fact was that in fifty years the cloth trade grew in volume by 150 per cent'.[2] (At this point a footnote, less often quoted or perhaps read than the sentence it qualifies, reminds the reader that 'neither the figures of provincial exports nor those of goods other than cloth sent out from London rose at anything like that pace, so that the London cloth statistics rather exaggerate the general growth in trade'.) The '150 per cent' is presumably arrived at by comparing the figure for 1550 (actually, the Michaelmas year 1549–50) with that for the first three years of the century. This in itself is a trifle misleading considering that 1549–50 was a boom year in which exports were substantially above the level of either the immediately preceding or the immediately following years. In our tables, London cloth exports for the five years 1547/8 to 1551/2 are seen to have averaged 115,571, which was about 135 per cent above Fisher's figure for the first three years of the century.

It is these partial calculations which lie behind the choice of such adjectives as 'meteoric'[3] and 'fantastic'[4] to describe the upward movement of exports in the first half of the sixteenth century, and already (in the writer's perhaps unusually unhappy experience) a generation of undergraduates has uncritically repeated such characterizations of the commercial trends of the period. Since 1947, at least, there has been no justification for this, for in that year Mr. (now Professor) Stone published his brilliant critique of Fisher's article in which he drew attention to the distorting effect of neglecting wool, worsteds, and the outports, and offered a table of woollen exports

[1] Fisher, 'Commercial Trends', p. 96.
[2] Loc. cit., p. 97.
[3] Loc. cit., p. 96.
[4] Van der Wee, op. cit. ii. 184.

which placed the statistics of the matter in a far truer light. Our own tables are little more than a chronological extension of Stone's figures. Unfortunately, Stone's article has been much less noticed than Fisher's, a fact which is partly at least to be explained by the circumstance that while Fisher's paper was rightly included in the first volume of reprints *Essays in Economic History*,[1] Stone's was indefensibly omitted not only from the first but from the two succeeding volumes. Not only has this meant that Stone's article has been several degrees less accessible to many students, but it has been denied the subtle suggestion of approval in high places which inclusion in these volumes—no doubt contrary to the intention of their editors and publishers—has seemed to some to imply. Regrettably, an incautious extension of Fisher's London cloth figures to the cloth trade or even to exports generally is a trap into which not only undergraduates but first-rate scholars have fallen. Even so careful a scholar as Dr. Bowden tells us that 'cloth exports practically trebled in volume during the first half of the sixteenth century'.[2] The actual expansion from 1500/1–1504/5 to 1547/8–1551/2 was barely two-thirds.

It is interesting and a little depressing to see how figures which are quite correct in themselves, but which require careful exegesis, can gradually, by a progressive and unconscious neglect of the qualifications which ought to remain attached to them, come to appear to support a broad characterization of a historical period which is certainly wrong. But it is time to turn to the more pleasant and constructive task of commenting briefly on other aspects of the pre-debasement trend in woollen exports.

First, we have noted that both outport exports and wool exports fell as a proportion of national woollen exports. Was the fall of the second the cause of that of the first—did the outports, that is to say, lose ground relatively *because* of the fall in wool exports? What makes this question seem worth asking is that the outports played relatively speaking a much more important role in wool exports than in exports of cloth: in 1488/9–1492/3 they accounted for less than 32 per cent of the latter but for over 54 per cent of the former. Perhaps, then, the well-known trend towards a monopoly of England's exports by the capital city was due at least in part to a change

[1] *Essays in Economic History*, ed. E. M. Carus-Wilson, for The Economic History Society (Edward Arnold, 1954).

[2] Bowden, op. cit., p. 43.

in the composition of exports which favoured London and prejudiced the outports? We can easily test this hypothesis by recalculating the share of the outports in woollen exports at some later date —say, 1538/9–1542/3—on the assumption that in that period the outports' shares in both cloth and wool exports were what they actually were at that time, but that the share of cloth and wool exports in the total had remained at the same level as in 1488/9–1492/3. The formula is

$$x = \left(\frac{a \times c}{100}\right) + \left(\frac{b \times d}{100}\right),$$

where

$x =$ outports' hypothetical share in woollen exports, 1538/9–1542/3;
$a =$ outports' share in cloth exports, 1538/9–1542/3;
$b =$ outports' share in wool exports, 1538/9–1542/3;
$c =$ cloth share in woollen exports, 1488/9–1492/3;
$d =$ wool share in woollen exports, 1488/9–1492/3.

Writing in the actual values we get

$$\begin{aligned} x &= \left(\frac{15{\cdot}6 \times 64{\cdot}7}{100}\right) + \left(\frac{22{\cdot}8 \times 35{\cdot}3}{100}\right) \\ &= 10{\cdot}09 + 8{\cdot}05 \\ &= 18{\cdot}14. \end{aligned}$$

The outports' share in woollen exports in the earlier period had been 39·7 per cent. We see that had the relative positions of cloth and of wool in the national total remained unchanged, the outports' share would have fallen to 18·1 per cent, instead of to 16·1 per cent as it actually did. In other words, the outports would have lost almost as much ground as they did compared with London had the relative positions of cloth and of wool remained unchanged. Only to a minor extent were they the victims of a change in the composition of exports which was disadvantageous to them; to a much larger extent their decline was the result of the fact that they lost ground to London in respect both of cloth exports and of wool.

They did not, however, lose ground steadily throughout the period under review. Column (8) of Table XII shows that during the reign of Henry VII the outports gained rather than lost ground, both absolutely and relatively. In commenting on this tendency, Mr. (now Professor) P. Ramsey suggested that it was largely 'illusory' in that it was caused by the short-lived boom of exports from Southampton, the trade of which was dominated by London merchants who used it only as an outport convenient in certain circumstances.[1] One might of course question whether this is an adequate reason for discounting the growth of trade in that port as an element in the recovery of the outports; the national distribution of trade might look very different in the twentieth century were trade to be allotted to places where the head offices of importing and exporting houses are located rather than to the ports through which it physically passes. From some points of view it is doubtless important that Southampton's revival was primarily the work of London merchants; but to the quayside worker loading cloth, to the chandler or the tavern-keeper fitting out the ships and entertaining their crews, that might have seemed irrelevant.

TABLE XIII

Southampton's role in woollen exports, temp. *Henry VII*

	Total	*London*		*Outports*	
			%		%
A. *Cloth exports*					
1. 1488/9–1492/3 (all ports)	278,048	190,002	68·3	88,046	31·7
2. do., excluding Southampton	267,651	190,002	71·0	77,649	29·0
3. 1503/4–1507/8 (all ports)	398,706	236,044	59·2	162,662	40·8
4. do., excluding Southampton	341,332	236,044	69·2	105,288	30·8
B. *Wool exports* (cloth equivalents)					
5. 1488/9–1492/3 (all ports)	151,732	69,198	45·6	82,534	54·4
6. do., excluding Southampton	119,016	69,198	58·1	49,818	41·9
7. 1503/4–1507/8 (all ports)	144,088	71,293	49·5	72,795	50·5
8. do., excluding Southampton	114,402	71,293	62·3	43,109	37·7
C. *Woollen exports*					
9. 1488/9–1492/3 (all ports)	429,780	259,200	60·3	170,580	39·7
10. do., excluding Southampton	386,667	259,200	67·0	127,467	33·0
11. 1503/4–1507/8 (all ports)	542,794	307,337	56·6	235,457	43·4
12. do., excluding Southampton	455,734	307,337	67·4	148,397	32·6

However, we can rearrange the statistics to test how much difference the exclusion of Southampton, were that on Ramsey's grounds thought desirable, would make. The figures are given in Table XIII. This table shows the five-yearly totals of cloth, wool, and woollen exports for the whole country, London, and the outports for the years 1488/9–1492/3 and 1503/4–1507/8. The London and outport figures are also translated (columns 3 and 5) into percentages of the total. In each case, all outports are included in the first instance (lines

[1] Ramsey, 'Overseas Trade', pp. 179–80.

1, 3, 5, 7, 9, 11) and then Southampton is omitted both from the national and from the outport columns (lines 2, 4, 6, 8, 10, 12). It can be seen that whereas when Southampton is included the outport share of woollen exports rises from 39·7 per cent to 43·4 per cent, without Southampton it falls from 33·0 per cent to 32·6 per cent. Inspection of the other entries in column 5 reveals that as far as cloth exports alone are concerned, the outports gained slightly even in the absence of Southampton, but not by quite enough to offset the fall in their share in wool exports—a fall which went on at about the same rate whether Southampton is included or not. Thus it is fair to say that it was the considerable expansion of cloth exports from Southampton which transformed the otherwise virtually unchanged position of the exports *vis-à-vis* London into a decided revival. On the other hand, it is also true to say that even without this local prosperity at Southampton the outports virtually held their own relatively, and shared almost equally with London—so far as cloth exports are concerned, more fully than London—in the very marked absolute growth of woollen exports which characterized the reign of the first Tudor. Not until the following reign did the outports as a whole have objective cause for the grievances about the concentration of trade in London to which they so often and so plaintively gave expression.

TABLE XIV

Growth of woollen exports, 1488/9–1492/3 to 1544/5–1550/1

	(1)	(2)	(3)	(4)
1488/9–1492/3	85,956	—	—	—
1499/1500–1503/4	111,501	(+) 29·7	(+) 2·4	(+) 2·4
1504/5–1508/9	113,533	(+) 1·8	(+) 0·3	|
1509/10–1513/14	115,425	(+) 1·7	(+) 0·3	↓
1514/15–1518/19	121,747	(+) 5·5	(+) 1·0	(+) 0·6
1519/20–1523/4	109,482	(−) 10·1	(−) 2·1	|
1524/5–1528/9	114,725	(+) 4·8	(+) 0·9	↓
1529/30–1533/4	107,333	(−) 6·4	(−) 1·3	(−) 0·8
1534/5–1538/9	120,005	(+) 11·8	(+) 2·2	↓
1539/40–1543/4*	136,969	(+) 14·1	(+) 2·7	(+) 2·4
1544/5–1550/1†	143,040	(+) 4·4	(+) 0·7	(+) 0·7

* Wool, four years only.
† Cloth, six years only; wool, two years only.

(1) = annual average.
(2) = percentage increase (+) or decrease (−) over preceding period.
(3), (4) = annual compound percentage rate of growth over preceding period (measured from mid point to mid point).

Our chief need, however, for the pre-debasement export figures is as a frame of reference into which to fit the expansion of the debasement years. Specifically, we want to know whether that expansion represented a marked change of trend when set alongside the values for the preceding decades. Table XII, already introduced to the reader, and Table XIV, which presents the more important figures in quinquennial periods, give a clear answer to this question. In the last five years before the Great Debasement, 1539/40–1543/4, the volume of woollen exports was some 60 per cent above the level of 1488/9–1492/3. It had attained this level not by a process of continuous expansion, but in two short periods of very marked growth, from early in the reign of Henry VII to the opening years of the sixteenth century, and then from about half-way through its fourth decade up to, and including, the debasement years. In between, woollen exports continued to advance very slowly in the first two decades up to a fairly high peak at the end of the second decade (the 1519/20 volume of exports was only three times exceeded during the whole period covered by this study), from which the trend was then definitely downwards for some twelve to fifteen years. Table XIV includes columns in which the percentage increase (or decrease) from one quinquennial period to the next is translated into a percentage annual rate of growth, counting from the mid point of one period to the mid point of the next. The average for the seven-year period 1544/5–1550/1, that is the debasement years, is also included; its derivation will be explained in the succeeding section. It should be noticed that estimates of the annual average of cloth exports during this last period are based on six of the seven years only, and for wool on only two out of seven. The unavailability of the seventh year (1546/7) for cloth probably matters little, since those figures which do survive (see Appendix C) agree with literary evidence in suggesting that this was an average year for its period, so that its inclusion would make very little difference to the cloth annual average. On the other hand, an annual average for wool exports based on only two years out of seven is clearly liable to be quite sadly astray, and here one can only console oneself with the reflection that since wool exports were little more than ten per cent of the total (where we know both) in the middle years of the century, any given percentage error in the wool estimate would have to be divided by about ten in assessing its probable effect on the average shown for woollen exports as a whole. Even a very large error in the wool average could therefore result in relatively small damage to the total.

It would not, perhaps, readily occur to anyone scrutinizing columns (3) and (4) of Table XIV to characterize the rate of growth of woollen exports in any part of this period as 'meteoric' or 'fantastic', but if there is any sub-period which merits that title the first part of the reign of Henry VII has as good a claim as any, and better than any period other than the immediate pre-debasement years. In summarizing his analysis of the trade of this reign, Mr. Ramsey contrasted its achievements with 'the more publicized triumphs of the following decades' and was content to refer to it as 'the initial phase of the great expansion of England's foreign trade in the early sixteenth century'.[1] This is really to make too modest a claim for it; in terms of rates of growth of woollen exports the middle years of Henry VII's reign were the most prosperous part of the whole period. From 1488/9–1492/3 to 1499/1500–1503/4, that is in eleven years, nearly 30 per cent was added to the total of woollen exports; in the next forty less than another 23 per cent was added. To discuss the reasons for this, to conjecture, in particular, how much must be credited to the Magnus Intercursus of 1496, would take us beyond the scope of this study and of its author's knowledge. But it is interesting, at least, that the most striking phase of the trade expansion should have occurred in a period for which no one, as yet, has claimed the benefit of exchange depreciation. (The fact that, as Mr. Ramsey notes, imports were rising even more rapidly than exports[2] would constitute prima facie evidence against such an explanation.)

The timing of the onset of the second phase of rapid growth of woollen exports can perhaps be disputed according to whether we choose to look on the high value for 1533/4 or on the lower one for 1534/5 as out of trend. At all events a pronounced and sustained rise in woollen exports did not begin until about the middle of the fourth decade of the century.[3] When it did start, this expansion was marked, but still barely as rapid as that of the earlier period. The quinquennial average values for 1534/5 to 1538/9 and for 1539/40 to 1543/4 (the latter based on only *four* years for wool) reveal annual compound rates of growth of respectively 2·2 and

[1] Loc. cit., p. 182.
[2] Loc. cit., p. 179.
[3] Schanz, op. cit. ii. 13, dates the upward turn of trade—he is considering imports as well as exports and basing his periodization primarily on customs yield—from 1538.

2·7 per cent over the preceding period. By contrast, the annual average for the seven years of debasement, 1544/5 to 1550/1—though as already explained its reliability is lower owing to gaps in the figures —is less than 4½ per cent above the average for the last pre-debasement quinquennium, an annual growth rate of only 0·7 per cent. Thus the second phase of expansion, which accelerates in the two pre-debasement quinquennia, seems clearly to lose momentum in the years of debasement and then to stagnate, save for one outstanding figure in 1553/4, after Edward VI's attempts to restore the coinage. At a first glance, then, there is little to suggest that the debasement of the coinage from 1544 onwards can explain at most anything more than the last and far from the most impressive phase of early Tudor export growth.

Nor does the hypothesis of export stimulation via exchange depreciation fare very well, at first glance, in the interval between the two great periods of early Tudor expansion. Fisher, it will be remembered, claimed that the expansion of cloth exports during the 1520s to which his table seemed to point was to be explained partly by the beginning of exchange depreciation. 'The fall of sterling [we read] began with the French war of 1522, and its first stage was crystallized by the reduction of the weight of coins in 1526 . . . During the 'thirties the exchanges probably weakened still further . . .'[1] In this scheme neither *explicandum* nor *explicans* survives closer scrutiny. In fact, Fisher's London cloth figures are nowhere more misleading than during the 1520s, a decade in which the shares of wool and of the outports in the national woollens total both fell exceptionally rapidly. The 1520s and early 1530s, so far indeed from witnessing a particularly rapid expansion of woollen exports, actually register a decline. As for the *explicans*, Van der Wee's graph[2] shows that apart from the undoubted and sudden fall following the coinage alterations of 1526, the London–Antwerp rate was in fact remarkably stable both in the 1520s and in the 1530s. The only probable influence on exports which one would be prepared to concede to exchange movements in this period is that of provoking the marked, but not sustained, rises in 1526/7 and 1527/8 (Table XII). The latter year, however, was followed by four years of substantial and successive decline to the second lowest export value since the start of the century. Since one naturally expects the expansionary impetus of

[1] Fisher, 'Commercial Trends', p. 99.
[2] Van der Wee, op. cit. iii, Graph 33, p. 79.

an exchange depreciation to be strongest in the immediately following years,[1] this seems difficult indeed to reconcile with the Fisher thesis. Whatever the causes of the second major expansion of exports from about the mid thirties onwards, it seems clear that one must look for them, at least until the debasement period itself is reached, elsewhere than in the foreign exchanges.

Thus it seems difficult to find in a first glance at the chronology of the export expansion of the late fifteenth and early sixteenth centuries much support for the view which ascribes that expansion to exchange depreciation. Closer scrutiny is called for, however, in analysing the effect on trade of the most pronounced decline in the London–Antwerp exchanges, that is, that which occurred during and was caused by debasement of the coinage from 1544 onwards. Such scrutiny demands a prior examination of the statistical evidence on trade, and we now turn to present such evidence as we have been able to unearth on this topic.

3. Exports during the Great Debasement

The Enrolled Customs Accounts on which Professor Carus-Wilson and Miss Coleman drew for their book *England's Export Trade 1275–1547* were summaries compiled in the Exchequer from the so-called 'Particular Accounts' submitted to the Exchequer by the officials at the various ports. Many of the Particular Accounts survive amongst the Exchequer records, and it is to this source that one must chiefly turn for information about exports and imports during the years of debasement, for which the Enrolled Accounts themselves have unfortunately not survived. Though the Particular Accounts are sufficiently numerous to afford us some partial insight into the pattern of English woollen exports in the years between the end of the Henrician Enrolled Accounts and the resumption of the series about the time of Elizabeth's accession, they are far from complete. One major gap can be filled from another source, namely the details of exports by the Hansards and other alien merchants resident in England, preserved amongst the Cotton manuscripts at the British

[1] In saying this, I am not unmindful of the view held by some economists that it took perhaps ten years for the full stimulus of the 1949 devaluation to be felt by British export industries. The capital-intensive nature of modern industry implies that a longer time-horizon must be adopted in scrutinizing the effects of the 1949 decision than would be called for in sixteenth-century conditions.

Museum. But our knowledge is still far from being as complete as we should wish.

I publish in Appendix C the information on exports of cloth and of wool which I have been able to discover in the Particular Accounts and elsewhere. Doubtless a few figures have escaped my notice. For the convenience of scholars wishing to effect comparisons between the debasement years and the period covered by the Carus-Wilson–Coleman volume, the cloth figures are presented in a similar format to that employed by those writers, save that a column has been added showing the total (of denizen, Hanse, and alien) exports for each port for each year. I also allow for the presentation of the over-all national total of cloth or of wool exports where, as happens in one or two cases, independent evidence of that figure chances to be available. From these statistics estimates of national cloth and wool exports have been made, where enough evidence is available to make that possible, by just the same procedures as were used to assemble the Carus-Wilson–Coleman evidence. However, for some years the gaps were too numerous and substantial to make a national estimate seem worth while, and in some of the instances where such an estimate has been possible, the amount of interpolation has been relatively greater than for the majority of the pre-debasement years.

The national estimates made from my own research on the Customs accounts are presented in Table XV. The reader who wants to see the full evidence on which these estimates are based can of course turn to Appendix C and consult the port-by-port figures. But to assist the reader who does not wish to go to this trouble I have included also in Table XV(A), dealing with cloth exports, a notation intended to show the degree of reliability which can be attached to the national estimate in question. Full details of this notation and of the methods used to compile the national estimates both of cloth and of wool will be found in Appendix C. Broadly, national estimates classified (1) are completely accurate (as accurate, that is, as the Customs records themselves), being based on accounts for all ports or on direct evidence of the national total. Estimates classified (2) are probably accurate (in the sense mentioned) to within about one per cent either way and are perfectly acceptable from the standpoint of our present purposes. Estimates classified (3) and (4) are progressively more hazardous but are still considered worth having for our present purposes. (The national cloth totals for the years before 1543/4 taken from the Carus-Wilson–Coleman volume would predominantly be classified (1) according to this scheme, 28 of the 50 estimates receiving this grading. All of the rest would be classified (2) save for 1528/9, which owing to the incomplete character of the London account would be classified (4).)

It will be seen that of the seventeen years from 1544/5 to 1560/1 inclusive, national estimates of cloth exports can be offered for eleven, and of wool exports for ten. Seven of these are years for which both cloth *and* wool exports can be estimated, so that a national woollens export figure can be presented. The remaining years are not, of course, complete statistical blanks, and the partial figures published in Appendix C together in some instances with 'literary' evidence permit some conjectures about export trends during them. It will be noticed that the least well-served period is the reign of Mary; for the debasement years proper, fortunately, our knowledge is reasonably good. What are the over-all impressions conveyed by these figures when considered against the background of pre-debasement trends?

It has been seen that during those years in which debased coinage was being issued and the exchange rate was moving against England —that is, the years 1544/5 to 1550/1—woollen exports averaged less than $4\frac{1}{2}$ per cent above the average for the immediate pre-debasement quinquennium. This, it has been suggested, is prima facie hard to reconcile with the view that the debasement acted, via the exchange rate, as a major stimulus to English exports. But looking more closely at values for individual years within this seven-year debasement period it is possible to attribute some expansionary influence to the induced fall in the exchanges. Estimates of wool exports are, regrettably, possible only for two of these years, namely 1544/5 and 1549/50. But the relatively small importance of wool at this time—it accounted for 5 per cent of total woollen exports in 1544/5 and for 9·1 per cent in 1549/50—makes it seem reasonable to look on the course of cloth exports as a safe enough guide to overall trends, and cloth estimates are possible for six years out of the seven. The remaining year (1546/7) is something of a puzzle, for what looks like the figure we are seeking survives in a State Paper which was reprinted in Tawney and Power's well-known volumes,[1] and it has been accepted by some scholars as in fact the true national total of cloth exports. Reasons are given in Appendix D for thinking that this figure cannot be relied upon, either being incorrect or having an

[1] SP 10/2, no. 13; Tawney and Power, op. cit. i. 178–84.

TABLE XV

A. *Cloth exports, 1544/5 to 1560/1*

Year	*Total*	*London*	%	*Outports*	%	*Index of reliability*
1544/5	121,017	109,613	90·6	11,404	9·4	(1)
1545/6	131,013	119,414	91·1	11,599	8·9	(1)
1546/7	—	—	—	—	—	—
1547/8	129,108	119,210	92·3	9,898	7·7	(2)
1548/9	138,605	128,200	92·5	10,405	7·5	(4)
1549/50	147,161	132,766	90·2	14,395	9·8	(1)
1550/1	128,148	112,710	88·0	15,438	12·0	(2)
1551/2	101,591	84,968	83·6	16,623	16·4	(3)
1552/3	—	—	—	—	—	—
1553/4	150,563	135,594	90·1	14,969	9·9	(1)
1554/5	—	—	—	14,932	—	—
1555/6	—	—	—	14,417	—	—
1556/7	125,431	113,696	90·6	11,735	9·4	(3)
1557/8	—	—	—	8,303	—	—
1558/9	—	—	—	9,077	—	—
1559/60	121,092	109,687	90·6	11,405	9·4	(2)
1560/1	95,433	81,847	85·8	13,586	14·2	(2)

NOTE. For method of computing index of reliability, see App. C, p. 171.

B. *Wool exports, 1544/5 to 1560/1*

Year	*Total*		*London*			*Outports*		
	Sacks	*Cloth equiv.*	*Sacks*	*Cloth equiv.*	%	*Sacks*	*Cloth equiv.*	%
1544/5	1,484	6,307	1,283	5,453	86·5	201	854	13·5
1545/9	—	—	No estimate made		—	—	—	—
1549/50	3,472	14,756	3,040	12,920	87·6	432	1,836	12·4
1550/1	—	—	No estimate made		—	—	—	—
1551/2	3,240	13,770	2,981	12,669	92·0	259	1,101	8·0
1552/3	5,846	24,845	4,830	20,527	84·5	1,016	4,318	15·5
1553/4	5,740	24,395	4,547	19,325	89·7	1,193	5,070	10·3
1554/5	3,109	13,213	2,324	9,877	74·8	785	3,336	25·2
1555/6	—	—	No estimate made		—	—	—	—
1556/7	1,387	5,895	911	3,872	65·7	476	2,023	34·3
1557/8	—	—	No estimate made		—	—	—	—
1558/9	4,257	18,091	3,518	14,951	82·6	739	3,140	17·4
1559/60	3,677	15,627	2,755	11,709	74·9	922	3,918	25·1
1560/1	4,075	17,318	2,970	12,622	72·9	1,105	4,696	27·1

C. *Woollen exports, 1544/5 to 1560/1*

Year	*Total*	*Cloth*		*Wool*		*London*		*Outports*	
	(1)	*Number* (2)	% (3)	*Cloth equiv.* (4)	% (5)	*Cloth equiv.* (6)	% (7)	*Cloth equiv.* (8)	% (9)
1544/5	127,324	121,017	95·0	6,307	5·0	115,066	90·4	12,258	9·6
1549/50	161,917	147,161	90·9	14,756	9·1	145,686	90·0	16,231	10·0
1551/2	115,361	101,591	88·1	13,770	11·9	97,637	84·6	17,724	15·4
1553/4	174,958	150,563	86·1	24,395	13·9	154,919	88·5	20,039	11·5
1556/7	131,326	125,431	95·5	5,895	4·5	117,568	89·5	13,758	10·5
1559/60	136,719	121,092	88·6	15,627	11·4	121,396	88·8	15,323	11·2
1560/1	112,751	95,433	84·6	17,318	15·4	94,469	83·8	18,282	16·2

uncertain chronological reference. The view which I much prefer is that suggested by literary evidence and by the partial statistics for London and the outports surviving in reputable sources, namely, that cloth exports in 1546/7 were at a level similar to that of the immediately preceding and following years, for which the totals were respectively 131,013 and 129,108 cloths. If this is so, then for the first four (Michaelmas) years of the debasement period cloth exports remained remarkably stable at a level a few per cent above the average for the immediate pre-debasement quinquennium, but below that of the pre-debasement peak in 1543/4. In the next two years, 1548/9 and 1549/50, there was, however, a very definite expansion to a hitherto unapproached peak of 147,161 cloths in the latter year. Following the peak of 1549/50, exports then fell off quickly in the two following years to a total of 101,591 cloths in 1551/2.

Can any relationship between the debasement and exports be hypothesized able to reconcile the pattern: stability–marked increase–sharp decline in cloth exports, with the fact that the London–Antwerp exchange rate was declining throughout the whole period (or, at all events, up to July 1551)? It does not seem impossible to proffer an explanation of this seeming paradox. In the first few years of the debasement, as Mr. Stone has rightly pointed out, the exchange rate did not in fact decline all that much.[1] According to the evidence presented in Chapter 5 the London–Antwerp rate stood in April 1544 at 26*s.* 8*d.*—very much the average level for the years immediately before the debasement—and had fallen only to 22*s.* 0½*d.* by November 1548. This was a decline of 17⅓ per cent in 55 months, or about one-third of one per cent per month. It fell rather more, however—to 18*s.* 0*d.*, or 18⅓ per cent—in the following 24 months, that is, to November 1550. This represented a rate of about 0·8 per cent per month. In the meantime, changes in mint price and mint equivalent had of course brought about an expansion in the money supply, but in stages which were quite the opposite of those in which the exchange rate fell. In Chapter 4 an attempt was made to estimate the money supply at various dates. Though those dates do not coincide exactly with the ones just chosen to measure movements in the exchanges the broad contrast which the estimates suggest is surely correct. It is that whereas the fall of the exchanges accelerated after late 1548, the money supply expanded much less rapidly after that date than before it. Table VIII (pp. 81–2) shows that from about £850,000 in 1542 the

[1] Stone, 'State Control', p. 106.

money supply expanded to about one and three-quarter million in early 1549. April 1544 would not have witnessed much expansion over 1542, nor would the estimate for November 1548 be much below that for early 1549. So we can say that in the first stage the money supply was roughly doubled while the exchanges fell by little more than a sixth. In the next two years, however, the money supply grew by only a little over 16 per cent, as Table VIII shows, compared with a fall of over 18 per cent in the foreign exchanges. Whereas therefore it would be legitimate to look for some expansionary influence on exports from late 1548 to late 1550, there is really no reason to entertain any such expectation in regard to the period before the former date, for during that time the internal inflationary impact of debasement considerably exceeded its weakening effect on the external value of the pound.

Clearly this conclusion accords perfectly well with the actual experience of exports in these two periods as revealed by the evidence presented in this chapter. It is as well, however, to point out explicitly that it is at variance with the arguments of earlier writers. Thus Fisher wrote: 'The fall in the external value of the pound began before inflation, and always kept ahead of it.'[1] This statement is buttressed by references to Feavearyear and—surprisingly at first sight—to Ricardo's *Principles.* The Feavearyear reference[2] turns out on inspection to be founded, in turn, upon Gresham's well-known letter extolling his own operations in the exchange market. As to the value of such evidence, silence is the most charitable commentary. The Ricardo reference is more interesting. It invokes that passage[3] in which Ricardo argues that it is the limitation of the quantity of a debased coinage which enables it to circulate at its fiat rather than its intrinsic value (the words 'fiat' and 'intrinsic' are my terminology, not Ricardo's). The truth of this assertion is not at present relevant to us, though it is historically highly vulnerable. But the more immediately relevant sentence which follows cannot be controverted by any evidence presented in the earlier chapters of this book: 'In the history [we read] of the British coinage we find, accordingly, that the currency was never depreciated in the same proportion that it was debased; the reason of which was, that it never was increased in quantity in proportion to its diminished intrinsic value.' At least as

[1] Fisher, 'Commercial Trends', p. 99.

[2] Feavearyear, op. cit., p. 50.

[3] D. Ricardo, *Principles of Political Economy* (Everyman Edition), p. 239.

far as the Great Debasement is concerned, this statement is both true and important. That it is true can easily be seen by confronting the figures in column 6 of Tables I and II on pp. 11–12 (showing the changing mint equivalent of silver and gold coins) with the estimates of money supply presented in Chapter 4. As to *why* it is true, it is hoped that the discussion of Chapter 2 has furnished an understanding of the determinants of mint output which would enable a satisfying explanation to be quickly put together. But the truth of Ricardo's sentence in this context does not justify the assertion that the external value of the pound must fall more rapidly than its internal purchasing power. Such an assertion would follow logically from Ricardo's true statement only if it were *also* true that the foreign-exchange rate moved proportionately with the intrinsic value (i.e. the reciprocal of the mint equivalent) of newly minted coins. Table XI and Graph A, read in conjunction with Tables I and II, column 6, show that this was not true. Chapter 5, which analyses the determinants of the exchange rate (or more accurately of the specie import and export points), shows *why* it was not true. For a fuller understanding of the reasons the reader is referred back to that chapter; but broadly it may be said that the specie import point fell less than the intrinsic value of new coinage because of the exaction of seignorage, and the specie export point fell less because of the coexistence of gold and/or silver coins whose *de facto* values differed less than their intrinsic values. Hence, while Ricardo's statement is true, it does *not* follow that the debasing of the coin should necessarily provoke a fall of the external value of the pound more rapid than the expansion of the money supply; both would be expected to, and did, proceed at a slower rate than the reduction of the intrinsic value of newly minted coins, but the second might outpace the first (as it did in the period to late 1548), or the first might outpace the second (as it did after that time).

We have now offered arguments which render theoretically attractive the contention that while the debasement of the coinage did not stimulate exports before late 1548, it did so in the two years following that date. We have also seen that the actual course of exports conforms well, up to late 1550, with the expectations aroused by such a contention, though it remains possible—as it so often does in causal analysis—that this consilience between expectations and events was fortuitous, the latter having been fashioned, in truth, by other, unexplored, influences. But what of the period after late 1550?

What, that is to say, of the unequivocal and steep decline of exports from the peak Michaelmas year 1549/50 to the pronounced trough of Michaelmas 1551/2? That our argument seems imperilled by this decline follows from a further confrontation of Tables VIII and IX, which shows clearly that from late 1550 to the high summer of 1551 the fall of the exchange rate proceeded much more rapidly than the continued expansion of the money supply, from which it of course follows that we should have expected, even more than in the period late 1548 to late 1550, an expansionary influence on English exports.

The non-monetary influences on exports, whose existence no one has ever doubted, can of course be invoked to explain this difficulty. The writer's inadequate grasp of the broader background of events prevents any novel interpretation here, but it seems entirely likely that other scholars have been justified in pointing to Charles V's renewed campaign against heresy in 1550, the plague of 1551, and the withdrawal of Hanseatic privileges in England in February 1552 as contributory causes of the progressive decline of exports in the early 1550s.[1] As regards the last of these, it might be noted that the decline of Hanseatic exports from London by some 26,000 cloths, from nearly 40,000 in 1550/1 to less than 14,000 in 1551/2, falls only about 2 per cent short of the over-all decline in cloth exports from England between those two years. Thus it may well be that as far as the second half of this two-year slump is concerned, economic nationalism in the form of the rivalry between the Merchant Adventurers and the Hanse is much the worst villain of the piece.

It is perhaps less certain whether we ought to follow earlier writers in nominating Edward's 'calling down' of the base silver in 1551 as a further cause of weakness.[2] Tables VIII and IX can be compared to show that the decrease in the money circulation which this brought about was proportionately much larger, and much prompter, than the recovery in the London–Antwerp exchange rate. *A priori* one would therefore have thought that the reductions in the fiat value of the silver coins should have alleviated, rather than aggravated, the inflationary pressures on export prices in terms of foreign currencies. If in fact, as seems certain, domestic prices did not decline following these reductions, as Edward's advisers clearly hoped, this is probably to be ascribed to institutional and psychological factors, and it seems

[1] P. Ramsey, *Tudor Economic Problems* (The Men and Ideas Series, I, Victor Gollancz, 1963), p. 68; Unwin, op. cit., p. 149.

[2] S. T. Bindoff, *Tudor England* (Penguin Books, 1950), pp. 140–1.

unfair to blame Edward's ministers or the measures they took. On the other hand, it is much easier to concur with the general agreement that Government measures in the monetary and exchange sphere in mid 1551 impeded trade by generating inconvenience to merchants and uncertainty and a loss of confidence amongst them. The 'calling down' of the coinage was not carried through swiftly and decisively at one stroke, but in a hesitating manner calculated to breed uncertainty and rumour-mongering.[1] Meanwhile the collapse of the exchange rate—misgivings over which were no doubt exploited by interested parties—had prompted the Government to make one of the periodic moves against freedom of private exchange transactions, which were suspended until further notice in June 1551.[2]

There is no doubt that these measures—in combination, of course, with other unfavourable or disquieting circumstances which included the sharp slide of the foreign-exchange rate—generated inconvenience and uncertainty which contributed to the decline of trade. The Johnson letters, for example, bear witness to the confusion in the City in the summer months of that eventful year.[3] The situation improved later; by the end of September the Johnson Letters show the exchanges operating again, though *sub rosa* and imperfectly,[4] as the continued 'gap' between London–Antwerp and Antwerp–London rates shows, while the Government's intentions for the coinage were made plain in the proclamation of 30 October 1551.[5] Yet it seems probable that the aftermath of these uncertainties continued to hamper business for several months, and thus they may have influenced the level of exports not only in the Michaelmas year 1550/1, but in 1551/2 also.

Yet one may question whether it was only because of such adventitious handicaps—many and varied though they were—that trade languished in 1550/1 and 1551/2. The truth seems to be rather that they aggravated difficulties which had already become apparent earlier in 1550, that is *within* the boom export year itself. As early as April 1550 the clothiers had complained that the Merchant Adventurers had acted collusively to depress cloth prices.[6] Such a complaint may seem a surprising one in the middle of a boom year for exports,

[1] Cf. pp. 42 and 85 above.
[2] Hughes and Larkin, op. cit., no. 375 (pp. 523–4).
[3] Winchester, op. cit., letters dated 10 June and 8 July 1551.
[4] Loc. cit. i. 403–4.
[5] Hughes and Larkin, op. cit., no. 382 (pp. 535–6).
[6] APC 1550–2, pp. 19–20.

but on this point the evidence of Gresham's daybook, to be discussed shortly, lends support to the allegation that cloth prices did indeed begin to turn downwards early in 1550, if not even before. In their reply the Merchant Adventurers made some play with the notion that standards of clothmaking had declined; such a decline is a familiar enough consequence of a strong pressure to increase the volume of output, and there is independent evidence that it occurred.[1] It also seems likely, however, that the Adventurers were right in another defence they offered, namely, that the fall in cloth prices reflected the increasing saturation of the market and the fact that large numbers of cloths were lying unsold at Antwerp. The intriguing possibility which this suggests is that the demand for English cloth was by now relatively inelastic upwards, in the short run at least, and that if the fall in the exchanges had stimulated cloth exports it was not so much by enlarging the market for them abroad as by increasing the profitability to the cloth exporter and lowering the cost to him of borrowing in London, on the promise of repayment abroad, the money with which he financed his shipments. In such circumstances it was natural that exporters should compete amongst themselves, contracting to purchase cloth from their suppliers weeks before it was actually made (as the Gresham daybook shows they did). The desire to take advantage of these favourable circumstances was doubtless strengthened by the fact that no one knew how long they would last; it seems plain that the decision to embark on the final stage of debasement, the issue of 3 oz. silver, was not made until the last moment, and for many months before that protestations of the new King's intentions to restore the coinage and some attempts, feeble and unsuccessful though they were, to initiate such a process must have kept alive uncertainty amongst the merchants as to how long they could count on a continuation of the fall in the exchanges, and a corresponding eagerness to take advantage of the situation while it lasted. If, however, the 'boom' in exports largely arose from anticipatory purchases of cloth which did not fundamentally change the conditions of relatively inelastic demand in Antwerp but merely emptied the pipeline, so to say, at the English end only to pile up inventories in Antwerp, a reaction was bound, and perhaps sooner rather than later, to set in anyway. That there is some validity at least in this interpretation is suggested strongly by the fact that the break in cloth prices occurred *before* any of the adverse circumstances which aggravated the slump

[1] Strieder, op. cit., *passim*.

of 1551/2 became manifest, and while the expansionary stimulus of exchange depreciation was still marked and, one would think, increasing.[1]

But it is quite clear that this mechanism accounts at most only in part for the crisis of the early 1550s. The fall of cloth exports from 1549/50 to 1551/2 was steeper than the rise from 1547/8 to 1549/50, and the unfavourable circumstances already discussed surely depressed exports below the level to which they would have dropped as a reaction from the anticipatory buying and inventory accumulation of the two preceding years. That being so, the stage was set for a further cyclical reaction, only this time in the reverse direction. Just as the accumulation of unsold cloths abroad arising from the buoyant exports of the late 1540s provoked a downswing which was to be the expected even in the absence of the *additional* depressive influences of 1551 and 1552, so may the *additional* shortfall of exports arising from those influences have prepared the way for a compensating 'boom' when those conditions disappeared. This they did by the beginning of Mary's reign. By then the temporary difficulties of 1550 and 1551 both in the Low Countries and in the City of London had disappeared; the coinage had become stabilized on a not unsatisfactory basis and with it the foreign-exchange rate; and the Hanse's privileges were restored, though conditionally, early in Mary's reign.[2] In such happier circumstances the cloth export boom of 1553/4 looks in part, at least, like a compensatory reaction from the abnormal trough of two years earlier. (It is worth note that Hanseatic cloth exports, at 27,903, were some 14,000 above the level of 1551/2, though still below their peak volume of the debasement period.)

Other writers have found other explanations for the high volume of cloth exports in 1553/4. Thus Dr. Bowden believes that this peak was achieved thanks to 'costs painfully adjusted and in response to the weakening of the exchange rate'.[3] It is difficult to know how to appraise this view. The data on exchange rates presented in Table IX and Graph A betray no evidence of this alleged further weakening of the exchanges, and one would have thought that the change in the valuation of the link money in the Low Countries in March 1553 would have tended rather to strengthen the London–Antwerp rate (as, indeed, the graph suggests it did). Admittedly, quotations are

[1] See below, p. 159.

[2] Rymer, *Foedera, Conventiones, Literae*, 2nd edn., xv (1728), 364.

[3] Bowden, op. cit., p. 155.

much more infrequent for Mary's reign, and there may have been some short-lived weakening of the exchanges which our own data have not recorded, though if so it is not clear what caused it, nor what evidence for it other scholars have found. As for the painful readjustment of costs, again it is difficult to know to what evidence this refers. Certainly the research on which this monograph is based has unearthed no evidence which would permit of precise statements about production costs during the debasement period; nor do we for this period have even the aid of a rough indication of the trend of cloth prices such as that which Gresham's daybook affords for the later 1540s. Perhaps, however, Dr. Bowden had in mind the low level of wool prices about the beginning of Mary's reign. The value shown for 1553 in his table testifies to this, and if the ratio of other costs to raw material costs was anything like that suggested by the cloth/wool price ratios discussed earlier, one would certainly expect some appreciable resultant decline in costs of production. Even though the organization of the market may have allowed clothiers rather than merchants to appropriate a good deal of this windfall, especially at a time of buoyant exports, still there may have been some element of price stimulation in the expansion of exports.

All this is very speculative. But if one is dealing in speculations, there is another line of thought which the combination of high cloth exports and low wool prices provokes. Why *were* wool prices low, in any event, at a time when the demand for it by the cloth workers must have been so high? It seems to have been the general belief of contemporaries that in the short run cloth exports and wool prices were positively correlated, and both of these negatively correlated with wool exports.[1] The argument was in essence that wool supply was price-inelastic in the short run—an eminently reasonable assumption—and that cloth for export was by now the largest single factor in the demand for wool and therefore constituted the 'price-setter' which largely determined the prospects for the export of raw wool. This argument seems to have gained at least the tacit approval of the most knowledgeable modern scholars, and a comparison of

[1] This, of course, was the basis of the recurring complaints by the Staplers against the growth of the cloth industry: cf. Bowden, op. cit., pp. 133 ff. and 'Movements in Wool Prices, 1490–1610', *Yorkshire Bulletin* iv (1952), 117; E. E. Rich, *The Ordinance Book of the Merchants of the Staple* (Cambridge U.P., 1937), pp. 13–14.

our cloth and wool export figures with Bowden's wool price index affords a good deal of, though by no means unequivocal, support for it. According to this scheme the years 1553 and 1554 were clearly out of line, for they witnessed a combination of high cloth exports, *low* wool prices, and (as Table XV shows) a simultaneous marked recovery, both relative and absolute, of wool exports.

The intriguing possibility which this combination opens up is that the high volume of cloth exports at the beginning of Mary's reign was partly induced by factors influencing the *supply* of wool. An abundant supply could, by reducing the price, stimulate the export both of wool and of cloth, the division of the increase between the two being determined of course by the differing effects on the prices of the two exports and the price-elasticity of demand for them at the time. Such a hypothesis consorts better with the combination of circumstances described than does an explanation turning solely upon factors influencing the *demand* for cloth exports alone, or even for all exports generally. It is worth while, indeed, looking backwards once again to the pre-debasement period to ask whether one can confidently reject the hypothesis that changes on the supply side influenced the trend of woollen exports earlier in the century.

It is, of course, perfectly clear that there was a secular trend towards the substitution of exports of wool manufactures for exports of raw wool. The over-all growth of cloth exports in the first half of the sixteenth century was made possible roughly as to two-thirds by the increase in the supply of wool available for exports and as to one-third by the diversion of wool from direct export to its use as an input for the cloth export industry. It is also true, as we have been, that in the short run an increase in the output of cloth for export was often achieved by diverting additional wool into the cloth industry and away from wool exports through an induced increase in its price. Yet it also seems possible to detect evidence pointing to some influences from the side of wool supply which at times stimulated the increase both of cloth *and of wool* exports. The most striking evidence of this is that the two periods of marked expansion in cloth exports, that is before the beginning of the sixteenth century and from about the mid 1530s onwards, were both marked by absolute increases *in the volume of wool exports* as well as in those of cloth. It is true that in both of these periods, as Table XII shows, the rise in wool exports (when transformed to a 'cloth equivalents' basis) fell short of that in cloth exports in absolute terms, though in proportionate terms wool exports grew substantially more than cloth in the decade beginning 1529/30–1533/4. Still, both periods of marked expansion in cloth exports saw wool exports increase too; wool's lost ground, in absolute terms, was lost entirely in the period from 1514/15–1518/19 to 1529/30–1533/4 when cloth exports were also virtually stagnant and woollen exports as a whole declining. It is as though two different mechanisms were superimposed on each other. On the one hand there was a secular trend, continuing more or less steadily throughout the period under review (and of course before it), towards the diversion of wool from export in its raw state to an input to the cloth export industry. On the other hand there were fluctuations in the total export of woollens or, so to look at it, in the total supply of wool for export, this increasing in the periods before 1499/1500–1503/4 and again after 1529/30–1533/4, and declining somewhat between these dates. In the first and third periods both influences combined to push cloth sharply upwards and at the same time largely offset each other so as to permit wool a small (absolute) rise, whereas in the intervening years they combined to push wool very sharply downwards while offsetting each other to keep cloth virtually stationary. Pursuing this approach the analyst of early Tudor exports might then think that he would have satisfactorily explained the trend and changing composition of woollen exports when he had accounted for (*a*) the long-term trend towards the substitution of cloth for wool exports, and (*b*) the postulated fluctuations in the total export of wool, raw and manufactured.

As to the first of these, there is nothing which causes the present writer any uneasiness in accepting as true and adequate the explanations already current amongst economic historians, especially those which turn on the improving technology of English cloth manufacture, the rise of Antwerp (specifically a *cloth* rather than a *wool* export outlet), and the much heavier incidence of taxation on wool than on cloth exports. It is not so clear that we can rest satisfied with current explanations of the second problem, that of the fluctuations in total woollen exports. It must be stressed that what is sought, conforming to the present line of inquiry, is some *generally* expansionary influence operating on exports as a whole, or at any rate on woollen exports as a whole, either on the demand or the supply side, or on both. Factors operating uniquely on *cloth* exports have already been taken into account under the first heading. One such general influence might well have been exchange depreciation, which of course would exert an influence, so to say, 'across the board'. But it has been argued that the first great wave of expansion (to *c.* 1500) can certainly not, and the second (from *c.* 1535) can for the most part probably not be ascribed to this cause. What is left? Fisher's characterization of the early sixteenth century as 'one of the great free-trade periods of modern English history'[1] is attractive, but has not been uniformly espoused by other scholars.[2] It is not yet firmly established that the increasingly oligopolistic organization of English trade was the cause, rather than the result, of the difficulties experienced by the traditional cloth exports in the later sixteenth century. But in any event it is not clear how this explanation can account for what we need it to account for, namely, two periods of increase in woollen exports *interrupted by thirty years or so of over-all stagnation.*

One other possibility which deserves very brief comment is that the total volume of exports may have been influenced by the equalization of duties on cloth exports by alien and denizen merchants between 1539 and 1546. The origins of this scheme are not important to us, but for a period of seven years from April 1539 alien merchants were required to pay only the same rate of duty as denizens, that is, 1*s.* 2*d.* on the cloth of assize, instead of their normal 2*s.* 9*d.*[3] At first glance the statistics seem to suggest that this change stimulated exports greatly, for exports of cloth by alien merchants were well above the usual level from 1538/9 to 1545/6 inclusive. It seems highly unlikely, however, that the reduction was large enough to make any great difference to the over-all level of cloth exports, and closer scrutiny of the figures suggests that its chief effect was to increase exports of cloth by aliens at the expense of those by denizens. This effect is particularly apparent at the end of the seven-year period, for alien exports rose to record levels in 1544/5 and 1545/6, clearly in an attempt to take maximum advantage of the concession while it lasted, but in doing so pulled down the level of denizen exports correspondingly. In 1547/8 (it will be recalled that the figure for 1546/7 is missing) alien cloth exports collapsed to an insignificant figure, the whole of their trade now being transferred to denizens.[4]

[1] Fisher, 'Commercial Trends', p. 101.

[2] Especially Stone, 'State Control', p. 109.

[3] For the text of the proclamation, see Schanz, op. cit. ii. 602–4.

[4] The following figures, which show London cloth exports by denizen and alien merchants as percentages of (national) woollen exports, illustrate the points made

These facts suggest that it may have been customary for what were in fact 'alien' exports to be shipped under the name of an English partner or agent so as to attract the lower rate of duty, and that, whether to escape detection of this deceit or to avoid the payment of *douceurs* to the English collaborator, this practice was temporarily abandoned during the period when customs duties were equalized and the financial incentive for it therefore disappeared. Thus the incident does not seem likely to suggest an important reason for the growth of woollen exports from the mid thirties onwards; but it *is* surely evidence which should be borne in mind in studies which give particular attention (as this study has not done) to the distribution of English trade between denizen and alien merchants.[1] It is scarcely too much to say that estimates of this distribution based on the Customs records alone may bear very little relation to reality.

It might perhaps be questioned whether the possibility of changing influences from the *supply* side has been adequately explored. Let us be clear what is in question. There can be no doubt that the supply of wool absorbed by exports (of raw wool as well as of cloth) *did* increase in the two periods of marked expansion we have identified. Except in so far as this enlargement of supply could have been met by reducing domestic consumption or stocks of wool, or by importing it—and none of these seems a plausible explanation save perhaps on a marginal scale and in the very short run—this logically implies an increase in domestic wool production in those periods, but not in between them. From this point of view it is relevant to note that the question of enclosure and conversion evoked much more discussion in the first two decades of the sixteenth century, and again near its middle, than in the intervening decades. It is also interesting to recall Professor Beresford's suggestion that most of England's lost villages died in the period 1450–1520, and that the investigation of 1517–18, which took cognizance only of cases of depopulation occurring after

in the text. (It should, of course, be borne in mind that London cloth exports increased markedly as a percentage of national woollen exports in this period.)

London cloth exports
(as percentage of national woollen exports)

	Denizens	*Aliens*
1536/7–1537/8	46·8	4·8
1538/9–1545/6	37·3	25·4
1547/8 and 1549/50	60·3	0·8

[1] It was sometimes alleged by contemporaries that the low rate of duty on Hanseatic exports led to similar deceptions; see, e.g., SP 11/15, fols. 18 ff., and cf. G. Sartorius, *Geschichte des Hanseatischen Bundes* (Göttingen, 1808) iii. 322–3.

1488, failed to catch the largest part of its potential haul.[1] The outcry of the middle years of the century turned on the questions not only of enclosure and conversion, but of the overstocking of the commons. It seems easy, then, to reconcile the chronology of enclosures and changing land use with the fluctuating course of woollen exports. What is in question is whether these variations in the rate of growth of wool production reflect simply changes in the relative profitability of sheep farming *induced uniquely* by influences bearing on the demand for wool, or whether factors on the supply side exerted an additional or indeed preponderant influence.

What makes the idea of such supply-side influences seem attractive is the difficulty we have had in identifying demand-side influences capable of explaining the chronological variations in the rate of growth of woollen exports. But would it be any easier to account for these variations in terms of supply-side influences? Here again it must rest with scholars better informed than the present writer to answer this question definitively. If, however, we have to account *somehow* for a decline after about 1519 in the rate of increase of wool supply—and therefore, since enclosure had in all likelihood been hitherto a major way of achieving such an increase, of the rate of enclosure too—it does not seem impossible that 'supply-side' influences should have been at least partly responsible. The impression left by a reading of Beresford's book, for example, is that the enclosures of the later fifteenth and early sixteenth century had typically occurred in settlements which for one reason or another had already become largely depopulated, or where the tenurial structure was favourable to the would-be encloser. The number of such settlements was of course limited (and perhaps would have tended to decline anyway as population began to rise once again), and as these so to say 'riper' villages disappeared opportunities for easy enclosure and conversion which did not arouse too much opposition must have become more restricted. Then again, it is perhaps wrong to dismiss too lightly the possible deterrent effect of Government regulation. It has become the fashion amongst modern historians to assume that much economic and social legislation and regulation was quite ineffectual in Tudor times, but the present writer counts himself amongst those who believe that this scepticism has been carried a good deal too far. The anxiety of those who conceived themselves likely to be harmed

[1] M. Beresford, *The Lost Villages of England* (Lutterworth Press, 1954), chapter v.

by a restrictive statute to be exempted from its provisions (as in the 'Halifax Act' of 1555); the eagerness of interested groups to repeal statutes they disliked as opportunity offered (as with the repeal of much of the anti-enclosure legislation in 1593); the desire to obtain explicit permission to do things capable of provoking legal action (as with the early private-enclosure bills and agreements enrolled in Chancery);[1] the willingness of groups or individuals to pay large sums of money to obtain exemption from actions prohibited by statute (for example, to get licences to export unfinished cloth); and the persistence of demands for Government to regulate economic activity—all these are inconsistent with the view that Government regulation was totally ineffective. What Government prohibition did—and does—was not to render the prohibited action totally impossible, but to increase the *cost*, and thus reduce the profitability, of doing it, by making it risky. An economist would wish, ideally, to appraise the effectiveness of restrictive legislation not by asking, did it make such-and-such acts impossible or not, but by asking, *how much* did it add to the cost of doing what was prohibited by making it risky, or riskier? From this point of view, we are not entitled to deny *some* cost-increasing, profit-reducing effect to the early anti-depopulation Acts, to Wolsey's 1517 enclosures commission, and to the brief period of more intense prosecution of offenders in the prerogative courts which followed this commission.[2]

Sceptics, however, will perhaps see a surer restraint on the growth of sheep-farming in relative movements of the prices of wool and wheat. For reasons which need not here be discussed, the third decade of the century saw a sudden jump in average wheat prices to a plateau fully one-third higher than that of the first two decades. Wool prices, on the other hand, which had gone up markedly in the cloth export boom of the second half of the second decade, fell back at the beginning of the 1520s to the slowly rising trend which they followed for the first forty years of the century. These divergent movements, which are shown in Table XVI, imply that for a time during the 1520s the financial incentive to convert arable to pasture and the relatively greater marginal profitability of enclosure for pasture must

[1] M. W. Beresford, 'Habitation versus Improvement: the Debate on Enclosure by Agreement', in F. J. Fisher (ed.), *Essays in the Economic and Social History of Tudor and Stuart England* (Cambridge U.P., 1961).

[2] Ramsey, *Tudor Economic Problems*, p. 39; I. S. Leadam, *The Domesday of Inclosures 1517–1518* (Longmans, Green & Co., 1897) i. 10–11.

have been quite sharply reduced. It is conceded, of course, that the fall of wool prices after about 1519 could be taken as evidence of a decline in demand for woollen exports. Yet the peak wool prices of 1515–17 apart, it was by the change in wheat prices rather than in wool prices that the shift in the ratio of wheat to wool prices came about.

TABLE XVI

Wool and wheat prices, 1488/92 to 1544/50

	(1) *Wool*	(2) *Wheat*
1488/92	96·8	6·07
1499/1503	91·4	7·05
1504/8	90·8	5·66
1509/13	107·0	6·17
1514/18	127·4	6·38
1519/23	112·4	8·40
1524/8	114·4	8·37
1529/33	116·4	8·62
1534/8	126·4	8·39
1539/43	151·8	8·63
1544/50	169·3	12·26

(1) = Bowden's index of wool prices (1450–99 = 100), in P. J. Bowden, op. cit., pp. 219–20.

(2) = Wheat price in shillings per quarter, from Beveridge material housed at the London School of Economics, and printed in W. G. Hoskins, 'Harvest Fluctuations and English Economic History, 1480–1619', *Agricultural History Review* xii (1964), 44–6.

In the light of all these factors it seems not impossible that the pace of enclosure and with it the increase in wool production which it was primarily intended to facilitate should have been restrained, in the twenties at least, by factors independent of those operating on the demand for exports of wool and cloth. What of the resumed expansion of wool production which must have set in during the 1530s? The last-mentioned influence—the sudden jump in wheat prices in the 1520s—lost impact gradually as wool prices slowly rose while those of wheat remained constant at the level to which they had jumped at the beginning of the twenties. One may think, too, that whatever deterrent effect the commission, legislation, and prosecutions of the period 1517–20 had had would gradually have evaporated. However, the evidence, such as it is, seems to discredit the idea of any marked resurgence of the rate of enclosure in the fourth and fifth decades of the century, the outcry and commission of the later 1540s notwithstanding.[1] It may rather be that the increase in wool production and (one must suppose) in flock numbers was accomplished by more intensive exploitation of the existing pastoral acreage. In this connection the more frequent complaints of the overstocking of commons which marked the agitation of the 1540s are surely significant. One wonders, too, whether the dissolution of the religious houses and the increased land transfers which this helped to promote are too much played down today as factors facilitating or prompting more efficient or more predatory land use.

The purpose of the foregoing digression into the pre-debasement period was to examine the possibility that influences bearing on the supply side carried at least a share of the responsibility for changes in the volume of woollen exports which occurred in that period. This does indeed seem plausible, but no definitive assessment of the relative importance of such influences is feasible at the present stage of knowledge. We return from this digression to our consideration of the reign of Queen Mary. If one concedes the possible importance of 'supply-side' factors in the period before 1544, it is surely even easier to imagine that they may partly account for the boom export volumes at the beginning of Mary's reign. One would not have expected the upward trend of wool production induced by the expansion from the mid 1530s onwards to have come abruptly to a halt with the contraction of 1551/2, even had sheepmasters been able to recognize that contraction for the decisive turning-point which later historians have often considered it. Sheep numbers, after all, cannot be either increased or reduced all that quickly, and one can perfectly well conceive that wool production should in any event have continued to increase for a few more years. Moreover, there is no reason why all sheepmasters should have promptly concluded that the downturn of 1550–2 spelled the end of the prolonged expansion of the preceding fifteen years. From the point of view of Governmental restraints upon enclosure, too, there is little difficulty in supposing that the trend towards sheep-farming should have continued, or indeed accelerated, in the early 1550s—not, at least, if we follow Tawney in seeing Warwick's administration as 'the bottom point in the con-

[1] Ramsey, op. cit., pp. 26–7.

dition of the sixteenth century peasantry . . . years during which an exceptional freedom from restraint was enjoyed by the great landlords'.[1] All this being so, it seems quite reasonable to suggest that the 'rebound' effect on exports following the abnormal contraction of 1551/2 should have been compounded by a further expansive influence from the side of wool supply. Such an interpretation is not only congenial to common sense but helpful in explaining the otherwise puzzling coexistence of high wool exports and low wool prices alongside high cloth exports in 1553/4.

It is unfortunate, however, that no estimates of cloth exports are available either for 1552/3 or for 1554/5 or 1555/6. This lack of adequate evidence for the surrounding years makes it impossible to be sure how far the high export figure for 1553/4 was a mere isolated peak representing the 'rebound' effect from the depression of two years earlier. Such partial evidence as is available suggests very tentatively that 1554/5 was probably also a good year, with woollen exports then falling away to the estimated volume of 131,326 cloth equivalents in 1556/7—a figure which, however, was still close to the average for the first few years of the debasement period. The next two years are again years for which no national woollen exports estimate is possible, the London cloth export figure being unavailable. (Can the administrative historian explain the paucity of quantitative evidence surviving from Mary's reign?—for it will be recalled that we have met similar gaps in the records not only of the Customs, but of the Mints and of foreign-exchange operations.) When an estimate is again possible, for 1559/60, the volume of woollen exports (136,719 cloth equivalents) is at about the level of the immediate pre-debasement years. In the following year it fell, with the difficulties in the Low Countries, by some 17½ per cent. Apart from this sharp fall in the last years of our study, it thus seems likely that the retreat from the peak of 1553/4 was fairly slow, as one might have expected if supply-side influences had something of the importance contemplated for them in this analysis.

The attempt to place the history of exports in the Great Debasement in perspective would ideally require some attention to the course of exports in the following decades. Certainly the emphasis which this study has placed on the need for a reconsideration of the earlier sixteenth century when exports of wool and of the outports

[1] R. H. Tawney, *The Agrarian Problem in the Sixteenth Century* (Longmans, Green & Co., 1912), pp. 372, 386.

are added to Fisher's London cloth figures makes a continuation of this broader coverage into Elizabeth's reign seem imperative. But that is a matter for a separate study. The present chapter can conclude with a few remarks about aspects of exports during the Great Debasement other than their over-all magnitude.

It can be seen from Table XV(C) that the shares both of wool and of the outports in national woollen exports fell to record low values during the debasement years. For the only two such years for which a national total can be estimated, 1544/5 and 1549/50, wool exports were respectively 5 and 9·1 per cent and outport exports respectively 9·6 and 10 per cent of the total. The outports had lost ground both in wool and in cloth exports; they accounted for only about one-eighth even of the former in the two years mentioned, while in the case of cloth exports the outport share fell to only some 7½ per cent in 1547/8 and 1548/9. These values all, of course, continue the trends of the pre-debasement period. In so far as they were intensified during the debasement years, this can be adequately explained by the pressure exerted on supplies of wool by the rise of cloth exports to peak levels in the later 1540s. Even though one may follow the argument of the present chapter in conceding some importance to supply-side influences on the volume of woollen exports, it does seem clear that the cloth boom of the later 1540s impinged on a wool supply which was somewhat inelastic in the short run, thus inducing a sharp rise in wool prices and a decline in exports of raw wool. The researches and comments of Dr. Bowden seem to indicate that in this respect, at least, the complaints of the Staplers were basically correct.[1] In so far as the outports had still been, in the pre-debasement years, relatively more oriented to wool than to cloth exports, the decline in wool exports naturally pulled down the outports' share in the national woollen total.

Table XV(C) appears to suggest, at first glance, that both wool and the outports made some recovery by the end of the period here under review. This may be, but it will require further analysis of the early part of Elizabeth's reign before any such trend can be regarded as established. What is certain is that the two years for which we have estimates of woollen exports and which were years of sharp contraction, 1551/2 and 1560/1, both witnessed a marked relative and even absolute recovery of such exports from the outports. That wool exports should recover as cloth exports declined is a familiar manifestation of the short-run inverse relationship between them which

[1] Bowden, op. cit., Appendix (pp. 219–20), pp. 112 ff.

has been noticed, and such a relative recovery of wool would to a minor extent account for the increase in the same year of the outports' share of the total. But only to a minor extent. The relative recovery of the outports in 1551/2 and in 1560/1 went well beyond what could have been expected from the relative rise in wool as compared with cloth; indeed, perversely enough, wool did not as it happens contribute to the relatively good outport showing in the former year. It may be that the outports' exports, in the short run and in absolute terms, tended to be more stable than those of London during the debasement period because they were less uniquely oriented to the Antwerp market, or perhaps because the outport merchants were a degree more ignorant of or phlegmatic towards the alarums and excitements which clearly influenced business expectations in the capital city. The greater short-run stability of outport exports thus caused would help to explain the tendency for the outports' share of total exports to rise in years of sharp downturn in London. It is necessary, however, to add that outport exports do *not* seem to have displayed any such greater stability in the years before the debasement; on the contrary, they seem in the twenties and thirties in particular to have been *more* liable to sudden fluctuations than London exports, and on two occasions at least, in 1521/2 and in 1534/5, to have suffered much more sharply than London in years of contracting trade, so that their percentage share in the total actually fell.

It remains to point out that nothing has been said here regarding the *value* of exports, much less the balance of payments, in the debasement period, though in Chapter 4 some heroic assumptions about the balance of payments, based more on the coinage records than on those of trade, were made to facilitate the calculations of the supply of money. Schanz, it may be recalled, made a crude attempt to assess the average balance of trade for Henry VIII's reign.[1] It has been generally assumed that the debasement, in stimulating the *volume* of exports, also generated a fall in the average price of cloth in terms of the foreign currency. The assumption of such a fall must, of course, be made if the orthodox argument alleging the stimulating effect of the debasement on exports is to enjoy cogency. Similarly, it is assumed—and with equal theoretical plausibility and the added support of much contemporary comment—that the fall in the exchanges increased the domestic price of imported goods. The

[1] Schanz, op. cit. ii. 30–6.

debasement, then, is supposed to have had an adverse effect on England's terms of trade. This is indeed likely, but the actual course of either cloth or import prices has not been charted.

The difficulty with cloth prices is not so much an absolute lack of evidence as that of finding a series of prices over time which one can reasonably take to relate to a homogeneous commodity. Not only were there many varieties of cloth, but the more popular varieties varied in price, and doubtless in size and quality, from one clothier to another. There are several general statements in contemporary documents which purport to summarize the average change in cloth prices over a given period, but most lack specificity and fail to convince of being reliable evidence. An exception is the deposition of the Drapers' Company of London reviewing the increase in the prices of certain specified types of cloth in the four years ending July 1551.[1] The document suggests increases ranging from about 65 to a little over 100 per cent. Another, continuous, series of prices is that which can be extracted from the Gresham daybook.[2] Though not all the purchases there recorded are suitable for our purposes, there are quite a large number of entries ranging over the period May 1546 to July 1550 which can reasonably be regarded as relating to a uniform commodity, the continuity of the name of the clothier from whom the cloths were purchased and of the description of the cloths, and the reasonable progression of the prices in question, all combining to lend authenticity to the resulting data. In addition, the quite large number of cloths involved in many cases and the fact that several of the transactions were contracts for future purchases enable one to feel a confidence that the prices relate to well-standardized products. Perhaps one should say, though, that these series represent the prices of what *purported* to be uniform types of cloth, for the frequency with which, especially in 1549, the daybook notes deductions from the going price 'for shortness'[3] lends support to the evidence one can find elsewhere[4] corroborating the contention of the Drapers' Company that 'the sayde clothe was never so yll and falsely made'.

It is extremely unfortunate that the systematic evidence on cloth prices to be found in the daybook should peter out in the summer of

[1] Tawney and Power (eds.), op. cit. ii. 191–2.
[2] See Chapter 5, fn. 2, p. 87.
[3] See, for example, entries no. 4190, 4197, 4231, 4498, 4580.
[4] Strieder, op. cit., *passim*.

1550, for as far as it goes it suggests a much more gentle rise in cloth prices than that claimed by the Drapers' Company. The two could of course be reconciled if most of the increase occurred in the last year of the debasement period, that is July 1550 to July 1551, on which the daybook is silent. But while it is indeed likely that the check to the domestic price of cloth experienced in early 1550 was overcome and the upward movement resumed in response to the sharper fall of the exchange rate which began in the summer of 1550, it also seems plausible that the sharp decline in cloth exports and the lower rate of expansion of the money supply should have combined to keep that upward movement below the proportionate fall in the exchanges. If that were indeed the case, it would be difficult not to suspect some conflict between the two pieces of evidence. True, the only type of cloth recognizably common to the two sources was the northern kersey, which in the Drapers' memorandum was shown as rising a good deal less than most varieties listed there. Even so, there is a big difference between the increase from £24 a pack about July 1547 to £38 in July 1551 suggested by this document, and that from 23*s*. 0*d*. or 23*s*. 4*d*. a piece in 1546 to only 29*s*. 0*d*. a piece at the end of 1549 suggested by the Gresham daybook. It may, of course, be to some extent that Gresham, as a big buyer with regular suppliers, was able to keep the buying price down a little, but in the hectic competition amongst merchants for cloth in 1549 it is unlikely that any buyer could have enjoyed much monopsonistic advantage.

The speculations to which this evidence gives rise, though remaining mere speculations owing to the inadequacy of the data, are indeed fascinating. The cloth prices extracted from the Gresham daybook are charted in Graph B (see end of book). That the over-all trend of the prices paid for cloth in England by Gresham's servants was not one, before mid 1550 at least, of runaway inflation, emerges clearly from this figure. Yet we have seen that in the earlier years of the debasement the movement of the exchange rate, too, was relatively muted, and up to the autumn of 1548, at least, the rise of cloth prices probably outpaced the fall in the external value of the pound. Though no exchange quotations are available between September 1546 and January 1547, the rate was probably declining throughout that period from the 25*s*. 0*d*. of the former month to the 23*s*. 3½*d*. of the latter. Throughout the summer and autumn of 1548 the rate was still hovering somewhat above the 22*s*. mark. Gresham's buying price for cloth, meanwhile, seems to have risen for different types of cloth and different suppliers in proportions ranging from about 15 to about 25 per cent between the end of 1546 and the late autumn of 1548. The supply price of English cloth in Antwerp, then, could actually have risen in this period—or, if we suppose the various costs incurred between buying in England and selling in Antwerp to have risen less than proportionately, could have remained at best more or less unchanged. Such a reconstruction agrees well enough with the conclusion extracted from our earlier analyses, that in the first part of the debasement period the internal inflationary impact of debasement was greater than its weakening effect on the external value of the pound. It is also consistent with this analysis that our export data give no sign, in this period, of any substantial expansion.

From November 1548 to March 1549 the exchange rate fell more sharply, from a little over 22*s*. to a little over 20*s*. It then stabilized about that level for most of the remainder of the year. Perhaps this fall, coinciding as it did with the end of the period of rapid monetary expansion, helped cause the marked increase in cloth exports which occurred, for the first time, in Michaelmas 1548/9. Within twelve months or little more, however, the Antwerp market showed signs of becoming saturated, and the prices at which Gresham's agents bought kersies from William Bennett, John Barksdale, and Thomas Dolman quite clearly show that there were some grounds for the concern manifested by the clothiers as to the course of cloth prices. Since this fall in buying prices in England occurred at a time when the exchanges were also still falling, though gently and somewhat fitfully, it is probable that Antwerp prices also turned downwards—a conclusion which, in turn, would lend support to the defence which the Merchant Adventurers made to the clothiers' allegations.

Though no consistent series of cloth prices between July 1550 and July 1551 is known to the writer, we have seen that the otherwise puzzling disparity between the evidence of the Gresham daybook and that of the Drapers' Company's memorandum can be explained if we suppose that the downturn in (English) cloth prices in early 1550 was halted and gave place to a marked rise between the summer of that year and the summer of the next. The hypothesis of such an upturn receives support from the apparent discontinuation of complaints about falling prices, from the contemporary evidence of a more 'literary' character in favour of such a rise (such as Lane's well-known letter to Cecil),[1] and (inferentially) from the very sharp rise of

[1] Tawney and Power (eds.), op. cit. ii. 182–6.

wool prices. (Bowden's index, which fluctuates with no clear trend between 150 in 1543 and 168 in 1549, then shoots up meteorically to 281 in 1550 and 268 in 1551.)[1] But how could the hypothesis of a sharp upward turn of English cloth prices in 1550/1 be reconciled either with the much slower progress of monetary inflation which our analysis suggests, or, even more, with the clear downturn in the volume of cloth exports in that year? The solution of this paradox is surely to be sought in the exchange rate, which about July 1550 entered on much the most pronounced fall which it experienced at any time during the debasement period. From 19*s*. 6½*d* (Fl.) to the pound in July 1550 the London–Antwerp rate fell to a (known) minimum of 12*s*. 9*d*. twelve months later. Even if cloth prices in Antwerp were falling appreciably under the impact of shrinking sales, this fall of the exchange of more than one-third in a year would have made it possible for the buying price in England to rise, and sympathetically with this the price of wool. Thus it may well be that in the short run at least the exchange rate was capable of exerting a stronger influence on the domestic price of goods entering into international trade than did the general monetary situation; and in insisting, as they so often did, on the primacy of the exchanges contemporary commentators may not have deserved the censure which the scholars of later ages have been too ready to bestow on them. To the extent, however, that the fall in the exchanges was so to say 'taken up' by higher prices and profits for merchants, clothiers, and wool-growers, it was not available to reduce the (foreign currency) price of English cloth in Antwerp. It may be that the short-run influence of the falling exchange rate on the volume of cloth sales was limited in this way, the selling price in Antwerp changing only relatively little and merchants, clothiers, and wool-growers dividing the spoils of the larger sterling equivalent of that price between them. Of course in the longer run the rise in profits accruing to these groups would prompt an expansion of cloth-making from the supply side. But in the short run this interpretation, highly provisional though it is, suggests a way of reconciling the otherwise puzzling coexistence of falling exchanges, falling cloth exports, and rising cloth and wool prices.

4. Some Shortcomings of the Analysis

In the foregoing pages we have attempted an 'explanation sketch' of changes in England's cloth exports by drawing on data collected and

[1] Bowden, op. cit., Appendix, p. 219.

hypotheses fabricated in earlier chapters of this book. The reader will hardly need to be convinced that this sketch falls far short of being a finished portrait. Far too much of the evidence, for one thing, is unsurely founded or deficient in coverage—the estimates of the money supply exemplify the former defect and the data on cloth prices the latter. *Annual* export figures, again, are a clumsy statistical basis where one is concerned with such short-period analysis. And some of the individual explanatory hypotheses are but frailly anchored to empirical data and rely too heavily on circumstantial evidence. (It seems fair, however, to claim that not all of our data are as suspect as this; there seems little doubt, for example, that the course of the exchange rate has been securely enough charted, and it may be hoped that the reader has been reasonably well convinced by the analysis of its determinants offered in Chapter 5.)

The greatest single deficiency of the preceding analysis, however—and this it shares with most earlier studies—is that no attention has been given to the import side. No study of the interaction of debasement, monetary inflation, and the exchanges could claim to carry conviction unless it helped to explain what happened to imports as much as what happened to exports. It is first in charting, and then in analysing, the course of imports that the most obvious hope for future progress in the understanding of trade trends during the Great Debasement, and indeed during the whole sixteenth century, resides.

APPENDIX A

THE DATING OF THE *MEMORANDUM* 'FOR THE UNDERSTANDING OF THE EXCHANGE'

IN a closely reasoned article in the *Economic History Review* Mrs. M. Dewar has argued that the *Memorandum* 'For the Understanding of the Exchange', which most historians, following Professor R. de Roover, have attributed to Sir Thomas Gresham and have dated from early in Elizabeth's reign, was in fact written in 1554 by Sir Thomas Smith.[1] It is not to the present purpose to adjudicate between these two claims, or to propound a third solution. But one error in Mrs. Dewar's argument which quickly becomes apparent to the student of the monetary history of the period may perhaps be drawn to the reader's attention.

Mrs. Dewar's strongest argument for dating the *Memorandum* in 1554 is her contention that a description of the state of the English coinage (presumably at the time of writing) contained in it does not, as De Roover had claimed, reflect the condition of the coinage in the early years of Elizabeth's reign. In her view this description would, however, be wholly accurate if applied to the period immediately preceding what she describes as Mary's attempt to reform the coinage. Mrs. Dewar places Mary's action in August 1554, a date which appears to lend support to the other evidence which she adduces in favour of May 1554 as the precise month in which the *Memorandum* was written.

Unfortunately, Mary's attempt to 'reform' the coinage in fact dates from August 1553. Perhaps Mrs. Dewar was confused by the complexity of the regnal years of Philip and Mary; she may have supposed that the '20 August anno primo Mariae' of the document in the Harleian MSS.[2] from which she took the text of the proclamation 'for the new severall moneys and coynes' means 20 August 1554. In fact it means 20 August 1553; August of the following year would

[1] M. Dewar, 'The Memorandum "For the Understanding of the Exchange": its Authorship and Dating', *Economic History Review*, 2nd Series xvii, no. 3 (Apr. 1965), 476–87.

[2] Harleian MSS. 660, fol. 60.

be 1 and 2 Philip and Mary. The date of this proclamation is correctly identified by Steele.[1] The mint indenture authorizing the striking of these new coins dates equally from 20 August 1553, not from 20 August 1554 as Mrs. Dewar claims. Her error here is even more puzzling since the authority on whom she draws for details of this indenture, the numismatist Henry Symonds, gives the correct year.[2] His ascription of it to 1553 is confirmed by scrutiny of the original in the Exchequer records,[3] and is placed beyond doubt by the mint account of the official concerned, Thomas Egerton, which is preserved amongst the Audit Office rolls.[4]

Mrs. Dewar, then, inadvertently postdates by one year what she calls the Marian attempt to reform the coinage. Does this signify? So far as her criticism of the ascription of the *Memorandum* to the early years of Elizabeth's reign is concerned, no; whatever force may reside in her argument that, by internal evidence, the *Memorandum* cannot have postdated the Marian 'reform' would be totally unaffected by the dating of those reforms in 1553 rather than in 1554. Either, she might contend, would be equally hard to reconcile with the claim made for the early years of Elizabeth. But August 1553 would by Mrs. Dewar's own arguments be equally fatal to the dating of the *Memorandum* in May 1554—indeed, rather *more* than equally so; for while one can conceive that a writer on exchange matters in, say, 1559 might possibly have overlooked Mary's rather unoriginal coinage indenture of six years earlier, it is not so easy to suppose that anyone writing only nine months later would not have had it in mind. Thus Mrs. Dewar is hoist with her own petard.

Two alternatives face us: either to regard her argument that the *Memorandum* cannot have postdated the Marian reforms as incorrect, or to argue for a date prior to 20 August 1553. The first alternative would greatly weaken her case for May 1554, the second demolish it. Can we decide between them? In fact, the second alternative would be difficult indeed to reconcile with the reference in the text to the *Memorandum* to 'the statute [*sc.* of apparel] thereof made of late by Quene Mary'. Mrs. Dewar, in seeking to establish May 1554 as the month of authorship, makes an attempt which her readers may think heroic rather than convincing to suggest that the word 'statute' refers to bills against 'excesse in apparel' which were before both Houses

[1] Steele, op. cit. i, no. 428.
[2] Symonds, 'The Coinage of Queen Mary Tudor', p. 180.
[3] E. 101/307/1.
[4] A.O. 1/1670/497.

of Parliament in April and May 1554, but which never became law. If we accept the second alternative propounded above, this explanation falls to the ground. Indeed there seems to be nothing, if we search for a date of writing prior to 20 August 1553, to which these words could possibly apply. Mary, after all, had only been on the throne some five weeks when her first coinage indenture was made, and her first Parliament did not meet until 5 October 1553.

There is, indeed, a further point. Mary's mint indenture of 20 August 1553 merely repeated, with the most trifling alterations, the provisions of her predecessor's last indenture, namely that of 5 October 1551.[1] It is this indenture of 1551, together with the 'calling down' of the base coins which preceded it, which most clearly deserve credit as the first serious attempt to 'reform' the coinage. Following, as they did, hard upon the last desperate bout of debasement and upon the two-stage 'calling down' of base silver to half its previous value, and heralded, as they were, by considerable discussion and by a proclamation announcing the new coinage, Edward's new mint provisions of late 1551 were an altogether more important and memorable (though not always remembered) event in the history of the currency than was Mary's routine indenture following her accession. Thus the argument that from its reference to the state of the coinage the *Memorandum* cannot have postdated 5 October 1551 would at first sight seem far more plausible than Mrs. Dewar's contention that it cannot have postdated 20 August 1553. Yet we *cannot* place the *Memorandum* earlier than 5 October 1551; the reference already quoted to Queen Mary suffices to make that certain.

There is thus the very strongest presumption in favour of the first, rather than the second, alternative—namely, that Mrs. Dewar's objections to a date of writing postdating the first Marian currency reforms cannot be sustained. That being so, May 1554 looks no more likely, or one may think (as argued above) perhaps less likely, than a later date when the 'reforms' may more easily be supposed to have slipped out of the writer's hand, and when their lack of success in getting rid of the mass of base coins, which could not have been so confidently predicted in 1551 or 1553, should have become apparent.

It may be pointed out that *in so far as* Mrs. Dewar's claims on behalf of Sir Thomas Smith as author of the *Memorandum* rest on the ascription of the work to May 1554—and this they do partly, but not wholly—to that extent these claims suffer a loss of cogency by

[1] Add. MSS. 18759, fols. 69^{v} ff.

virtue of the weakening of the evidence in favour of that month as the date of composition.

One final comment may be made. In a recent article Professor D. R. Fusfeld has suggested that neither Gresham nor Smith but the mint official, Richard Martin, may have been the author of the *Memorandum*.[1] The argument presented above has nothing whatever to say for or against this ascription, save for the minor and negative consideration mentioned in the last paragraph. However, the writer might perhaps take the opportunity to point out that the actual form of presentation of the *Memorandum*, that is, highly schematic and articulated by the use of braces, is not one which, as De Roover supposes,[2] necessarily supports the claims of Gresham as against Martin. Such a layout was common in many sixteenth-century accounts, and notably in the mint accounts. For what it is worth this evidence would point to Martin at the very least as much as to Gresham. As to the date which Fusfeld suggests—'between 1553 and 1576'—the present argument finds both the implication that we cannot yet point to a particular year, and the naming of 1553 as the *earliest* possible date of composition, highly congenial. The suggestion that the *Memorandum* could have been written as late as 1576 is, however, more difficult to accept, for it is not quite so easy to agree that the document can have postdated Elizabeth's recoinage. Thus the conclusion is that the *Memorandum* was probably written between August 1553 and September 1560, with perhaps a very slight preference for a later rather than an earlier date within this period, and leaving open a distinctly lower possibility for some date between September 1560 and 1576.

[1] D. R. Fusfeld, 'On the Authorship and Dating of "For the Understanding of the Exchange" ', *Economic History Review*, 2nd Series xx, no. 1 (Apr. 1967), 145–50.

[2] R. de Roover, loc. cit., pp. 150–2.

APPENDIX B

GAPS IN THE MINT ACCOUNTS

THE first gap in the calculations of the output of coinage inflicted by the absence of mint records concerns the output of Tower II after the end of Thomas Knight's period of control there in December 1547. An estimate of output for the period January to September 1548 can be made by drawing on the evidence of Peckham's accounts. As explained in the text, Sir Edmund Peckham's office of High Treasurer of the Mints was set up to control the activities of the various individual Mints during the debasement period, and to act as accounting superior to them. The bulk of the profits of the individual establishments were paid over to Peckham. In the early years of the debasement there was a close similarity between the sums received by Peckham from each individual establishment and the amounts levied by it in seignorage. Seignorage was by far the largest component of mint income, and payments to Peckham the chief channel for the disposal of profits. Mint expenses in these years of high seignorage rates were relatively small compared with seignorage receipts, and tended to be somewhat offset by smaller sources of income (such as allowances arising from the so-called 'remedies'). It was natural, therefore, for payments to Peckham (with a lag of a month or two) to coincide fairly closely with receipts from seignorage.

In the case of Tower II, receipts from seignorage to the end of 1547 totalled £94,826.[1] Payments to Peckham by the Under-Treasurer during that period, Thomas Knight, totalled £91,824.[2] In the period April to October 1548 Peckham is recorded as having received from Knight's successor, Steven Vaughan, payments totalling £16,500. The next such payment was not made until 10 January 1549, and I therefore take this £16,500 as corresponding roughly to the amount of seignorage levied at Tower II during the coinages of 1 January to 30 September 1548. I then divide this sum between seignorage on silver and seignorage on gold in the ratio 30 to 1. This ratio, in the last resort, is arbitrarily chosen, but it has regard to the facts that in the period October 1547 to September 1548 the ratio of silver to gold

[1] E. 101/302/29. [2] E. 351/2077.

seignorage at Tower I was about 13 to 1, and that in the year or two before October 1547 the silver/gold seignorage ratio had been about twice as high at Tower II as at Tower I. I thus attribute £550 to seignorage on gold and the remaining £15,950 to that on silver. From the data in Tables I and II it is then simple arithmetic to translate these figures into a gold output of £16,500 and a silver output of £28,710.

Regrettably, Peckham's accounts cannot with any confidence be used after 1548 for calculating missing coinage figures in this way. Partly this is because it became increasingly common for the Under-Treasurers to be instructed to make various sorts of payments which bypassed Peckham's accounts, as for example when Sir John York of the Southwark Mint paid over £26,000 to the Fuggers and others in Flanders 'for the King's use'.[1] The fact that several of the Under-Treasurers became increasingly behindhand in their accounting is an additional difficulty. Finally, the operation by which testons were recoined into smaller pieces obscures the accounting during 1549. This operation was not primarily designed to make a profit; those delivering testons at the Mints were repaid in smaller pieces to a similar value, the King bearing the costs of the recoining. The Under-Treasurers were accordingly debited with the full value of the small pieces struck from the melted-down testons, and credited with that of those paid out to the subject. But these two amounts did not necessarily coincide, since the surrendered testons contained a proportion of 6 oz. coins of the 1545–6 issue, which had an intrinsic value higher than that of the majority of the surrendered testons, those of 4 oz. fineness, and also than that of the small coins into which they were transformed. Hence the face value of any given batch of small coins was generally higher than that of the testons from which they were fabricated. In addition, quantities of fine silver were added to bring the silver/alloy mix up to the required standard when 6 or 8 oz. coins were being struck, and this again may have contributed an unknown amount of 'profit' at those Mints (Tower II and Durham House) for which the relevant accounts have not survived.[2] For all such reasons we cannot assume, in and after 1549, that rough equivalence between payments to Peckham from these two Mints and the seignorage gathered at them which made possible an approximate estimate of the output at Tower II in 1548.

[1] E. 159/41.

[2] For a more detailed discussion, see Appendix E below.

One other gap in the accounts can be filled with some degree of confidence. It concerns the 3 oz. silver of 1551. It seems certain that only the three surviving London Mints—Tower I, Tower II, and Southwark—ever produced this coin, and relevant accounts are extant for the first and third of these.[1] Tower I produced in round figures £81,000 of 3 oz. silver, and Southwark £92,000. We know from Peckham's accounts that Tower II was generating income during this period; the amounts paid over to the High Treasurer by Throckmorton, Under-Treasurer at Tower II, are about two-thirds of what Peckham received from York in respect of each of the other two London Mints. We have seen, however, that by this time it is impossible to assume any close equivalence between the sums paid to Peckham and the level of mint activity, so that too much should not be made of this. The evidence of Elizabeth's recoinage[2] suggests that something upwards of a quarter of a million pounds worth of 3 oz. coins were originally produced, which would leave about £80,000 to be accounted for at Tower II—not an unlikely figure in the light of the rate of output at the other two Mints. Then again there is the infuriatingly obscure evidence of Edward VI's *Journal.* (The obscurity springs in perhaps equal measure from the unsuitability of the elliptic style for explaining technical problems, and the incapacity of the boy King to understand them.) Feavearyear, whose interpretation of the literary evidence relating to the 3 oz. silver was highly imaginative, took from the entry in Edward's *Journal* on 6 September 1551 the phrase 'many also three ounces, 130000 l. now of late', reading this to mean (since the minting of 3 oz. silver had stopped in July) that £130,000 of such coins had been produced in all.[3] But, as we have seen, some £173,000 was produced at Tower I and at Southwark alone, so that Feavearyear's interpretation is clearly wrong. Nor could the entry mean 130,000 pounds weight, which would be far too much. The solution seems to be that Feavearyear overlooked the significance of the words 'of late'. The original intention in embarking on the coining of 3 oz. silver, according to Edward's *Journal*, was to make a profit 'by which the dette of the realm might be paid, the country defended from any suddain attempt, and the coin be amended'—an astonishing array of benefits to hope for from

[1] Both on Sir John York's account, E. 159/41.

[2] See p. 68 above.

[3] Feavearyear, op. cit., p. 66. For the stopping of 3 oz. coinage in July, see APC 1550–2, p. 316.

so restricted an experiment! Towards the end of May these intentions seem to have been abandoned, and the Council ordered the minting of 3 oz. silver to be stopped. It was resumed in June, however, in deference to the pressing needs of defence.[1] Despite the obscurity of the language it seems from the *Journal* and the Privy Council records that some £120,000 may have been coined before the temporary cessation was ordered; the accounts for Tower I and Southwark reveal an output of about £92,000 by the end of May, which seems to be not inconsistent, allowing on the one hand for the output from Tower II and on the other for the Council's information being perhaps a little out of date. The significance of the words 'of late' would then be to relate the output of the £130,000 referred to to the time *since the order stopping coinage was countermanded.* The £120,000 coined *before* added to the £130,000 coined *after* resumption would then lead us again to the total 3 oz. output of about a quarter of a million pounds, which from all points of view looks about right. In deference to this line of reasoning an estimated output of £80,000 of 3 oz. coins at Tower II is therefore included in the coinage table.

What remains? Apart from the gaps in the records of Tower I (and perhaps of York) from 1551 onwards, our information is now complete save for the following: (*a*) the output of Durham House throughout its existence; (*b*) the output of gold and of 6 oz. silver at Tower I from November 1550 to March 1551 inclusive; (*c*) the output of gold and of 4 oz. and of 6 oz. silver (and perhaps of converted testons) at Tower II from October 1548 to March 1551, inclusive. We can be fairly sure that most, probably all, of these omissions were of small importance. Thus, gold output from October 1548 at Tower II (where it had never been nearly as important as at Tower I) and at Tower I from November 1550 was almost certainly of negligible proportions, given the over-all trend in the output of that metal. So for similar reasons would have been the output of 4 oz. silver from October 1548 at Tower II. As for Durham House, all evidence agrees that its over-all level of activity was quite unimpressive. Peckham received only £9,100 from the Under-Treasurer of this Mint, John Bowes, and although in this period Peckham's accounts have ceased to be reliable evidence of seignorage receipts, this adds to the general impression of an insignificant level of output. It is unlikely, in view of the general decline in the minting of gold after 1548, that Durham House coined much if any of that metal, and £9,000 seignorage on

[1] See the *Journal* entry for 30 May 1551, and APC 1550–2, p. 305.

silver at 1549 rates would imply an output of only £18,000. There remains the question of the output of 6 oz. silver at Tower II, and, during the last five months of that issue, at Tower I also. The amounts received by Peckham suggest, for what this evidence is worth, that activity at those Mints was far smaller than the simultaneous activity at Southwark. The view that they produced only small amounts of 6 oz. coin is, however, more powerfully suggested by the evidence of the recoinage, which points to an original production of 6 oz. coins very closely corresponding (with the usual allowances for the counterfeiter and the Irish coinage) to the quantities produced at other Mints and by the 'converting testons' operation.

APPENDIX C

WOOLLEN EXPORTS, 1544/5–1560/1

THE data on the basis of which Tables XV(A) and XV(B) have been constructed were taken chiefly from the surviving Particular Accounts (E. 122) amongst the Exchequer records at the Public Record Office, and are presented in full in the tables in this Appendix. For the first two years most of the figures are reproduced from Carus-Wilson and Coleman's volume (which, however, missed one or two available figures for those years), while for the last two some of the entries are to be found in the Enrolled Accounts which start again in 1559/60. Hanseatic and alien cloth exports from London for the years 1543/4 to 1550/1 are to be found amongst the Cotton MSS. at the British Museum; they were printed by J. M. Lappenberg in *Urkundliche Geschichte des Hansischen Stahlhofes zu London* (Hamburg, 1851), *Urkunden*, pp. 175–6. Detailed references are given in the footnotes to the tables which follow. The cloth total for Exeter in 1553/4, for which no account appears to have survived, is estimated by subtracting the totals for London and all the other outports, which are available, from the national total which is independently known.

In order to facilitate the task of scholars who wish to make comparisons with pre-debasement years, the data relating to cloth exports have been presented in the same format as that adopted by Carus-Wilson and Coleman, save that a column has been added to show the total (of denizen, Hanseatic, and alien exports) for each port for each year and provision has also been made to show the national total which, as it happens, is independently known (from E. 122/175/4) for three years. The national total is also shown for 1545/6, for which, all the accounts being extant, no estimating is involved.

It is from this table that Table XV(A) has been constructed. Years for which the London figures are missing have been omitted; for other years the known London total is given while a total for the outports is estimated by exactly the same procedure as was adopted in aggregating from the Carus-Wilson–Coleman figures for the years before the debasement period. The exceptions are the years 1544/5,

1549/50, and 1553/4, for which the national totals are given independently in E. 122/175/4. For the first of these years the London total (London denizen exports in 1544/5 being unknown) was derived by subtracting the outport estimate (only Chichester, as it happens, was missing here) from the national total, while for the two later years the outport total was similarly derived by subtracting the (known) London total from the national figure as given in the document referred to.

In presenting the estimates of cloth exports in Table XV(A) a notation has been used to alert readers to the approximate degree of reliability (in the sense of conformity to the figures which the Customs Accounts would show, were they all available) which can be attached to the estimate for each year. The notation (1) indicates that accounts are complete for all ports or that the national total is independently available; (2) signifies: accounts extant for London and for outports generally accounting for 50 per cent or more of the outport total (this would justify the expectation of only a very slight margin of error in the national total, considering that the outports generally accounted in this period for barely 10 per cent of cloth exports); (3) signifies: accounts extant for London and for outports generally accounting for less than 50 per cent of the outport total (even here the margin of error in the national estimate is probably only one or two per cent either way at most); (4) applying to 1548/9 only, means that the London account is incomplete, the London (denizens) figure being taken as the average of 1547/8 and 1549/50 (this is much more hazardous, particularly since the outport accounts are by no means all extant).[1] For the other years, for which the

[1] As a partial check on the accuracy of this system of notation, national totals were estimated by the usual procedure for 1549/50 and for 1553/4 and then checked against the actual national total as recorded in E. 122/175/4. Both estimates would have received a (2) notation, and they were in fact respectively only 0·12 per cent and 0·88 per cent below the actual total. An estimate, which would have been graded (4), was also made for 1544/5, for which the national total is again independently known but the London (denizen) figure is not. This would have been far more badly out (over 26 per cent above the actual figure). However, this year was exceptional in that it immediately preceded the end of the experiment of equalizing denizen and alien Customs duties, and following the logic of the analysis of the effects of this experiment offered earlier (Chapter 6, p. 147 and fn. 4), a safer estimating procedure would have been to have assessed denizen +alien exports in 1544/5 as equal to half the sum of denizen+alien exports in 1543/4 and 1544/6. Recalculating in this way, the estimated national total—still, of course, graded (4)—would have been 11·96 per cent above the actual total; a much better result, but still one which underlines the need to view the grade (4) estimate for 1548/9 very cautiously.

London accounts are completely missing (save 1546/7) and the national total is unknown, estimates for the outports only are given. For 1552/3 the extant accounts are so scanty that even this was not attempted. For 1546/7 no estimate has been made, in view of the uncertainty surrounding the year (cf. Appendix D), though in fact just about as much information survives as for 1548/9.

For wool, the breakdown between denizen, Hanseatic, and alien merchants has not been persevered with because of the smaller importance of the trade, the small number of outports involved, and the fact that denizen merchants now accounted for by far the largest part of wool exports. Apart from the small and very occasional shipments from Chichester, only five ports outside London—Boston, Hull, Newcastle, Sandwich, and Southampton—were now active in the wool trade; the only other port recorded as shipping wool at any date since 1523/4 was Ipswich, which last exported the commodity in 1538/9. In constructing Table XV(B) wool exports in the years 1544/5 to 1560/1 have therefore been estimated by interpolating figures, where missing, only for the five ports named, Chichester shipments being added where recorded. The national wool total, like that for cloth, is given for 1544/5, 1549/50, 1553/4 in E. 122/175/4. In the case of wool, it is respectively the London, London and outport totals which have been estimated for those years by a process of subtraction. Otherwise the procedure of estimation has been exactly the same as for cloth. The index of reliability has been omitted, however, since if founded on the same criteria it would have carried a rather different implication from the one for cloth, owing to the fact that the outports' share of the wool market was still rather greater than their share of the cloth market.

CLOTH EXPORTS, 1544/5–1560/1

NOTE. A blank space signifies: no account found
— signifies: nil exports

	1544/5				*1545/6*			
	Denizens	*Hanse*	*Aliens*	*Total*	*Denizens*	*Hanse*	*Aliens*	*Total*
LONDON		33,963	50,359	[1]	45,857	31,550	42,007	119,414[1]
Boston	—	—	4	4	—	—	—	—
Bridgwater	56	—	152	208	76	—	115	191
Bristol	504	—	1,321	1,825	1,558	—	1,006	2,564
Chichester					327	—	—	327
Exeter	1,684	—	2,100	3,784	2,197	—	388	2,585
Hull	186	202	172	560	1,113	—	77	1,190[2]
Ipswich	2,662	18	320	3,000	1,996	—	125	2,121
Lynn	6	—	9	15	6	6	—	12
Newcastle	7	4	6	17	15	—	—	15
Plymouth	18	—	143	161	34	—	26	60
Poole	219	—	5	224	150	—	63	213
Sandwich	—	—	—	—	—	—	—	—
Southampton	1,043	1	104	1,148	769	—	1,499	2,268
Yarmouth	24	—	8	32	53	—	—	53
TOTAL				121,017[2]				131,013

1544/5:
[1] Cotton MSS., Claudius E. VII, fols. 99–100.
[2] E. 122/175/4.
All other entries, Carus-Wilson and Coleman, op. cit.

1545/6:
[1] E. 351/607.
[2] E. 122/164/12.
All other entries, Carus-Wilson and Coleman, op. cit.

CLOTH EXPORTS, 1544/5–1560/1 (*cont.*)

	1546/7				*1547/8*			
	Denizens	*Hanse*	*Aliens*	*Total*	*Denizens*	*Hanse*	*Aliens*	*Total*
LONDON		29,689	14,793	[1]	79,331	38,816	1,063	119,210[1]
Boston	—	—	—	—	—	—	—	— [2]
Bridgwater	222	—	49	271	130	—	21	151[3]
Bristol	2,144	—	128	2,272	1,839	—	166	2,005[4]
Chichester	201	—	11	212[2]	231	—	2	233[5]
Exeter	2,467	—	432	2,899	2,395	—	96	2,491[6]
Hull					474	64	—	538[7]
Ipswich					1,497	—	3	1,500[8]
Lynn								
Newcastle	1	—	—	1	9	—	—	9[9]
Plymouth	66	—	7	73[3]	17	—	4	21[10]
Poole	484	—	95	579	773	—	45	818[11]
Sandwich					11	—	7	18[12]
Southampton					1,859	18	63	1,940[13]
Yarmouth								
TOTAL								

1546/7:
[1] Cotton MSS., Claudius E. VII, fols. 99–100.
[2] E. 122/37/1. [3] E. 122/117/1.
All other entries, Carus-Wilson and Coleman, op. cit.

1547/8:
[1] E. 122/84/4 and 5. [2] E. 122/12/17.
[3] E. 122/28/13 (to 28.8.1/548).
[4] E. 122/22/2. [5] E. 122/37/2.
[6] E. 122/44/2. [7] E. 122/65/1.
[8] E. 122/166/2. [9] E. 122/166/1.
[10] E. 122/117/3. [11] E. 122/122/3.
[12] E. 122/131/1 and 2. [13] E. 122/144/1.

	1548/9				*1549/50*			
	Denizens	*Hanse*	*Aliens*	*Total*	*Denizens*	*Hanse*	*Aliens*	*Total*
LONDON		43,583	1,361	[1]	87,181	44,402	1,183	132,766[1]
Boston					—	—	—	— [1]
Bridgwater	157	—	103	260[2]				
Bristol	2,029	—	173	2,202[3]	3,677	—	594	4,271[1]
Chichester	136	—	—	136[2]	140	—	—	140[2]
Exeter	1,502	31	80	1,613[4]	2,358	—	219	2,577[3]
Hull	828	252	60	1,140[5]	747	107	17	871[1]
Ipswich					2,200	—	4	2,204[1]
Lynn					—	—	—	— [1]
Newcastle	36	—	1	37[6]				
Plymouth	108	—	10	118[2]				
Poole	474	—	24	498[2]				
Sandwich	—	—	—	— [2]	10	—	12	22[1]
Southampton					1,393	4	1,250	2,647[1]
Yarmouth					256	—	—	256[1]
TOTAL								147,161[4]

[1] Cotton MSS., Claudius E. VII, fols. 99–100.
[2] E. 122/166/2. [3] E. 122/212/16.
[4] E. 122/167/4. [5] E. 122/65/4.
[6] E. 122/110/1.

[1] E. 122/167/4. [2] E. 122/37/4.
[3] E. 122/44/5. [4] E. 122/175/4.

CLOTH EXPORTS, 1544/5–1560/1 (*cont.*)

	1550/1				*1551/2*			
	Denizens	*Hanse*	*Aliens*	*Total*	*Denizens*	*Hanse*	*Aliens*	*Total*
LONDON	69,859	39,854	2,997	112,710[1]	65,690	13,824	5,454	84,968[1]
Boston	23	—	—	23[1]	—	—	—	—[1]
Bridgwater	374	—	30	404[1]	209	—	10	219[1]
Bristol	3,920	—	333	4,253[1]				
Chichester								
Exeter	2,781	—	333	3,114[2]				
Hull	1,460	48	109	1,617[1]				
Ipswich	1,837	—	3	1,840[1]	1,717	—	—	1,717[1]
Lynn	147	—	—	147[1]				
Newcastle								
Plymouth	145	—	1	146[1]	196	—	16	212[1]
Poole	901	—	72	973[1]	1,031	—	14	1,045[1]
Sandwich	62	—	10	72[1]				
Southampton	2,366	—	283	2,649[1]	2,410	—	48	2,458[1]
Yarmouth	23	—	—	23[1]	109	—	—	109[2]
TOTAL								

1550/1: [1] E. 122/166/8. [2] E. 122/44/7.

1551/2: [1] E. 122/166/1. [2] E. 122/154/4.

	1552/3				1553/4			
	Denizens	Hanse	Aliens	Total	Denizens	Hanse	Aliens	Total
LONDON					96,988	27,903	10,703	135,594[1]
Boston					60	—	—	60[2]
Bridgwater					59	—	84	143[3]
Bristol					3,335	—	155	3,490[4]
Chichester	1,291	—	57	1,348[1]	1,611	—	77	1,688[5]
Exeter								3,915[6]
Hull					2,066	—	—	2,066[7]
Ipswich	2,514	—	—	2,514[2]	1,572	—	—	1,572[8]
Lynn	601	—	10	611[3]	405	—	2	407[9]
Newcastle					80	—	—	80[10]
Plymouth					72	—	—	72[11]
Poole	1,051	—	2	1,053[4]	1,390	—	2	1,392[12]
Sandwich					40	—	—	40[13]
Southampton					—	—	—	—[14]
Yarmouth	—	—	—	—[5]	44	—	—	44[15]
TOTAL								150,563[16]

1552/3: [1] E. 122/37/8. [2] E. 122/53/37. [3] E. 122/100/10. [4] E. 122/122/8. [5] E. 122/166/15.

1553/4: [1] E. 122/87/4. [2] E. 122/13/4. [3] E. 122/28/14. [4] E. 122/23/2. [5] E. 122/38/3. [6] Deduced by subtraction. [7] E. 122/66/4. [8] E. 122/166/15. [9] E. 122/100/12 and 122/101/4. [10] E. 122/110/12. [11] E. 122/117/14. [12] E. 122/122/9. [13] E. 122/131/7. [14] E. 122/145/6. [15] E. 122/154/8. [16] E. 122/175/4.

CLOTH EXPORTS, 1544/5–1560/1 (*cont.*)

	1554/5				*1555/6*			
	Denizens	*Hanse*	*Aliens*	*Total*	*Denizens*	*Hanse*	*Aliens*	*Total*
LONDON								
Boston	32	—	8	40[1]	52	—	—	52[1]
Bridgwater	198	—	65	263[2]	104	—	8	112[2]
Bristol	2,314	—	28	2,342[3]	141	—	1,433	1,574[3]
Chichester	1,030	—	15	1,045[1]	827	—	30	857[4]
Exeter	2,580	—	5	2,585[1]	3,123	—	156	3,279[5]
Hull	3,316	60	11	3,387[1]	2,924	—	—	2,924[6]
Ipswich								
Lynn	640	—	—	640[1]	596	10	9	615[7]
Newcastle					143	—	—	143[8]
Plymouth	223	—	—	223[1]	109	—	2	111[9]
Poole								
Sandwich	106	—	—	106[1]	47	—	6	53[10]
Southampton	637	—	226	863[4]	1,222	—	111	1,333[11]
Yarmouth	363	—	—	363[1]	428	—	—	428[12]
TOTAL								

1554/5:
[1] E. 122/168/3. [2] E. 122/200/3.
[3] E. 122/23/5. [4] E. 122/209/7.

1555/6:
[1] E. 122/13/11. [2] E. 122/28/18.
[3] E. 122/199/5. [4] E. 122/38/8.
[5] E. 122/45/4. [6] E. 122/66/9.
[7] E. 122/100/16. [8] E. 122/110/14.
[9] E. 122/117/19. [10] E. 122/131/12.
[11] E. 122/145/12. [12] E. 122/154/11.

	1556/7				1557/8			
	Denizens	*Hanse*	*Aliens*	*Total*	*Denizens*	*Hanse*	*Aliens*	*Total*
London	88,489	11,157	14,050	113,696[1]				
Boston	147	—	—	147[2]	—	—	18	18[1]
Bridgwater								
Bristol					973	—	58	1,031[2]
Chichester	425	—	7	432[3]	236	—	—	236[3]
Exeter					1,881	—	8	1,889[3]
Hull					404	—	12	416[3]
Ipswich	1,636	—	22	1,658[4]	1,726	—	180	1,906[3]
Lynn	352	—	—	352[5]	54	—	—	54[3]
Newcastle	225	—	—	225[6]	37	—	2	39[3]
Plymouth					176	—	—	176[4]
Poole	1,250	—	28	1,278[7]	798	—	—	798[3]
Sandwich					—	—	—	—[3]
Southampton	1,244	—	315	1,559[8]	1,178	—	379	1,557[3]
Yarmouth	247	—	—	247[9]	60	—	—	60[3]
Total								

1556/7:
[1] E. 122/86/5. [2] E. 122/13/13.
[3] E. 122/38/9. [4] E. 122/54/3.
[5] E. 122/100/17. [6] E. 122/110/15.
[7] E. 122/207/9. [8] E. 122/145/14.
[9] E. 122/154/12.

1557/8:
[1] E. 122/13/14. [2] E. 122/199/6.
[3] E. 122/168/7. [4] E. 122/117/22.

CLOTH EXPORTS, 1544/5–1560/1 (*cont.*)

	1558/9				*1559/60*			
	Denizens	*Hanse*	*Aliens*	*Total*	*Denizens*	*Hanse*	*Aliens*	*Total*
London					89,863	8,380	11,444	109,687[1]
Boston	6	—	1	7[1]	6	—	2	8[2]
Bridgwater					132	—	3	135[3]
Bristol	491	—	38	529[2]	1,413	—	11	1,424[1]
Chichester					646	—	9	655[4]
Exeter	2,527	—	33	2,560[3]	2,889	—	19	2,908[1]
Hull	1,086	—	39	1,125[4]	1,434	94	6	1,534[5]
Ipswich	2,449	—	149	2,598[5]				
Lynn	28	—	—	28[6]	53	—	—	53[6]
Newcastle	33	—	—	33[7]	42	—	—	42[7]
Plymouth					12	—	—	12[9]
Poole	987	—	8	995[8]	1,109	—	11	1,030[8]
Sandwich					44	—	—	44[10]
Southampton	306	—	153	459[9]				
Yarmouth	33	—	—	33[10]				
Total								

1558/9:
[1] E. 122/13/15. [2] E. 356/28.
[3] E. 122/45/12. [4] E. 122/66/14.
[5] E. 122/54/4. [6] E. 122/101/1 (to 29.5.1559).
[7] E. 122/111/1. [8] E. 122/123/1.
[9] E. 122/146/1. [10] E. 122/155/1.

1559/60:
[1] E. 356/28. [2] E. 122/14/1.
[3] E. 122/29/1. [4] E. 122/38/14.
[5] E. 122/67/1. [6] E. 122/101/5.
[7] E. 122/111/2. [8] E. 122/123/3.
[9] E. 122/118/1 (to 23.9.1560).
[10] E. 122/132/2.

	1560/1			
	Denizens	*Hanse*	*Aliens*	*Total*
LONDON	59,556	16,425	5,866	81,847[1]
Boston	33	—	2	35[2]
Bridgwater	88	—	4	92[3]
Bristol	1,168	—	155	1,323[1]
Chichester	647	—	16	663[1]
Exeter	4,282	26	83	4,391[1]
Hull				
Ipswich	2,997	155	55	3,207[4]
Lynn	164	—	—	164[1]
Newcastle				
Plymouth	168	—	8	176[5]
Poole	1,065	—	34	1,099[6]
Sandwich	36	—	—	36[7]
Southampton	582	—	207	789[1]
Yarmouth	29	—	6	35[8]
TOTAL				

[1] E. 356/28. [2] E. 122/14/3.
[3] E. 122/29/3. [4] E. 122/54/5.
[5] E. 122/118/2. [6] E. 122/123/4.
[7] E. 122/132/4. [8] E. 122/155/8.

WOOL EXPORTS (SACKS), 1544/5–1560/1

	London	*Boston*	*Hull*	*Newcastle*	*Sandwich*	*Southampton*	*Chichester*
1544/5*		—[1]	20[1]	142[1]	8[1]	31[1]	
1545/6		237[1]	6[2]	54[1]	10[1]	208[1]	
1546/7		70[1]		30[1]			4[3]
1547/8			35[4]	59[5]			8[6]
1548/9			19[7]	49[8]			4[9]
1549/50*		305[10]	73[10]		5[10]	—[10]	
1550/1		175[11]	28[11]		6[11]	—[11]	
1551/2	2,981[5]	176[5]					
1552/3	4,830[12]						129[13]
1553/4*	4,547[14]	754[15]	361[16]				
1554/5	2,324[17]	375[18]	344[18]		19[18]		
1555/6		245[19]	348[20]				
1556/7	911[21]	75[22]					
1557/8		162[23]	197[24]	47[24]	—[24]	82[24]	
1558/9	3,518[25]	203[26]	235[27]			254[28]	
1559/60	2,755[29]						
1560/1	2,970[30]	569[31]					

SOURCES:

[1] Carus-Wilson and Coleman, op. cit.
[2] E. 122/164/12.
[3] E. 122/37/1.
[4] E. 122/65/1.
[5] E. 122/166/1.
[6] E. 122/37/2.
[7] E. 122/65/4.
[8] E. 122/110/1.
[9] E. 122/166/2.
[10] E. 122/167/4.
[11] E. 122/166/8.
[12] E. 122/86/1.
[13] E. 122/37/8.
[14] E. 122/87/3.
[15] E. 122/13/4.
[16] E. 122/66/4.
[17] E. 122/87/8.
[18] E. 122/168/3.
[19] E. 122/13/11.
[20] E. 122/66/9.
[21] E. 122/86/11.
[22] E. 122/13/13.
[23] E. 122/13/14.
[24] E. 122/168/7.
[25] E. 122/86/13.
[26] E. 122/13/15.
[27] E. 122/66/14.
[28] E. 122/146/1.
[29] E. 122/88/5.
[30] E. 122/88/10.
[31] E. 122/14/3.

* Signifies national total available in E. 122/175/4.

APPENDIX D

WOOLLEN EXPORTS, 1546/7

FEW Particular Accounts survive to give us details of cloth and wool exports for 1546/7, though the most important gap, that for London, is partially filled by the figures for Hanseatic and alien cloth exports given in the Cotton Manuscripts at the British Museum.[1] A document exists, however, amongst the State Papers Domestic at the Public Record Office which purports to offer a comparison of Customs duties on wools, wool fells, and cloths collected in the 28th year of King Edward the Third and in the 38th year of Henry the Eighth.[2] The object of the paper is to demonstrate that given the heavier incidence of Customs duty on wool, the King had lost revenue by the growth of cloth exports at the expense of those of wool. This paper was reprinted by Tawney and Power in their well-known volumes.[3]

If the data contained in this paper could be regarded as authentic, they would fill an awkward gap in our knowledge of trade during the debasement period. But can they? The provenance of the document is unknown; it carries a simple endorsement 'customs for Wolles'. We know, of course, that its theme—the loss of revenue arising from differential taxation and the change in the composition of exports—was one which caused increasing concern amongst the Government's advisers in the middle years of the sixteenth century, and that the Book of Rates of 1558, which provided for a sharp increase in the rate of duty on cloth, sought to remedy the defect of which it complained. The document in question might, then, at first sight be some official memorandum prepared in connection with the consideration of this problem, or it might equally well be a submission, by some more or less interested busybody, of the sort which such political and economic issues often evoked—a 'project', in short, similar to many others to be found amongst the State Papers of the sixteenth and early seventeenth centuries.

Whatever the origins of the paper, there are a number of pieces both of external and of internal evidence which lead one to doubt

[1] Cotton MSS., Claudius E. VII, fols. 99–100.
[2] SP 10/2, no. 13.
[3] Tawney and Power, op. cit. i. 178–84.

the authenticity of its data for 'the xxxviiith yere of the Raigne of Kinge Henry theight'. First, what year—that is, what period of twelve months—is in fact referred to? There was of course no such complete year as 38° H. VIII, Henry dying before the end of his thirty-eighth regnal year (which began on 22 April 1546). Apart from the twelve months 22 April 1546–21 April 1547, '38° H.VIII' could conceivably refer to calendar 1546, or (remembering that the Exchequer still used the Michaelmas year) to Michaelmas 1545/6 or Michaelmas 1546/7. (Calendar 1547 is impossible if only because the document is dated 6 October 1547.) Of these four possibilities, the first two are both highly unlikely, since they would have involved a great deal of arithmetical labour in extracting and adding up from the Particular Accounts exports and imports over a period different from that (i.e. the Michaelmas year) conventionally used for accounting by the Exchequer of the day and in respect of which annual totals were therefore compiled by the Exchequer officials themselves. (Only such officials, one would think, would have had access to these Accounts anyway.) Beyond this general consideration, the first possibility (regnal 38°) seems unlikely because it never in fact existed, and the second (calendar 1546) unlikely because the known total of cloth exports for Michaelmas 1545/6 is so far below the total suggested by the document that exports in the missing three months (29 September to 31 December 1546) would have needed to be quite impossibly high to account for the discrepancy between the two. The third possibility, Michaelmas 1545/6, turns out to be no possibility at all, since complete accounts have been discovered for cloth exports in that year and the national total is far below that suggested by the document.

We are compelled to believe that the document refers to the Michaelmas year 1546/7. But at once the authenticity of its figures seems suspect because it is dated 6 October 1547. It seems quite incredible that the often-dilatory port officials should have completed their books for 1546/7 and have sent them up to London, and that someone should there have extracted and totalled them in this memorandum, all in the space of one week. We are driven to the conclusion that the figures for '38° H. VIII' were not taken from the official returns but were estimated, from some source or sources unknown, sometime before the year to which the figures purport to relate had ended.

This conclusion is buttressed by a number of other obstacles to believing the document to have been a transcript of, or based upon, the customs records. First, neither the partial figures which *do* survive (for some of the outports and for Hanseatic and alien exports from London) nor contemporary comment suggest that 1546/7 was anything like the boom year which cloth exports of 172,017 would have made it. Secondly, there are at least two pieces of internal evidence which tell against such a belief: (*a*) three of the four separate amounts of Customs duty shown for 38° Henry VIII are not correctly calculated, that is, the sum shown does *not* in fact quite equal the number of sacks, fells, or cloths shown multiplied by the rate of duty given (the Customs Accounts themselves, however, were generally quite accurate in this respect); and (*b*) no distinction is made between denizen, Hanseatic, and alien merchants in the rate of duty on cloth paid, shown as 1*s*. 2*d*. for the whole 172,017 cloths (in fact, of course, only denizens paid 1*s*. 2*d*., the Hanseatic merchants paying 1*s*. 0*d*. and alien merchants 2*s*. 9*d*. at this time). A direct transcript from Exchequer records would inevitably have incorporated such a distinction.

The data for 28° Edward III, with which the figures referred to above are compared, show cloth and wool exports which are of the right order of magnitude, but which do not agree precisely, when compared with the figures for 28°/29° Edward III (i.e. Michaelmas 1354/5) in Carus-Wilson and Coleman's book. It is clear that the figures for 28° Edward III were taken from one or other of the three abstracts of Customs for that year known to have existed in the Exchequer records in the sixteenth century.[1] These abstracts were used by Tudor and Stuart writers on several occasions for purposes of comparison, for example by John Hales in his 1548 report on *Causes of Dearth*[2] and by Edward Misselden in *The Circle of Commerce*.[3] There is thus no proof here that the writer of the document under discussion had access to the Exchequer records, but it may be legitimate to claim that he was at least close to official circles. There is some support, too, for the view that the paper was of the nature of a 'project' rather than an official memorandum in the sentence: 'Remembrancces to my lorde protectours grace for the profe of this boke . . .' Historians acquainted with the ways of project-mongers will have

[1] Cf. A. Beardwood, 'Alien Merchants and the English Crown in the later Fourteenth Century', *Economic History Review* ii (1930), 235–7.

[2] E. Lamond (ed.), *A Discourse of the Common Weal of this Realm of England* (Cambridge U.P., 1954), p. xliii.

[3] E. Misselden, *The Circle of Commerce* (London, 1623), pp. 119–20.

no difficulty in recognizing the marks of the beast in the choice of the word 'boke' (frequently used to refer to 'projects' but rarely, if ever, to official papers), the desire to offer 'profe' of its argument, and the eminence of the person (evidently Somerset) for whom it was intended.

Our conclusions must therefore be that the document is of unknown provenance and of uncertain chronological reference, and that the cloth and wool figures for 38° Henry VIII which it contains cannot be accepted as authentic.

APPENDIX E

THE CONVERSION OF TESTONS, 1548/9

THIS book has eschewed comment on the fiscal aspect of the debasement of the coinage, since the interested reader will find admirable guidance on this subject in an article in the *Economic History Review* by Dr. C. E. Challis.[1] Only in one respect do Dr. Challis's conclusions seem to call for revision, and that is in his handling of what one might call the 'converting testons' operation. Though this topic is of relatively small significance from the fiscal point of view, a somewhat detailed critique of Dr. Challis's treatment of it may be worth while for the incidental light it throws on the problems of interpreting the mint accounts, on the motives of the Government, and on several other matters connected with the coinage.

A proclamation was issued on 10 April 1548 declaring that testons would no longer be current after the end of the year.[2] Though this deadline was subsequently postponed, and though a considerable number of testons probably survived until Elizabeth's reign, a large proportion of these debased testons were in fact brought to the Mints and there converted into groats and smaller coins. Dr. Challis is reluctant to accept the Government's own account of the motives which it claimed had led it to the decision to demonetize the testons, and interprets the move instead as a 'fiscal device': 'The old testons [he writes], ranging in fineness from 9 oz. to 4 oz., were to be converted into groats and small moneys 4 oz. fine, and in the process the king was to take his inevitable cut.'

Dr. Challis further suggests that this 'device' suggested itself to the Government because the supply of bullion to the Mints was declining as 'the inducement of higher mint prices' became less effective. The Tables which conclude the article appear to show that the 'converting testons' operation yielded at those Mints for which the relevant accounts are extant a profit of some £92,000—a figure sufficiently impressive (bearing in mind that some relevant accounts

[1] C. E. Challis, 'The Debasement of the Coinage, 1542–1551', *Economic History Review*, 2nd Series xx, no. 3 (1967), 441–66.

[2] Hughes and Larkin, op. cit., no. 302.

are missing) to lend support to his interpretation of the Government's motives.

Dr. Challis does not make clear just how, in the case of the recoined testons, the Crown took its 'inevitable cut'. Both the sections of the accounts relating to the recoining of testons and the proclamation announcing their coming demonetization make clear that seignorage was not claimed in this operation; and indeed Dr. Challis does not suggest that it was. How then could any profit arise? While Dr. Challis is not explicit on this point, I think it is fair to claim that he leads the reader to infer that the King gained because the *average* intrinsic value (that is, fine-silver content) of the testons brought in was higher than that of the groats and smaller coins which the subject got in exchange. Both the sentence from the text of his article already quoted and the relevant sentence in his *Appendix*[1] lead one to believe that this is Dr. Challis's explanation of the puzzle.

But this explanation is surely inadequate. It is highly unlikely on *a priori* grounds that the proportion of testons other than those of the then lowest standard (4 oz.) could have been sufficiently high to provide the margin of additional silver which Dr. Challis's figures would call for. It is unlikely, in the first place, that the testons surrendered at the Mints included an appreciable number of coins of any issue richer than the 6 oz. coins of 1545/6. This is partly because by 1549 very few such coins survived, as can be seen from Diagrams I and II on page 73, but also because by 1549 earlier silver issues were more valuable, given the current mint price for silver, as bullion than in coined form. For example, 64 testons of the 9 oz. issue of 1544–5 would have been repaid, if surrendered as required by the proclamation announcing the demonetization of testons, by but £3. 4*s*. 0*d*. in smaller coins. But melted down these 64 testons contained one pound of fine silver, which in early 1549 fetched £3. 8*s*. 0*d*. at the Mints. Only the 6 oz. and 4 oz. coins minted from April 1545 onwards would have been worth surrendering as coins rather than as bullion.

Now at the Tower Mint Dr. Challis's method of calculating net profit puts the profit of reworking the testons at some 32 per cent over and above the cost of purchasing and reminting them. The intrinsic value of the small coin produced from the melted down

[1] This sentence, to be found on pp. 455–6, reads in part '. . . such profit as the King made depended on the amount of fine silver contained in the money brought to the mint . . .'

testons, whether made to the 4 oz., 6 oz., or 8 oz. standard, was the same in all cases—differences in fineness being precisely cancelled out by offsetting differences in weight—and was the same as that of the 4 oz. testons which formed the bulk of the base silver in circulation on the eve of the 'converting testons' operation. The intrinsic value of the 6 oz. coins of 1545/6 had been just half as great again as that of the later 4 oz. issues. So to achieve the average margin of 32 per cent silver content above that of the 4 oz. coins, the incoming testons would have had to be mixed in the proportion of nearly two 6 oz. coins to one 4 oz. (Allowing for the surrendered testons being rather underweight and for losses in manufacture, the ratio would in fact have had to be rather *more* than two to one.) But in early 1549 the 4 oz. testons far outnumbered the 6 oz. in the circulation. If *all* testons had been surrendered, 4 oz. coins would therefore necessarily have predominated; whereas, if only a proportion of the total number of testons in circulation were delivered, the King's loyal subjects would scarcely have tendered their best testons to be recoined while retaining the worst for their own use. The 2:1 ratio indicated seems therefore inconceivable.

But to call Dr. Challis's explanation in question it is not necessary to resort to such *a priori* arguments; careful consideration of the mint accounts themselves shows it to be inadequate. Take the Tower account again.[1] Some 22,018 lb. of 6 oz. small coins were produced which, if faithfully made, must have contained 11,009 lb. each of alloy and of silver. The account shows that in their manufacture, 4,058 lb. of fine silver had been added to the mixture resulting from the melting-down of the 18,004 lb. weight of testons from which the 6 oz. small coins were to be made. Hence the original silver contained in those testons must have weighed 6,951 (= 11,009−4,058) lb. They must therefore have been $\frac{6{,}951}{18{,}004}\times 12$ or 4·63 oz. fine. This implies that the testons surrendered would have comprised 6 oz. and 4 oz. coins in a proportion of slightly less than 1 to 2—a far more likely ratio than that called for by Dr. Challis's explanation. But had such a proportion held over the whole Tower intake, it would have made possible a 'profit', in Dr. Challis's sense, of only about £12,000, which is less than half the sum his Tables suggest. (Again losses and the matter of the weight of the testons are ignored.)

Clearly Dr. Challis's explanation is at best inadequate. Can another

[1] E. 101/303/5.

be provided? As soon as one re-examines the problem with fresh eyes, it is seen to be strikingly simple. In the course of transforming the surrendered testons into small coins at the Tower quantities of alloy and fine silver were added at various times. The former was necessary to bring the silver/alloy mix resulting from the melting-down of the surrendered testons *down* to the 4 oz. standard, when 4 oz. coins were being produced; the latter to bring it *up* when 6 oz. and 8 oz. coins were being fabricated. Let us forget the alloy, whose value was trifling. The 4,970 lb. of fine silver added in making 6 oz. and 8 oz. coins at the Tower was valued at 68 shillings a pound weight, and the Under-Treasurer was accordingly 'allowed' some £16,900 as the cost of purchasing it. This sum is of course rightly included by Dr. Challis under the heading 'coinage charges' in respect of the 'converting testons' operation. The figure of 68/- a pound weight was chosen because this was the current price which the Mints paid for bullion in the open market in early 1549. But at that time the pound of fine silver, with added alloy, was coined in the course of 'normal' production into silver coins with a face value of £7. 4*s*. 0*d*. (see Table I). Of this, £3. 16*s*. 0*d*. was deducted as seignorage, leaving the balance of £3. 8*s*. 0*d*. to pay to the person bringing the silver to the Mint. Now the small coins of 4, 6, and 8 oz. struck from the melted-down testons were made to this standard, £7. 4*s*. 0*d*. to the pound of fine silver, and it is at *this* value that our 4,970 lb. reappears —or rather does *not* appear, for it is effectively concealed—in the recorded output of small coins. In other words, the silver added during conversion was valued at one price on the expenditure side, and implicitly valued (though not itemized) at more than twice the price on the income side. The larger part of Dr. Challis's 'profit' was, in effect, seignorage at the usual rate on this silver. Now, it would surely be misleading to credit this profit to the demonetization of testons; for once this silver had been purchased, it could perfectly well have been made into the coin of current production, and yielded the same profit, had the 'converting testons' operation never been embarked upon.

How important was this source of profit at the other Mints for which we have the relevant accounts? At York it did not operate at all, for here only 4 oz. small coins were made and there was no need to add any silver. But at all other Mints silver 'commyxed', as the accounts put it, with the molten testons to make 6 oz. or 8 oz. small coins was the *major* source of profit, accounting for over three-quarters of the 'profit' at Southwark and at Bristol, well over half at the Tower, and four-fifths at Canterbury. Altogether, at the five Mints for which we have records, some 63·5 per cent of Dr. Challis's total 'profit' of about £92,000 came from this source.

This may be the appropriate point at which to remark that in referring hitherto to 'profit' I have had in mind the remainder left by subtracting in respect of each Mint Dr. Challis's item (10), 'Coining charges: Testons' from item (8), 'Gross Profit'. This is in fact an over-generous definition of net profit, for it fails to attribute to the 'converting testons' operation any part of item (12), 'General Mint Expenses' (chiefly salaries and wages). This would surely be appropriate, for at most Mints recoining testons was the major, or even the only, activity for a good part of 1549. Were the 'gross profit' reduced to allow for these overheads, the gain arising from the addition of silver would of course be seen to be an even larger percentage of the total, and the net profit truly attributable to the 'converting testons' operation correspondingly reduced.

Before going on to comment on the implications of this, however, a few more words about the source of the 'profit' are in order. Can we say that all that part of the gain which did not come from the addition of silver arose in the way which what we may call the 'Challis mechanism' describes? This is probably largely true, but not wholly true. Were the accounts complete, it would be possible in each case to calculate the average fineness of the surrendered testons, as was done in respect of the 6 oz. production at the Tower, and thus to know for certain where the 'profit' came from. But in some instances, some of the relevant figures are missing, notably the *weight* of the surrendered testons or of alloy added. Such gaps frustrate the calculation referred to save in the case of 6 oz. production at the Tower, where the surrendered testons averaged, as we have seen, some 4·63 oz. fine, and in that of 8 oz. production at the same Mint, where the fineness works out at 4·52 oz. In the case of the 4 oz. production at the same Mint, the weight of *alloy* added to bring the mixture down to the 4 oz. standard is omitted, doubtless because its cost was so small, and a similar omission mars the Canterbury account.

We could, however, *estimate* the amount of alloy added in these two cases by assuming that the same weight of metal should appear on both the 'input' and 'output' sides of the accounts. That is to say, the *weight* of testons received, *plus* that of any silver and/or alloy added and *minus* that of material lost in the melting house should equal the weight of small coins issued *plus* that of material lost in the process of striking the new coin. Both sides of this equation would show the quantity of raw material, in other words, at the point where it was ready to undergo the final phase of transformation into new coins. At the Tower Mint and in respect of 6 oz. and of 8 oz. production the two sides do in fact agree in this way. If we could assume that the unspecified addition of alloy was the only missing item, a value for it could of course readily be deduced and a similar calculation of the fineness of the original testons could then be performed. Treated in this way the Tower (4 oz.) and Canterbury records suggest finenesses, respectively, of 5·12 oz. and of 4·43 oz. Unfortunately, we cannot be sure that the alloy 'commyxed' *is* the only item missing. That this is so is proven by the Southwark account, on which *all* the items mentioned, including alloy added, are to be found, and which yet does not 'add up'. The 'output' side shows a total production (including 'wastes' and 'remains') of 46,670 lb., whereas on the 'input' side we can account for but 44,108 lb. Clearly something is missing from the latter. But what?

While the work of the Mint chiefly consisted of working into coin bullion sold to it by private subjects, there was always, as has been discussed in the text, some minting 'on government account'. A government office might cause to be reminted coin which came into its hands in the normal course of fiscal activity. The King's debtors might be persuaded or required to satisfy him by delivering coin or plate to the Mint. Queen Mary's dower consisted in part of 97 chests of Spanish treasure which were taken to the Mint to be coined into Sterling money. There is no reason to suppose that such deliveries played no part in furnishing the raw material for the 'converting testons' operation; on the contrary, the proclamation of 22 May 1549[1] specifically provided that the King's debtors might satisfy their obligations by proffering testons to the Mints. How would such transactions be recorded in the accounts recording the 'converting testons' operation?

The answer is that they would not. These accounts were far from giving a full financial description of mint activity; their purpose was solely to establish the residual indebtedness of the Under-Treasurer to the King. Accordingly, they itemized on one side sums with which the Under-Treasurer was 'charged', i.e. his income, which in this case chiefly consisted of the face value of the small coins produced, and

[1] Hughes and Larkin, op. cit., no. 332.

on the other side sums 'allowed', i.e. authorized offsetting expenditure, which included the payment of salaries and wages, working expenses including the purchase of silver and alloy, sums paid to the public in return for surrendered testons, together of course with any profits already impressed to the High Treasurer. The residual indebtedness of the Under-Treasurer was then taken to be the difference between the totals of 'charges' and 'allowances'.

It can be seen that there is no place in this scheme of accounting for transactions of the type discussed. If a subject owing money to the King discharged his debt by delivering testons to the Mints, this transaction (though doubtless itemized elsewhere in the Mint's working records) was not, and could not be, included on the 'input' or 'allowances' side of these summary accounts, since the purpose of this side was to list out-payments by the Under-Treasurer, and no such payment was here involved. A subject came into the Mint, settled his debt to the King by surrendering testons to the receiving officer, and got nothing back. There was thus no 'allowance' to be recorded. But the testons in question *did* figure, though covertly, on the 'output' or 'charges' side, for they were simply thrown into the melting-pot with the rest and ultimately emerged as an (unitemized) part of the production of small coins. Swelling, therefore, the 'charges' without any corresponding inflation of the 'allowances', the debt thus honoured simply formed part of what the Under-Treasurer owed the King. The system of financial reporting might not commend itself to a modern accountant, but it achieved the right result in the end. To the historian reconstructing this mint activity, however, the only clue that such transactions had occurred might be a tell-tale discrepancy between the *weight* of output recorded on one side and the *weight* of input recorded on the other. Where such a discrepancy is clear, as at Southwark, we cannot tell how much of the profit beyond that earned by the addition of silver came from the excess silver content of the recorded input of testons, and how much from this 'hidden' input on government account, for of course we do not know what it was an input of—of testons (and if so of what fineness?), of sterling coins, even of plate? And where the figure of alloy 'commyxed' is missing, as at the Tower Mint in respect of the 4 oz. coins and at Canterbury, we cannot be sure whether it is in fact the *only* missing figure, or whether there had also been some unitemized transaction on government account to account for part of the missing weight.

We cannot therefore be sure that the estimated average finenesses of 5·12 oz. and 4·43 oz. for testons surrendered at the Tower (4 oz.) and at Canterbury are correct. But there is reason to place more reliance on the latter figure than on the former. One minor pointer to this is that there is no obvious reason why testons surrendered at the Tower and made into 4 oz. coins should have been so markedly richer than those made into 6 oz. or 8 oz. coins. It may also seem plausible *a priori* that transactions on government account would have been more frequent at the Tower than at a provincial Mint. But there is stronger positive evidence for preferring the somewhat lower figure for Canterbury. For a fineness comparable to the 4·6 oz. which seems to have prevailed at the Tower, combined with the gain arising from the known quantity of silver 'commyxed' with the molten testons, would *more* than explain the 'profit' of the Canterbury Mint. Since the second item—the 'gain' from the silver—is known with certainty from the account, it must be that the first source of profit was not as large as a 4·6 oz. richness in the surrendered testons would have made possible—that their fineness, in other words, was in fact *below* this figure. Nor is an explanation of such a difference far to seek. For the Canterbury Mint had only begun work in June 1545, and the ratio of 6 oz. coins of the 1545–6 issue to 4 oz. coins of later issues struck at Canterbury was substantially lower than the London ratio. If then we suppose, as is entirely congenial, a degree of geographical inertia in the circulation of coins, the circulating medium in the neighbourhood of Canterbury would have been expected to contain a lower proportion of 6 oz. and a higher proportion of 4 oz. testons than in the London area.

Such an explanation fits the Bristol case even more clearly. The Bristol account lacks both the weight of testons received and any reference to alloy added. But if we assume that at Bristol the testons surrendered weighed about the same as, on average, they did at the three Mints for which their weight can be calculated,[1] a little arithmetic shows that the two sides of the 'weight' equation approximately balance, and thus suggests that little alloy *was* added. Performing

[1] At three Mints—the Tower, Southwark, and Canterbury—the weight as well as the face value of surrendered testons is recorded on the account. From this it is easy to calculate how far the actual (average) weight of these testons fell short of their authorized weight. At the Tower the first was found to be 98·3 per cent of the second, at Southwark 98·6 per cent, and at Canterbury 98·4 per cent. In my calculations for Bristol and York I have assumed that their testons averaged 98·5 per cent of the authorized weight.

the usual calculation we then arrive at a value of little more than 4·05 oz. for the Bristol intake of testons. This value is seen on reflection to be highly plausible. For the 'profit' at Bristol was almost negligible, and more than 80 per cent of it can be accounted for anyway by the addition of silver. There is therefore virtually nothing left for the 'Challis mechanism' to explain beyond counteracting the tendency for the surrendered testons to be slightly below their authorized weight. Moreover, the Bristol Mint did not start work until after the 6 oz. issue of 1545–6 had been discontinued and superseded by the 4 oz. coins, and the Bristol Mint had never produced any base testons but those of the latter fineness. Given the same assumption of a degree of geographical inertia in the circulation—an even easier assumption here because of the greater distance from any other Mint—there is no reason to have expected anything other than a very small admixture of better coins which may have found their way to the West Country in the normal course of trade and travel.

The case of York is different again. Here the rate of 'profit', though lower than at the London Mints, was still appreciable. Yet only 4 oz. small coins were produced, so that only alloy, and no silver, had been added. The whole burden of accounting for the profit is therefore thrown on the other two sources discussed. The *weight* of testons surrendered is not given, but applying the same multiplier a value of 32,647 lb. is suggested. Since the weight of alloy added *is* given in the account, the usual calculation can then be performed and it points to an average richness of some 4·7 oz. However, this is not the sole source of profit here since the estimated weight of testons surrendered would leave the 'input' side some 525 lb. lighter than the 'output' side, suggesting a little activity on government account and some probably minor contribution to the profit from that source. (Some such activity would not be surprising given York's political and administrative importance.) Still, at York, alone amongst the five Mints, the 'Challis mechanism' does seem to explain the larger part of the observed profit. Why should the testons surrendered here have been relatively so rich?

In the first place the ratio of 6 oz. testons to 4 oz. testons struck at York, though lower than in the London area, was higher than at Canterbury (and of course than at Bristol where none of the former were minted). Then again, it is quite plausible that the 6 oz. testons should have survived somewhat better in the northern city than in London, for the speed with which bad money drives out good is a function of the financial sophistication of the community in which it circulates.[1] From this point of view we can readily believe that in the London area a higher proportion of the 6 oz. coins had been reminted or otherwise withdrawn from circulation before the 'converting testons' exercise started. Thus if the ratio of 6 oz. to 4 oz. testons had originally been somewhat higher in London than in York, this disparity may have been reversed by 1549.

It can be seen, then, that not only did the rate of 'profit' from converting testons vary from one Mint to another, but so did its source. Regrettably, the omissions from the accounts which have been explained make it impossible to provide a complete breakdown of the relative contributions of the three sources we have identified: the 'Challis mechanism', the addition of silver, and unrecorded 'inputs' on government account. The following points can, however, be made. First, the second of these sources of profit, the addition of silver, was undoubtedly the chief one, accounting for some 63·5 per cent of the total; the third accounted for the smaller, but not a negligible, part of the remainder, and the 'Challis mechanism' for an intermediate amount (which I should very tentatively assess at rather less than a third of the total).[2] Only this intermediate source of profit could truly be said to be dependent on the decision to demonetize the testons, since the other two could equally well have operated had that decision never been taken. When we remember, moreover, that the word 'profit' is being used in a sense which does not allow for the allocation of a share of mint overheads to the recoining testons operation, as would be proper, it can be seen that the fiscal contribution of the decision to demonetize the testons was much smaller than Dr. Challis leads his readers to suppose.

This conclusion has a bearing upon the Government's motives in deciding to demonetize the testons. Dr. Challis, as we have seen, takes a cynical view of these. But it has been argued that the operation was much less significant fiscally than he supposed; and it might

[1] If Canterbury's 6 oz. testons did not survive in their 'home' area quite as well as those of York, this is perhaps because the former city was not *quite* so well insulated, commercially speaking, from London, so that Gresham's Law may have operated to a greater extent in Kent than in the North.

[2] There is of course a semantic difficulty here, since if no silver had been added (and only 4 oz. small coins had been produced) the total of expenses would have been lower as well as that of output. The 'third of the total' in the text means *third of the recorded profit* (i.e. including the silver on both the expenses and the output side).

be added that so far as I am aware there is no evidence that the Government's motives for demonetizing the testons were other than what it said they were. Certainly it seems difficult to accept Dr. Challis's contention that the specific reason for this policy was to increase the profitability of the Mints at a time when their revenue-earning potential was threatened by the waning of the attraction of higher mint prices and a fall in supplies of bullion.

The document authorizing the reminting of testons dates from 16 February 1548.[1] Yet at this time the general level of activity at the Mints, bearing in mind gold as well as silver, was in aggregate but little below its peak level, and indeed the converting of testons did not really get under way until 1549 partly because the Mints were too busy with their other work.

The explanation which I prefer and tentatively offer is that the demonetization of testons was intended as the first stage in the introduction of a 'two-tier' system of coinage, the debased coins being confined to smaller denominations with a superstructure of 'good' gold and silver coins in denominations suitable for the conduct of overseas and wholesale trade. As we have seen, some such compromise as this was eventually achieved by the 50 per cent reduction of the value of the base coins in the summer of 1551[2] and the provision to resume minting 'good' gold and silver coins in October of that year.[3] It is perfectly true that before that compromise was achieved, two further issues of debased coins intervened: the 6 oz. coins of 1549–51, and the 3 oz. coins of 1551. But the first of these represented no further debasement of the currency, the 6 oz. coins holding the same intrinsic value as their 4 oz. predecessors of 1546–9. The rush of activity arose rather from reductions in the rate of seignorage and a consequent fall in the silver/gold ratio (inducing a bimetallic flow) which there is no evidence the Government intended or indeed understood.

The 3 oz. coinage of 1551 is doubtless a more serious stain on the reign's monetary record, but it was decided on, begun, temporarily halted, resumed, and terminated in a typically indecisive fashion and the total output was relatively modest. It has been well said that the keynote of policy in the reign of Edward VI was vacillation, and of no

[1] I have not found this document, but its purpose and date are made clear from several references to it in the mint accounts.

[2] Hughes and Larkin, op. cit., nos. 372, 376, 379.

[3] Ibid., no. 382; Add. MSS. 18759, fols. 69v ff.

aspect of policy is this more true than of the handling of the currency. If Edward's ministers must be condemned for continuing and aggravating the debasement which Henry VIII had begun, they must also be given credit for eventually halting it after exploring, gropingly and irresolutely, but not wholly insincerely, the path to a solution. It seems on present evidence uncharitable not to see the plan to remint the base testons into small coins as a first step along that path.

GRAPHS

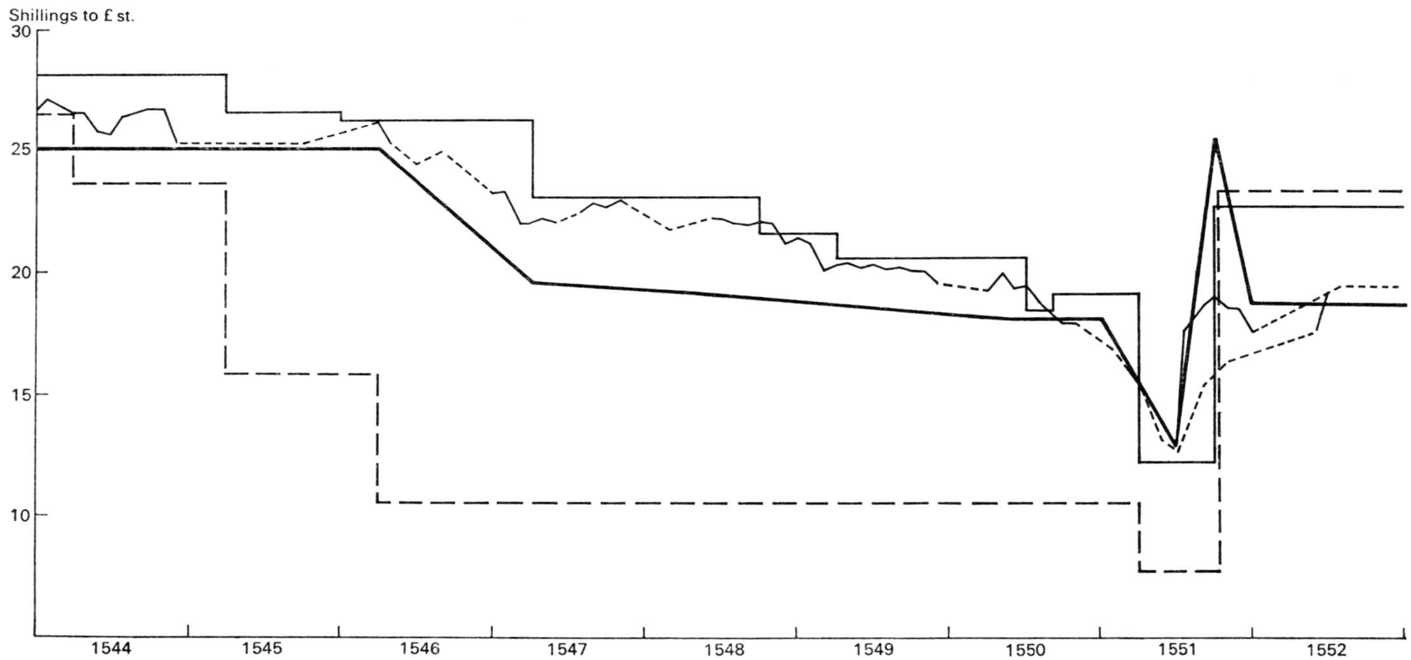
Shillings to £ st.
30
25
20
15
10
1544
1545
1546
1547
1548
1549
1550
1551
1552

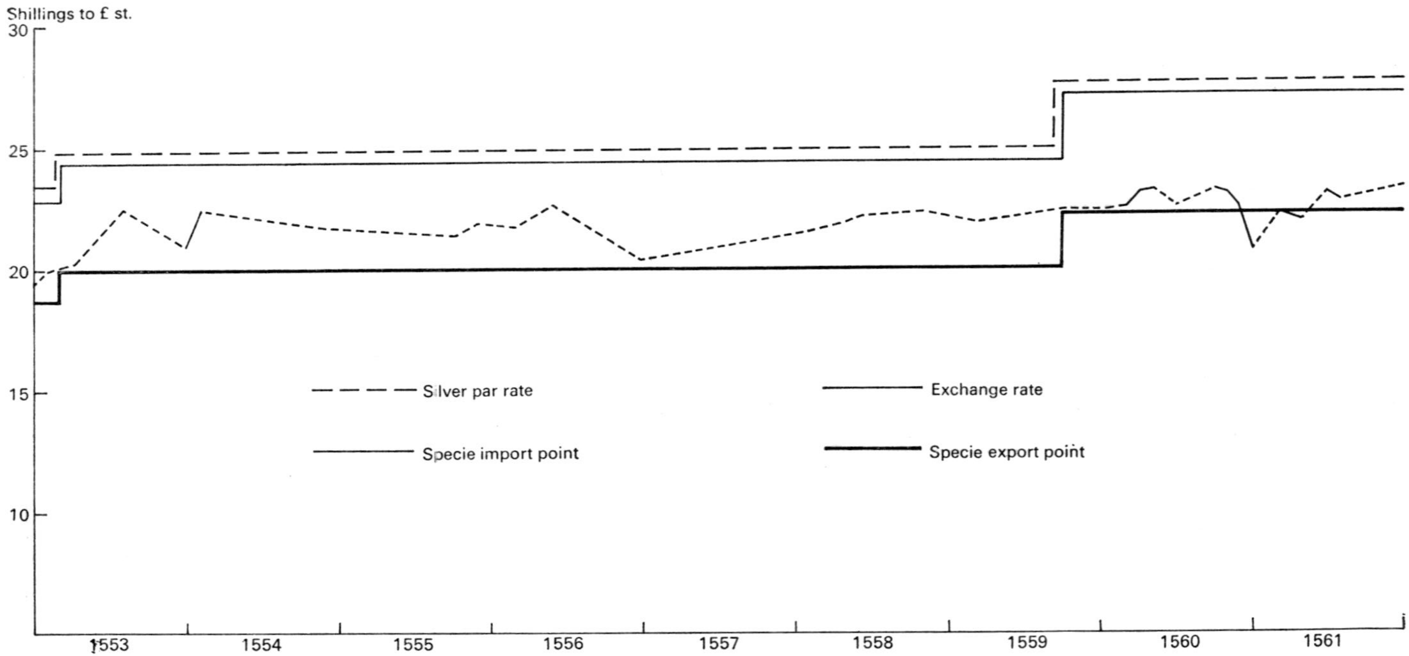

GRAPH A. The London–Antwerp Exchange Rate, 1544–61

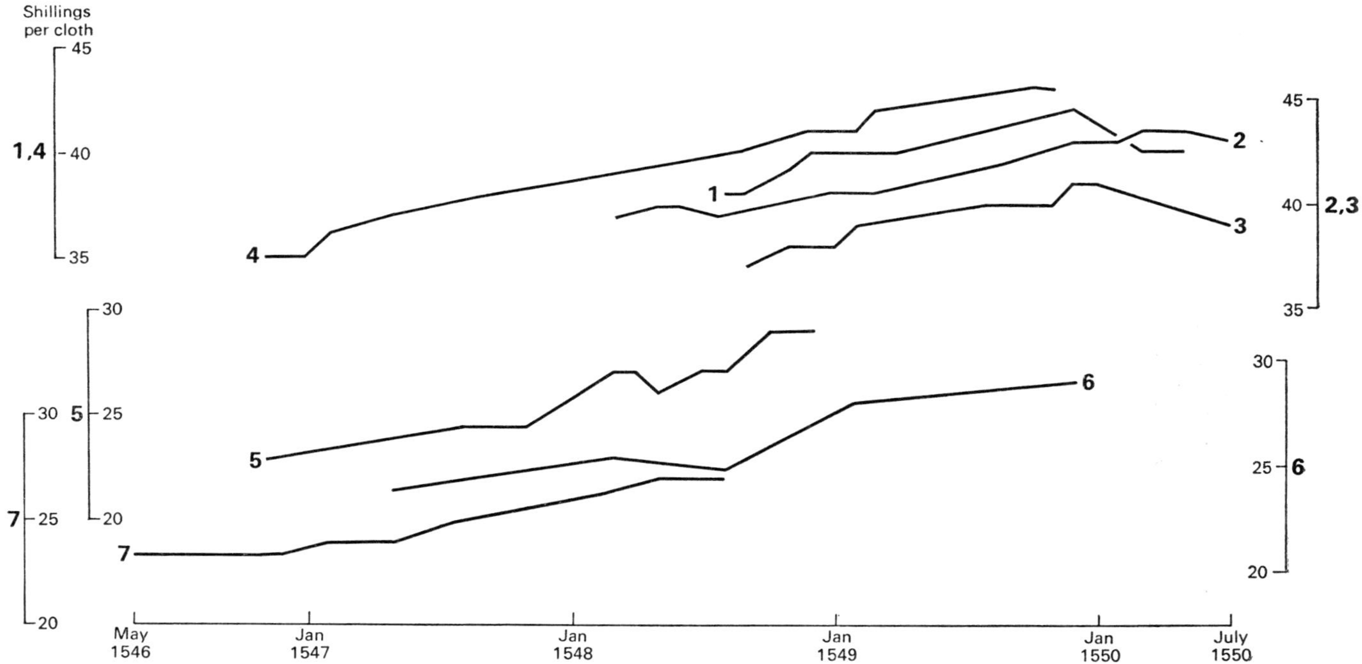

GRAPH B. Cloth Prices, 1546–50

1 = William Bennett
2 = Thomas Dolman
3 = John Barksdale
4 = John Winchcombe
} Kersies

5 = Gilbert Ramsden
6 = George Foxcroft
7 = John Dighton and Richard Wilkinson
} Northern Kersies

PRINTED IN GREAT BRITAIN
AT THE UNIVERSITY PRESS, OXFORD
BY VIVIAN RIDLER
PRINTER TO THE UNIVERSITY